# READING
## EXPLORER

5

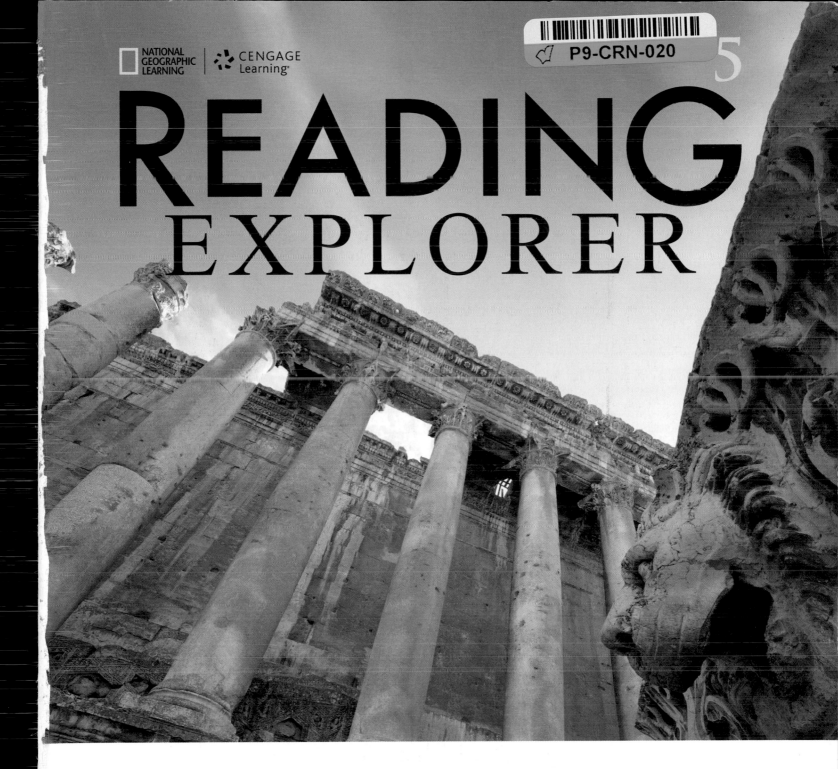

NANCY DOUGLAS • DAVID BOHLKE

HELEN HUNTLEY • BRUCE ROGERS • PAUL MACINTYRE

Second Edition

**NATIONAL GEOGRAPHIC LEARNING** | **CENGAGE Learning**

Australia • Brazil • Japan • Korea • Mexico • Singapore • Spain • United Kingdom • United States

**Reading Explorer 5**
**Second Edition**

**Nancy Douglas, David Bohlke, Helen Huntley, Bruce Rogers, and Paul MacIntyre**

**Publisher:** Andrew Robinson

**Executive Editor:** Sean Bermingham

**Senior Development Editor:** Derek Mackrell

**Development Editor:** Christopher Street

**Associate Development Editor:** Michelle Harris

**Director of Global Marketing:** Ian Martin

**Product Marketing Manager:** Anders Bylund

**Senior Director of Production:** Michael Burggren

**Senior Content Project Manager:** Tan Jin Hock

**Manufacturing Planner:** Mary Beth Hennebury

**Compositor:** SPi Global

**Cover/Text Design:** Creative Director: Christopher Roy, Art Director: Scott Baker, Senior Designer: Michael Rosenquest

**Cover Photo:** Sasha Gusov/Axiom Photographic Agency/Getty Images

Student Book with Online Workbook:
ISBN-13: 978-1-305-25451-0

Student Book:
ISBN-13: 978-1-285-84704-7

**National Geographic Learning**
20 Channel Center Street
Boston, MA 02210
USA

Cengage Learning is a leading provider of customized learning solutions with office locations around the globe, including Singapore, the United Kingdom, Australia, Mexico, Brazil, and Japan. Locate your local office at: **international.cengage.com/region**

Cengage Learning products are represented in Canada by Nelson Education, Ltd.

Visit National Geographic Learning online at **NGL.Cengage.com**

Visit our corporate website at **www.cengage.com**

Printed in the United States of America
Print Number: 03     Print Year: 2016

# Contents

| | | |
|---|---|---|
| Scope and Sequence | | 4 |
| Introduction | | 6 |
| Unit 1: | **Collapse** | 7 |
| Unit 2: | **Beyond Earth** | 29 |
| Unit 3: | **Health and Genes** | 51 |
| Unit 4: | **Vanishing Cities** | 73 |
| Unit 5: | **Eco-Living** | 95 |
| Unit 6: | **Wildlife in Trouble** | 117 |
| Unit 7: | **Human Body** | 139 |
| Unit 8: | **Social Behavior** | 161 |
| Unit 9: | **Creativity** | 183 |
| Unit 10: | **Elements and Toxins** | 205 |
| Unit 11: | **Islam and the West** | 227 |
| Unit 12: | **Wealth and Finance** | 249 |
| Credits | | 271 |

# Scope and Sequence

| Unit | Theme | Reading |
|------|-------|---------|
| 1 | **Collapse** | A: Secrets of the Maya<br>B: The Collapse of Angkor |
| 2 | **Beyond Earth** | A: Cosmic Dawn<br>B: Planet Hunters: Are We Alone? |
| 3 | **Health and Genes** | A: Mending Broken Hearts<br>B: The War on Allergies |
| 4 | **Vanishing Cities** | A: City Under Siege<br>B: Rising Seas |
| 5 | **Eco-Living** | A: Carbon Footprint<br>B: Plugging into the Sun |
| 6 | **Wildlife in Trouble** | A: Quicksilver<br>B: Building the Ark |
| 7 | **Human Body** | A: Secrets of the Brain<br>B: Human Bionics |
| 8 | **Social Behavior** | A: The Genius of Swarms<br>B: Of Ants and Humans |
| 9 | **Creativity** | A: Decoding Leonardo<br>B: The Power of Writing |
| 10 | **Elements and Toxins** | A: Hidden Hazards<br>B: Element Hunters |
| 11 | **Islam and the West** | A: The World of Süleyman the Magnificent<br>B: When the Moors Ruled Spain |
| 12 | **Wealth and Finance** | A: From Clams to Credit Cards<br>B: Gold Fever |

| Reading Skill | Vocabulary Building | Video |
|---|---|---|
| **A:** Understanding Infographics<br>**B:** Evaluating the Strengths of Arguments | **A:** Word Partnership: *sacrifice*<br>**B:** Word Link: *reg-* | Temples in the Jungle |
| **A:** Determining the Main Idea of Paragraphs<br>**B:** Understanding Cause and Effect Relationships | **A:** Word Link: *mit*<br>**B:** Word Link: *com-* | Comet Watchers |
| **A:** Scanning for Details (I)<br>**B:** Using Concept Maps | **A:** Usage: *exacerbate* and *compound*<br>**B:** Thesaurus: *tolerate* | Fighting Malaria |
| **A:** Recognizing Literal vs. Figurative Language<br>**B:** Reading a Text Critically | **A:** Usage: *complement* and *compliment*<br>**B:** Word Link: *poli* | Time and Tide |
| **A:** Distinguishing Main Ideas and Supporting Information<br>**B:** Identifying Similarities and Differences | **A:** Word Partnership: *obstacle*<br>**B:** Word Partnership: *premium* | Eco-Detectives |
| **A:** Identifying Homonyms<br>**B:** Understanding Root Words of Greek and Latin Origin | **A:** Word Link: *turb*<br>**B:** Thesaurus: *imminent* | Life on Ice |
| **A:** Understanding the Use of the Passive Voice<br>**B:** Distinguishing Fact from Opinion | **A:** Word Partnership: *unprecedented*<br>**B:** Word Link: *val* | Bionic Mountaineer |
| **A:** Understanding Inference<br>**B:** Scanning for Details (II) | **A:** Usage: *code* and *protocol*<br>**B:** Word Partnership: *fatal* | Monarch Migration |
| **A:** Relating Textual Information to a Map<br>**B:** Understanding Chronological Sequence | **A:** Word Partnership: *deny*<br>**B:** Word Link: *man/manu* | The Birthplace of Writing |
| **A:** Identifying Theory and Fact<br>**B:** Understanding Long Sentences | **A:** Usage: *albeit*<br>**B:** Word Link: *counter-* | Secrets of Toothpaste |
| **A:** Creating a Mental Map of a Text<br>**B:** Inferring an Author's Attitude | **A:** Word Link: *bi-*<br>**B:** Word Partnership: *violate* | Heritage of Spain |
| **A:** Applying Information from a Text<br>**B:** Identifying Coherence Devices | **A:** Word Partnership: *obligation*<br>**B:** Word Link: *-ship* | The Art Smuggler |

# Welcome to Reading Explorer!

**In this book,** you'll travel the globe, explore different cultures, and discover new ways of looking at the world. You'll also become a better reader!

## What's new in the Second Edition?

### New and updated topics

Explore the ruins of ancient civilizations, the effects of rising seas, and join the race to discover new elements.

### New Reading Skills section

Learn how to read strategically—and think critically as you read.

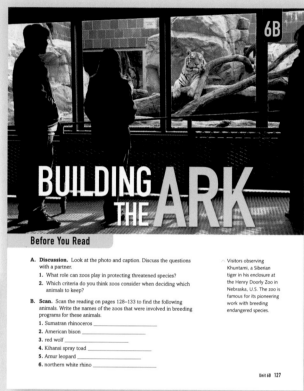

### Expanded Viewing section

Apply your language skills when you watch a specially adapted National Geographic video.

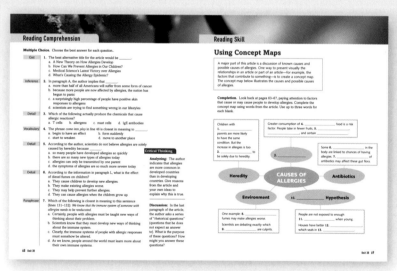

# Now you're ready

## to explore your world!

# COLLAPSE

Moai are huge humanlike figures carved from rock by the Rapa Nui people of Easter Island.

## Warm Up

**Discuss these questions with a partner.**

1. Can you name any societies or civilizations that were once powerful but no longer exist today?

2. Why do you think some societies and civilizations have not lasted?

3. What do you think are the main pressures affecting societies today?

# Before You Read

**A. Discussion.** Read the information on this page. Then answer these questions.

    **1.** What do you think is Guillermo de Anda's profession? Why do you think he is descending into the cenote?

    **2.** What do you think is the importance of cenotes in the Maya civilization? What could be the significance of light shining directly down into a cenote?

**B. Scanning.** Scan the reading on pages 9–14 and write a definition of these words.

    **1.** Chichén Itzá _____

    **2.** Chaak _____

    **3.** *milpa* _____

    **4.** *hmem* _____

Guillermo de Anda descends into the Holtún cenote[1] of Mexico's Yucatán. The roof is an enormous dome ringed by stalactites[2] that reach down toward the groundwater. When the sun is at its zenith,[3] light falls vertically into the water. These cenotes were an important part of the Maya civilization.

---

1 A **cenote** is a naturally formed deep hole in limestone.

2 **Stalactites** are rock formations hanging from cave ceilings, slowly formed by dripping water.

3 The **zenith** is a point directly above a particular location.

# SECRETS OF THE MAYA

The study of caves and wells in Mexico's Yucatán Peninsula is shining new light on the beliefs of the ancient and modern Maya.

## 1 | Gateway to the Rain God

**A**  From deep in a well near the ruins of the Mayan city of Chichén Itzá, archeoastronomer[4] Arturo Montero shouts to his colleague on the surface, "I saw it, I saw it! Yes, it's true!" Leaning over the mouth of the well, archeologist
5  Guillermo de Anda hopes to hear what he has suspected for many months. "What is true, Arturo?" he shouts. And Montero yells up again, "The zenith light! It really works! Get down here!"

**B**  The two archeologists are anxious to confirm whether this cenote could have acted as a sacred sundial[5] and timekeeper for the ancient Maya. On two
10  days every year—May 23 and July 19—the sun reaches its zenith over this part of Mexico. At those moments, the sun is vertically overhead and there is no shadow. On the morning of their descent, on May 24, Montero and de Anda see that the sun's rays come very close to vertical. The day before, they realized, a beam of light would have **plunged** straight down into the water.

4  An **archeoastronomer** is someone who studies archeological artifacts to determine what ancient people or civilizations believed and understood about astronomy.

5  A **sundial** is a device used for telling the time when the sun is shining. The shadow of a pointer falls onto a flat surface that is marked with the hours, and points to the correct hour.

**C** 15 Beneath its narrow mouth, the walls of the cenote open up to become a giant dome. It looks like a cathedral, except for the roots of trees that **penetrate** the rock as they reach for the water. The beam of sunlight dances like 20 fire on the surrounding stalactites, and it turns the water a beautiful **transparent** blue. The archeologists were probably the first people in centuries to watch the sun move slowly across the cenote's water.

**D** 25 Did Maya priests wait in this well—known as the Holtún cenote—to observe and correct their measurements of the sun's angle when it reached the zenith? Did they come here during times of drought to make offerings to 30 their water god, and at other times to give thanks for a good harvest? These and other questions involving the Mayan religion and extraordinarily accurate calendar are what the two explorers were investigating.

**E** 35 In recent years, archeologists have been paying more attention to the meaning of caves, the zenith sun, and cenotes in the beliefs of the ancient and modern Maya. Archeologists already knew that the ancient 40 Maya believed caves and cenotes to be doors to a world inhabited by Chaak, the god of life-giving rain. However, the significance of this fact has only recently started to become clear.

**F** De Anda began exploring Holtún in 2010. 45 One day, **inspecting** the walls of the cenote a few meters below the surface, he emerged from the water and felt something above his head. He was **astonished** to find a natural rock shelf holding an offering of human and 50 animal bones, pottery, and a knife—probably used for **sacrifices**—all neatly placed there centuries earlier. Below the water, he saw broken columns and Mayan stone carvings. The well was clearly a sacred site.

## Key to Survival

55

**G** Three years later, in the cornfield on the surface above the cenote, a crew of Maya farmers is working hard in the **grueling** Yucatán heat to pull the explorers out of the 60 well. The crew's leader is Luis Un Ken, an optimist with an easy smile who is respected by everyone in his nearby village. "There was a good rain the other day," he says, wiping the sweat off his face. "The Chaak moved."

**H** 65 For men like Un Ken, the old gods are still very much alive, and Chaak—ruler of cenotes and caves—is among the most important. For the benefit of living things, he pours from the skies the water he keeps in jars. Thunder is 70 the sound of Chaak breaking a jar open and letting the rain fall. The Chaak had moved, Un Ken said, and that meant the planting season would soon arrive.

**I** Chaak's absence can cause disasters for the 75 Yucatán Maya, possibly the **demise** of the ancient Maya civilization itself. Their land is an endless limestone shelf. Rain sinks through the porous[6] limestone down to groundwater levels, and consequently no river or stream 80 runs through the land. From the air, one sees a green sea of dense jungle. At ground level, however, the tropical forest appears very thin. Wherever there is enough soil, the Maya plant corn or *milpa*, a combination of the corn, 85 beans, and squash that constitutes their basic source of protein. But corn is a hungry crop; it sucks lots of nutrients from the soil. For thousands of years, milpa farmers have kept

---

**6** Something that is **porous** has many small holes in it, which water and air can pass through.

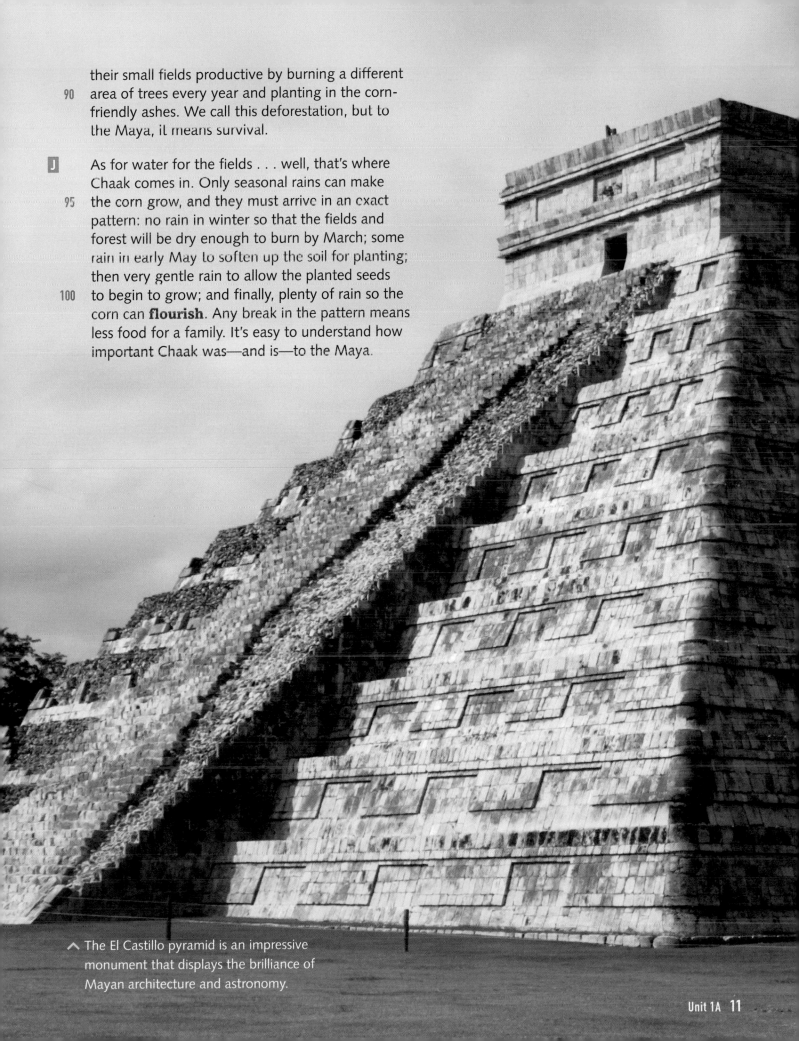

their small fields productive by burning a different
area of trees every year and planting in the corn-
friendly ashes. We call this deforestation, but to
the Maya, it means survival.

**J** As for water for the fields . . . well, that's where
Chaak comes in. Only seasonal rains can make
the corn grow, and they must arrive in an exact
pattern: no rain in winter so that the fields and
forest will be dry enough to burn by March; some
rain in early May to soften up the soil for planting;
then very gentle rain to allow the planted seeds
to begin to grow; and finally, plenty of rain so the
corn can **flourish**. Any break in the pattern means
less food for a family. It's easy to understand how
important Chaak was—and is—to the Maya.

90

95

100

∧ The El Castillo pyramid is an impressive
monument that displays the brilliance of
Mayan architecture and astronomy.

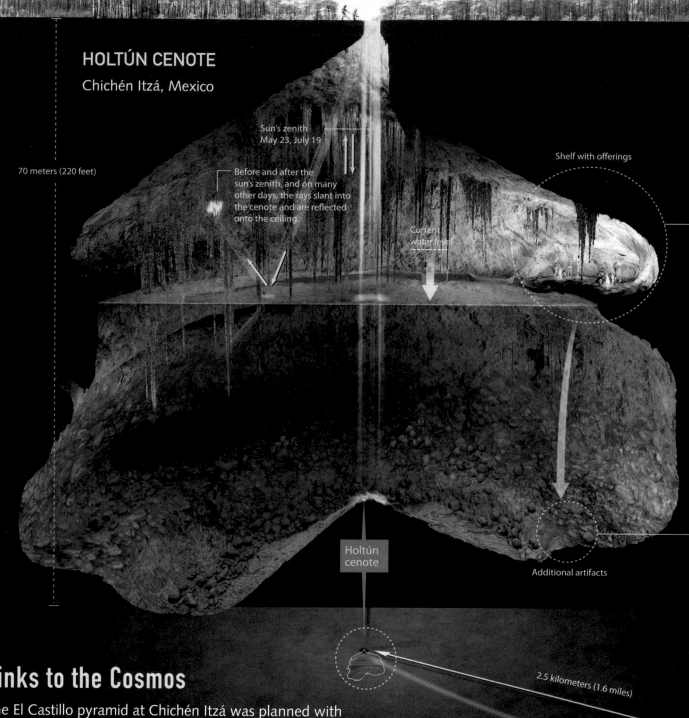

## HOLTÚN CENOTE
### Chichén Itzá, Mexico

70 meters (220 feet)

Sun's zenith
May 23, July 19

Before and after the
sun's zenith, and on many
other days, the rays slant into
the cenote and are reflected
onto the ceiling.

Shelf with offerings

Current
water level

Holtún
cenote

Additional artifacts

2.5 kilometers (1.6 miles)

# Links to the Cosmos

The El Castillo pyramid at Chichén Itzá was planned with
precision. Experts believe it is aligned to the March and
September equinoxes[7] when the sun's passage makes a
serpentlike shadow slither down its side. Guillermo de Anda
recently discovered that the structure also stands in the
middle of four cenotes (where the white lines cross, right),
probably symbolizing the sacred mountain at the center of
the Maya universe. It was also oriented to the moments
when the sun reaches its highest point in the sky (far right),
further connecting the cycles of the heavens.

---

7 The **equinoxes** are the two days of the year when the day and night are
  equal length.

# A PLACE OF PRAYER

Desperate for water for their crops, the Maya prayed to the rain god Chaak from deep inside the cenote. On a rocky shelf exposed during droughts, they laid out offerings and performed rituals, which may have included human and animal sacrifices. Archeologists found artifacts scattered on the floor of the cenote. They believe the Maya sometimes sacrificed objects such as ceramic pots or sculptures by breaking them.

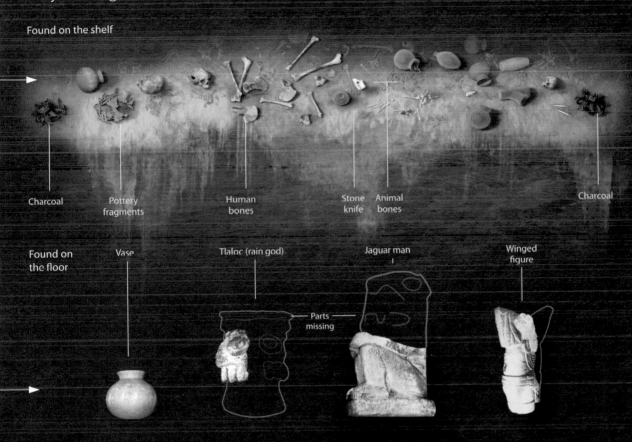

Found on the shelf

Charcoal | Pottery fragments | Human bones | Stone knife | Animal bones | Charcoal

Found on the floor

Vase | Tlaloc (rain god) — Parts missing | Jaguar man | Winged figure

# IN LINE WITH THE SUN

Twice a year, the sun rises directly to the northeast of El Castillo and travels over its peak (right). It then moves in an arc to the northwest (yellow line below), where it passes over the Hollún cenote before sinking to the horizon.

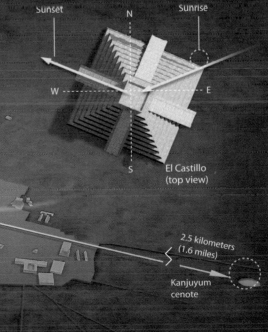

Sunset

Sunrise

N

W — E

S

El Castillo (top view)

Sacred cenote

Chichén Itzá

El Castillo

2.5 kilometers (1.6 miles)

Kanjuyum cenote

Sun's zenith
May 23, July 19

When the sun reaches its highest point in the sky—the solar zenith—its rays fall vertically to the ground.

Xtoloc cenote

# Pleasing the Rain God

**K** 105 In the village of Yaxuná, 20 kilometers (12 miles) south of Chichén Itzá, many people still depend on milpa, and an annual ceremony is held there to please the rain god. The villagers and their spiritual leaders
110 work without rest or sleep to persuade Chaak to come to them. They walk a long way through the forest to a sacred cave—on a fragile rope system—and climb down to its center to bring up the water the
115 ceremony requires. They raise the altar, dig a large cooking pit, and go to enormous expense to provide 13 fat chickens for the ritual meal. They make corn-and-squash-seed breads and cook them in the open pit
120 so that the steam can rise directly to the rain god as an offering.

**L** One recent such ceremony in Yaxuná was guided by Hipólito Puuc Tamay, a Maya holy man called a *hmem*. In a red baseball
125 cap and much washed shirt, he stood in front of an altar praying for the holy blessing of rain for the surrounding Maya communities. On instructions from the hmem, one of the villagers crouched on a
130 rock near the altar, keeping very still, only blowing from time to time into one of the gourds[8] in which Chaak stores the wind. He was just one of the neighbors, but he was also the rain god, and he sat with his eyes
135 closed so as not to harm the ceremony with his terrible glance. Two other participants brought him to the altar, facing backward, to receive a blessing from the hmem.

**M** There were little frogs, too, five slightly
140 **abashed** boys crouching at the foot of the altar, one boy at each corner and one at the center. Four of them said, *hmaa hmaa hmaa*, and the fifth, *lek lek lek lek lek*. The resulting blended sound was remarkably
145 like that of frogs in the evening rain.

In this harsh region with no rivers, the limestone cenotes, are the only permanent sources of fresh water. More than 3,500 hold rainwater that has been collecting for thousands of years.

**N** Out of nowhere, a wind came up in the clearing. Thunder could be heard in the blue distance. As the ceremonial meal of chicken and the corn-and-seed bread was
150 being distributed, the rain started—a light, refreshing summer shower. A sign, the hmem said, that Chaak had received his offering and was pleased with his people's prayer. Soon, perhaps, the earth would be
155 ready for planting.

---

8 A **gourd** is a container made from the hard dry skin of a gourd fruit. Gourds are often used for carrying water or for decoration.

# Reading Comprehension

**Multiple Choice.** Choose the best answer for each question.

Reference

1. What does *it* refer to in *I saw it. I saw it!?* (lines 3–4)
   a. the cenote
   b. the zenith light
   c. the stone sundial
   d. the mouth of the well

Figurative Language

2. What does the author compare the cenote to in paragraph C?
   a. a column
   b. dancing fire
   c. a cathedral
   d. a pool of water

Detail

3. What are Arturo Montero and Guillermo de Anda NOT investigating in the cenote?
   a. whether the ancient Maya had depleted the cenote's water from overuse
   b. whether the ancient Maya went there to give thanks and offer sacrifices
   c. whether the ancient Maya used the cenote as a sundial and timekeeper
   d. whether ancient Maya priests used the cenote to correct their measurements of the sun's angle when it reached the zenith

Inference

4. What did Luis Un Ken mean when he said, "The Chaak moved" (line 64)?
   a. It had rained.
   b. It was very hot.
   c. Chaak had prayed.
   d. Chaak was important.

Detail

5. Why is farming particularly difficult for the Maya?
   a. Rivers flood regularly.
   b. Rain does not sink into the ground.
   c. Crops like corn suck nutrients from the soil.
   d. There are not enough farmers during harvest time.

Sequence

6. To get the best crops, what must happen immediately after the fields are burned?
   a. Seeds are planted.
   b. The fields dry out.
   c. Heavy rain soaks the fields.
   d. Some rain softens the ground.

Purpose

7. What is the main purpose of paragraphs K and L?
   a. to explain a long-forgotten cultural practice
   b. to explain how one villager became the new Chaak
   c. to explain how a village prays to Chaak for rain
   d. to explain what villagers do during the milpa ceremony

## Critical Thinking

**Inferring:** Why do you think the author mentions that Luis Un Ken is an optimist? What significance does this have?

**Discussion:** The Maya civilization eventually collapsed. What do you think contributed to this collapse? Could it have been avoided?

# Understanding Infographics

An infographic is a visual representation of textual information or data. It condenses a large amount of information into a combination of images and text. This lets the reader quickly grasp essential information. Infographics can include text, photos, illustrations, captions, charts, graphs, and so on.

**A. Matching.** Look back at the infographic on pages 12–13. Match the descriptions (**a–d**) to the relevant sections on the infographic.

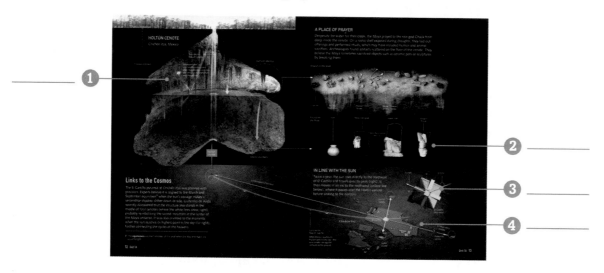

**a.** There are four cenotes surrounding El Castillo: Holtún cenote, Xtoloc cenote, Sacred cenote, and Kanjuyum cenote.

**b.** On days other than the sun's zenith, the sun rays are reflected onto the cenote's walls.

**c.** The pyramid at Chichén Itzá is oriented to the moments when the sun reaches its highest point in the sky.

**d.** A vase and a winged figure were some of the artifacts discovered on the floor of the cenote.

**B. True or False.** Mark these statements about the infographic **T** (True), **F** (False), or **NG** (Not Given).

| | | | |
|---|---|---|---|
| **1.** The Maya entered the cenote by jumping into the water below. | T | F | NG |
| **2.** During the sun's zenith, its rays are reflected onto the cave walls. | T | F | NG |
| **3.** The surface of the water is 220 feet below the cenote mouth. | T | F | NG |
| **4.** During droughts, the Maya put offerings on an exposed rock shelf. | T | F | NG |
| **5.** No offerings to the gods were ever made on May 23 and July 19. | T | F | NG |
| **6.** A broken Jaguar man was found on the rock shelf. | T | F | NG |

# Vocabulary Practice

**A. Completion.** Complete the information with the correct form of words from the box. Three words are extra.

| | | | |
|---|---|---|---|
| abashed | demise | flourish | grueling |
| inspect | penetrate | plunged | transparent |

With their sophisticated concepts of architecture, astronomy, and mathematics, the Maya were among the greatest of all ancient civilizations. They **1.** _____ for centuries, and at their peak, around A.D. 800, totaled 15 million people ranging from present-day Mexico to Honduras. Then, suddenly, their society collapsed. Consequently, people abandoned the cities and left immense pyramids in ruins. What caused the collapse of the Maya civilization?

Researchers now believe that climate change may be the answer. According to one study, a long period of dry climate, with three **2.** _____ droughts, led to the Maya's end. Researchers who **3.** _____ sediment from the Yucatán Peninsula found that these droughts matched downturns in the Maya culture. It is believed that the Maya were particularly at risk because their population depended wholly on lakes, ponds, and rivers that provided a supply of water for drinking and agriculture for just 18 months. Even when rain did come following a drought, water could not **4.** _____ the soil because it was so dry and hard.

Believers of the climate change theory say the droughts sparked a chain of events that led to the **5.** _____ of the Maya. "Sunny days, in and of themselves, don't kill people," says Richardson B. Gill, author of *The Great Maya Droughts: Water, Life, and Death*. "But when people run out of food and water, they die."

∧ The Mayan calendar was remarkably complex and accurate.

**B. Words in Context.** Complete each sentence with the correct answer.

1. If someone **plunges** into a lake, he or she _____.
   a. enters slowly and carefully   b. jumps in suddenly

2. You _____ see through something that is **transparent**.
   a. can                          b. cannot

3. If you are **astonished** to see someone, you feel very _____.
   a. frightened                   b. surprised

4. The **sacrifice** of an animal during a religious ceremony means the _____ of it.
   a. killing                      b. decorating

5. If you are **abashed**, you feel _____.
   a. confident and proud          b. embarrassed and ashamed

> **Word Partnership**
> Use **sacrifice** with: (*adj.*) **ultimate** sacrifice, **heroic** sacrifice, **animal** sacrifice; (*v.*) **entail** sacrifices, **endure** sacrifices; (*n.*) sacrifice **your weekend**, sacrifice **your social life**.

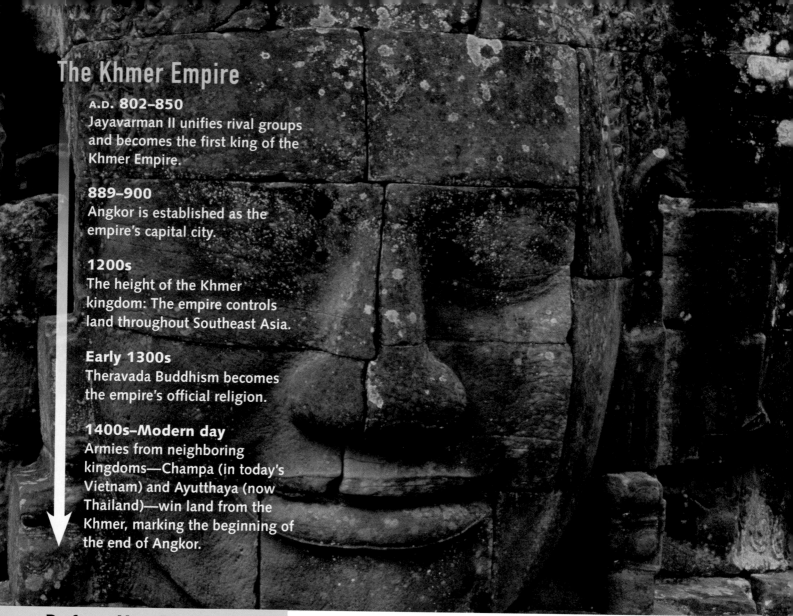

## The Khmer Empire

**A.D. 802–850**
Jayavarman II unifies rival groups and becomes the first king of the Khmer Empire.

**889–900**
Angkor is established as the empire's capital city.

**1200s**
The height of the Khmer kingdom: The empire controls land throughout Southeast Asia.

**Early 1300s**
Theravada Buddhism becomes the empire's official religion.

**1400s–Modern day**
Armies from neighboring kingdoms—Champa (in today's Vietnam) and Ayutthaya (now Thailand)—win land from the Khmer, marking the beginning of the end of Angkor.

## Before You Read

**A. Completion.** Use the information on this page to complete the notes about the Khmer Empire.

Empire founded by: _____

Capital city: _____

Religion(s): _____

Name of famous landmark: _____

Start of empire's decline: _____

The temples of Angkor remain a symbol of classic Khmer (Cambodian) architecture.

**B. Skimming and Predicting.** Skim the first page of the article (page 19). Predict what you think caused the decline of Angkor. Then read the rest of the article to check your ideas.

_____

_____

# THE COLLAPSE OF ANGKOR

After rising to sublime¹ heights, the sacred city may have engineered its own downfall.

## 1 | An Empire's Fall

**A** Almost hidden amid the forests of northern Cambodia is the scene of one of the greatest vanishing acts of all time. This was once the heart of the Khmer kingdom, which lasted from the 9th to the 15th centuries. At its height, the Khmer Empire dominated much of Southeast Asia, from Myanmar (Burma) in the west to Vietnam in the east. As many as 750,000 people lived in Angkor, its magnificent capital. The most extensive urban complex of the preindustrial world, Angkor stretched across an area the size of New York City. Its greatest temple, Angkor Wat, is the world's largest religious monument even today.

**B** Yet when the first European missionaries arrived in Angkor in the late 16th century, they found a city that was already dying. Scholars have come up with a list of suspected causes for Angkor's decline. These include foreign invaders, a religious change of heart, and a shift to maritime trade. But it's mostly guesswork: Roughly 1,300 inscriptions survive on temple doors and monuments, but the people of Angkor left not a single word explaining their kingdom's collapse.

¹ If you say something is **sublime**, you mean it has a wonderful quality.

At the edge of the Srah Srang reservoir in Angkor, Cambodia, stone lions stand guard over the ruins of the Khmer Empire.

**C** Some scholars **assume** that Angkor died the way it lived: by the sword. The historical records of Ayutthaya, a neighboring state, claim that warriors from that kingdom "took"
20 Angkor in 1431. If so, their motive is not difficult to guess. No doubt Angkor would have been a rich prize: Inscriptions boast that its temple towers were covered with gold. After its rediscovery by Western travelers just
25 over a century ago, historians deduced from Angkor's ruins that the city had been looted[2] by invaders from Ayutthaya.

**D** Roland Fletcher, co-director of a research effort called the Greater Angkor Project, is
30 not convinced. Some early scholars, he says, viewed Angkor according to the sieges[3] and conquests of European history. "The ruler of Ayutthaya, indeed, says he took Angkor, and he may have taken some formal regalia[4] back
35 to Ayutthaya with him," says Fletcher. But after Angkor was captured, Ayutthaya's ruler placed his son on the throne. "He's not likely to have smashed the place up before giving it to his son."

**E** 40 A religious shift may also have contributed to the city's decline, by diminishing royal authority. Angkor was a regal-ritual city; its kings claimed to be the world emperors of Hindu mythology and erected temples
45 to themselves. But in the 13th and 14th centuries, Theravada Buddhism gradually took over from Hinduism. Its principles of social equality may have threatened Angkor's elite. "It was very subversive,[5] just like Christianity
50 was subversive to the Roman Empire," says Fletcher.

**F** The regal-ritual city operated on a moneyless economy, relying on tribute[6] and taxation. The kingdom's main currency was rice, the staple
55 food of the laborers who built the temples and the thousands who ran them. For one temple complex, Ta Prohm, more than 66,000 farmers produced nearly 3,000 tons of rice a year. This was then used to feed the temple's priests,
60 dancers, and workers. Scholars estimate that farm laborers comprised nearly half of Greater Angkor's population. A new religion that promoted ideas of social equality might have led to rebellion.

**G** 65 Or maybe the royal court simply turned its back on Angkor. Angkor's rulers often erected new temple complexes and let older ones decay. This may have **doomed** the city when sea trade began to develop between Southeast
70 Asia and China. Maybe it was simple economic opportunism that, by the 16th century, had caused the Khmer center of power to shift: The move to a location closer to the Mekong River, near Cambodia's present-day capital,
75 Phnom Penh, allowed it easier access to the sea.

**H** Economic and religious changes may have contributed to Angkor's downfall, but its rulers faced another foe. Angkor was powerful
80 largely thanks to an advanced system of canals and reservoirs. These enabled the city to keep **scarce** water in dry months and **disperse** excess water during the rainy season. But forces beyond Angkor's control
85 would eventually bring an end to this carefully constructed, rational system.

**I** Few ancient sites in southern Asia could compare to Angkor in its ability to guarantee a steady water supply. That reliability required
90 massive feats of engineering. The first scholar to appreciate the scale of Angkor's waterworks was French archeologist Bernard-Philippe Groslier. In 1979, he argued that the great

---

2 If a store or house is **looted**, people have stolen things from it, for example, during a war or riot.

3 A **siege** is a military or police operation in which soldiers or police surround a place in order to force the people there to come out.

4 **Regalia** is the ceremonial jewelry, objects, or clothes that symbolize royalty or high office.

5 Something that is **subversive** is intended to weaken or destroy a political system or government.

6 A **tribute** is something you give, say, do, or make to show your admiration and respect for someone.

reservoirs, or *barays*, served two purposes: to
95  symbolize the Hindu cosmos[7] and to irrigate
the rice fields. Unfortunately, Groslier could
not pursue his ideas further. Cambodia's civil
war,[8] the brutal **regime** of the Khmer Rouge,[9]
and the **subsequent** arrival of Vietnamese
100 forces in 1979 turned Angkor into a no-go
zone for two decades.

**J** In the 1990s, Christophe Pottier followed up
on Groslier's ideas and discovered that the
south part of Angkor was a vast dispersed
105 landscape of housing, water tanks, shrines,
roads and canals. Then, in 2000, Roland
Fletcher and his colleague Damian Evans—as
part of a collaborative study with Pottier—
saw some NASA radar images of Angkor. The
110 researchers marveled at the sophistication of
Angkor's infrastructure. "We realized that
the entire landscape of Greater Angkor is
artificial," Fletcher says. Teams of laborers
constructed hundreds of kilometers of canals
115 and dikes[10] that diverted water from the rivers
to the barays. Overflow **channels** bled off
excess water that accumulated during the
summer monsoon months. After the monsoon,
irrigation channels dispensed the stored
120 water. "It was an incredibly clever system,"
says Fletcher.

**K** Fletcher was therefore baffled when his team
made a surprising discovery. An extraordinary
piece of Angkorian workmanship—a vast
125 structure in the waterworks—had been
destroyed, apparently by Angkor's own
engineers. "The most logical explanation is
that the dam failed," Fletcher says. The river
may have begun to erode the dam, or perhaps
130 it was washed away by an unusually heavy
flood. The Khmer broke apart the remaining
stonework and modified the blocks for other
purposes.

**L** Any weakening of the waterworks would
135 have left the city vulnerable to a natural
phenomenon that none of Angkor's engineers
could have predicted. Starting in the 1300s,
it appears that Southeast Asia experienced a

period of extreme climate change which also
140 affected other parts of the world. In Europe,
which endured centuries of harsh winters and
cool summers, it was known as the Little
Ice Age.

**M** To an already weakened kingdom, extreme
145 weather would have been the final blow.
Decades earlier, Angkor's waterworks were
already struggling. "We don't know why the
water system was operating below capacity,"
says Daniel Penny, co-director of the Greater
150 Angkor Project. "But what it means is that
Angkor . . . was more exposed to the threat of
drought than at any other time in its history."
If inhabitants of parts of Angkor were starving
while other parts of the city were hoarding a
155 finite quantity of rice, the most likely result
was social instability. "When populations in
tropical countries exceed the carrying capacity
of the land, real trouble begins," says Yale
University anthropologist Michael Coe. "This
160 inevitably leads to cultural collapse." A hungry
army weakened by **internal** problems would
have exposed the city to attack. Indeed,
Ayutthaya's invasion happened near the end
of a long period of drought.

**N** 165 Add to the climate chaos the political and
religious changes already affecting the
kingdom, and Angkor's prospects were bleak,
says Fletcher. "The world around Angkor was
changing. Society was moving on. It would
170 have been a surprise if Angkor persisted."

**O** The Khmer Empire was not the first civilization
brought down by climate catastrophe.
Centuries earlier, loss of environmental stability
likewise brought down another powerful
175 kingdom halfway around the world. Many

---

7  The **cosmos** is the universe.

8  A **civil war** is a war fought between different groups of
   people who live in the same country.

9  The **Khmer Rouge** was a radical communist movement
   that ruled Cambodia from 1975 to 1979 after winning
   power through a guerrilla war.

10 A **dike** is a wall built to prevent flooding.

scholars now believe that the fall of the Maya city-states in Mexico and Central America followed a series of droughts in the 9th century. "Essentially, the same thing happened to Angkor," says Coe, who in the 1950s was the first to detect similarities between the Khmer and Maya civilizations.

P In the end, the tale of Angkor is a sobering[11] lesson in the limits of human **ingenuity**. "Angkor's hydraulic[12] system was an amazing machine, a wonderful **mechanism** for regulating the world," Fletcher says. Its engineers managed to keep the civilization's achievement running for six centuries—until a greater force overwhelmed them.

180
185
190

---

11 A situation that is **sobering** is one that seems serious and makes you become thoughtful.
12 **Hydraulic** equipment or machinery involves or is operated by a fluid that is under pressure, such as water or oil.

∨ Intricate carvings depicting an ancient battle on the walls of the Banteay Srei temple located in Angkor

# Reading Comprehension

**Multiple Choice.** Choose the best answer for each question.

**Purpose**

1. What was the author's main purpose in writing this article?
   a. to offer various explanations for the fall of Angkor
   b. to trace the history of Angkor from the 9th to the 15th century
   c. to explain the inscriptions left in the temples by the people of Angkor
   d. to describe the irrigation system that allowed Angkor to flourish

**Detail**

2. According to the information in the first and second paragraphs (A–B), which of the following is NOT true about Angkor?
   a. It once ruled a large part of Southeast Asia.
   b. It was at one time the largest urban center in the world.
   c. It once held as many people as New York City does today.
   d. It was in decline when Europeans arrived in the 16th century.

**Vocabulary**

3. The phrase *by the sword* (line 17) is closest in meaning to _____.
   a. suddenly
   b. unexpectedly
   c. violently
   d. secretively

**Reference**

4. The word *it* in line 38 refers to _____.
   a. the kingdom of Ayutthaya
   b. the destruction of Angkor
   c. the formal regalia
   d. the city of Angkor

**Inference**

5. We can infer from information in paragraph F that the greatest number of people in Angkor worked as _____.
   a. construction workers
   b. dancers
   c. priests
   d. agricultural workers

**Detail**

6. How did the climate in Angkor change in the 1300s?
   a. Winters became too cool to grow rice.
   b. Rising temperatures caused great discomfort.
   c. There were terrible storms and constant flooding.
   d. Weather conditions became more extreme.

**Rhetorical Purpose**

7. Why does the author mention the Little Ice Age in paragraph L?
   a. to show that climate change caused more cultures to fail in Europe than in Asia
   b. to emphasize the extent and significance of climate change in the 1300s
   c. to explain why European cities were not as advanced as Angkor
   d. to show how Angkor's climate in the 1300s was similar to Europe's

## Critical Thinking

**Evaluating:** According to the article, what kinds of challenges did the kingdom of Angkor face? Which of these continue to threaten modern civilizations?

**Discussion:** Angkor Wat today is an important symbol of the modern nation of Cambodia. What place or monument in your country do you think best symbolizes your country? Why?

## Reading Skill

# Evaluating the Strengths of Arguments

An argument is a statement put forward by a writer that is supported by reasons or evidence. A writer may present one or more arguments in a text. As a reader, you need to evaluate the arguments to decide which are the strongest. One way to do this is to ask yourself questions as you read.

- Is the evidence a fact or an opinion?
- Is the evidence a fact or an unproven theory?
- Is the evidence supported by data or research?
- Is the evidence relevant and up to date?
- Are the sources that are cited credible?
- Does the writer provide enough evidence to support the argument?
- Is the author biased or prejudiced in any way?

**A. Analyzing.** Match each argument for why Angkor declined (**1–5**) with pieces of evidence (**a–e**).

1. _____ Invaders conquered Angkor.
2. _____ A religious shift contributed to the city's decline.
3. _____ The royal court turned its back on Angkor.
4. _____ The water management system broke down.
5. _____ A weakened Angkor was further hurt by climate change.

**a.** In the 1300s, Southeast Asia experienced a period of severe drought.
**b.** A shift to Theravada Buddhism diminished the kings' royal authority.
**c.** Angkor's own engineers seem to have destroyed a dam.
**d.** Angkor's rulers often built new temple complexes and let older ones decay.
**e.** Historical records of Ayutthaya claim their warriors took Angkor.

**B. Evaluating.** Find other evidence in the reading passage that support the arguments above. Which argument for Angkor's decline do you think is most likely?

# Vocabulary Practice

**A. Definitions.** Read the information below. Then match each word in **red** with its definition.

During the past century, California has built a sophisticated **mechanism** for delivering water. Thousands of kilometers of pipes and **channels** cross the state, **dispersing** water for farms, factories, and homes. However, the state's water resources are now severely stretched.

Some reasons for the crisis are environmental. A three-year drought has drained most of the state's reservoirs to low levels. California's largest **internal** storehouse of surface water—the Sierra Nevada mountain range—has less snow due to warming temperatures, leaving the state more reliant on external sources.

Some experts argue that California is vulnerable to the same fate of ancient civilizations, such as the Khmer and the Maya. These civilizations collapsed when water resources became **scarce**.

Recently, laws have been introduced to promote water conservation in major cities. However, water experts say that to solve their water problems, Californians should learn to live within the water resources of a dry landscape.

1. _____: spreading over a wide area

2. _____: passageways along which water flows

3. _____: very small in amount; not plentiful

4. _____: located on the inside of something

5. _____: a machine or system for doing something

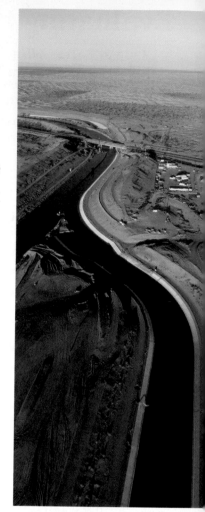

∧ Californian communities are dependent on water pumped in from the Colorado River.

**B. Words in Context.** Complete each sentence with the correct answer.

1. If someone shows **ingenuity** when solving a problem, he or she shows _____.
   a. skill or cleverness       b. lack of creativity

2. An event that **doomed** a civilization _____ it.
   a. helped                    b. destroyed

3. If you ate **subsequent** to your arrival at the hotel, you ate _____ arriving at the hotel.
   a. before                    b. after

4. A **regime** is a system of government, especially one that is _____.
   a. lenient                   b. harsh

5. If you **assume** something, you _____.
   a. believe something to be true without knowing it's true
   b. are sure of something even when others tell you the opposite

**Word Link** The word root **reg** means "rule" or "guide of," e.g., *regime, regalia, regal, regulate, regimented, region.*

# VIEWING Temples in the Jungle

## Before You Watch

**A. True or False.** What do you remember about Angkor from reading 1B? Mark the statements **T** (True) or **F** (False).

1. Angkor Wat is a symbol of classic Khmer (Cambodian) architecture.     **T**   **F**

2. Angkor Wat was originally built in honor of Buddha, but it later became a Hindu temple.     **T**   **F**

3. The first Europeans to arrive in Angkor found a healthy, thriving city.     **T**   **F**

4. Archeologists and historians are not sure why exactly Angkor collapsed.     **T**   **F**

5. Today, Angkor Wat is the world's largest religious monument.     **T**   **F**

⟨ Angkor Thom means "Great City." This temple complex, the Bayon, is a well-known and richly decorated Khmer temple there.

**B. Definitions.** Read these extracts from the video, and match each word(s) in **bold** with its definition.

1. This is Angkor, the capital of a **sophisticated** civilization that . . .

2. And more than five hundred years ago, they **fled** this grand city . . .

3. . . . prized for both its history and its **intrinsic** beauty . . .

4. Its story has been **pieced together** by archeologists and historians . . .

5. . . . developing **ingenious** irrigation systems to channel water . . .

a. _____ : original and clever     d. _____ : reconstructed

b. _____ : natural     e. _____ : ran away from

c. _____ : highly developed and complex

## While You Watch

**A. Noticing.** Check (✓) the topics that are mentioned in the video.

☐ the size of Angkor        ☐ the meaning of *Angkor* in Khmer

☐ when the Khmer fled Angkor        ☐ a visit by a French naturalist

☐ how long it took to build Angkor Wat        ☐ war between Angkor Wat and Angkor Thom

☐ attacks on Angkor        ☐ tourists who visit today

**B. Correction.** The captions below are not accurate. Use the information in the video to correct each caption.

1. When Henri Mouhot visited the ruins of Angkor, he found pictures of the city.

_____

_____

2. Angkor Wat served as a palace, a meeting place, and a funerary temple.

_____

_____

3. After the Chams attacked, Angkor Wat was abandoned and the king built Angkor Thom.

_____

_____

4. A huge battle early in the 14th century almost destroyed the Khmer people.

_____

_____

## After You Watch

**Discussion.** Discuss these questions with a partner.

1. What additional information did you learn from the video that is not mentioned in the passage on pages 19–23?

2. Does the information in the video contradict any of the information in the passage?

# BEYOND EARTH

A view of colliding galaxies, 70 million light-years away from Earth, combines visible light (blue) captured by the Hubble Space Telescope with never before seen swirls of gas revealed in a test image from the ALMA telescope.

## Warm Up

**Discuss these questions with a partner.**

1. What are some ways we can learn about what lies beyond Earth, or beyond our solar system?

2. How has astronomy helped human societies? How might it help us in the future?

3. The astronomer Galileo Galilei (1564–1642) said, "Doubt is the father of invention." What do you think he meant?

High in the Andes Mountains, a telescope larger than many cities reveals the secrets of the universe.

## Before You Read

**A. True or False.** Read the caption on page 31 and circle **T** (True) or **F** (False) for each sentence.

1. Traditional telescopes can see only a limited part of the spectrum of electromagnetic radiation.      **T**     **F**

2. ALMA is a traditional type of telescope.      **T**     **F**

3. ALMA can detect electromagnetic radiation of longer wavelengths than the human eye can.      **T**     **F**

4. Traditional telescopes are able to see deep-space gas clouds and other dark, cold areas.      **T**     **F**

**B. Skimming and Predicting.** Quickly skim the section headings on pages 31–36. What do you think each section will be about? Note your predictions. Then read the passage to check your ideas.

a. An Eye on the Heavens _____

b. The Perfect Location _____

c. Assembling the Array _____

d. Early Discoveries _____

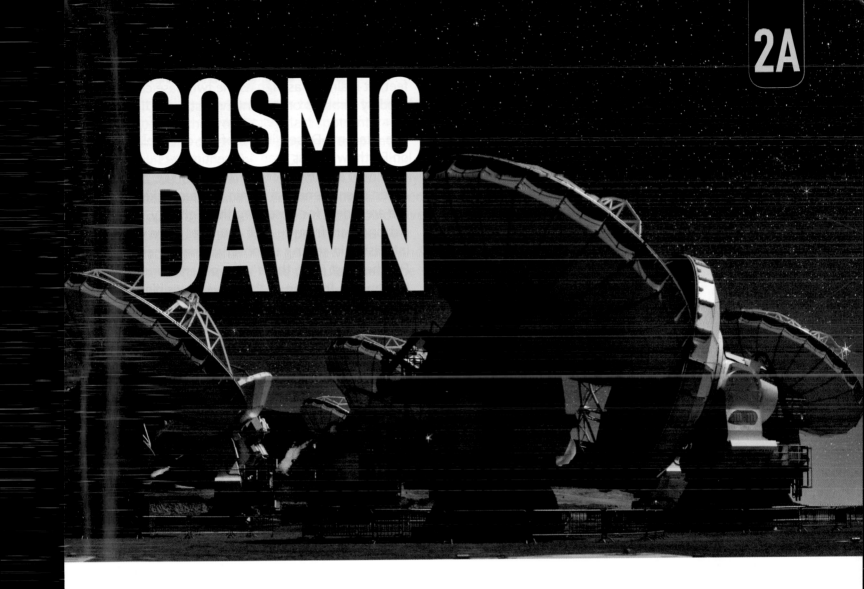

# COSMIC DAWN

## 1 An Eye on the Heavens

**A** Telescopes have come a long way since the first ones were invented early in the 17th century. Traditional telescopes allow astronomers to view objects in space thanks to the visible light
5 those objects **emit**, or reflect. However, for modern telescopes, any electromagnetic radiation will suffice for the purpose of viewing objects in space. Extremely hot objects, such as stars, emit not only visible light but also high-energy gamma radiation. Specialized telescopes—such as NASA's space-based Chandra X-ray
10 Observatory—are built to detect such radiation. Cold objects—like comets and asteroids—emit low-energy radiation, which is invisible to the naked eye. Much of the universe is even colder than this. The clouds of dust and gas of which stars are made are only slightly warmer than absolute zero—the temperature at which atoms stop
15 moving. To capture images of cold objects, astronomers use radio telescopes.

∧ Traditional telescopes are able to detect only visible light, which is a very small part of the spectrum of electromagnetic radiation. A new type of telescope, called ALMA (pictured above) can detect radiation of long wavelengths. ALMA has revealed to astronomers the dark, cold areas of space and the most distant galaxies invisible to traditional telescopes.

# ALMA's Ten-Mile-Wide Zoom

Elevation: 5,000 meters (16,400 feet)

Rearranging antennas on the wide plateau is like adjusting a camera's zoom. When the antennas are far apart, the telescope focuses on tight sections of the sky and fine details. Grouping the antennas closer together is like using a wide-angle lens and takes in wider areas of the sky.

ALMA consists of two telescope arrays working together. Two massive transporters relocate antennas in the main array with submillimeter precision. The Morita Array (right), a separate group of 16 antennas built by Japan, targets large-scale structures in the universe.

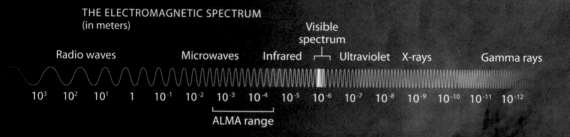

THE ELECTROMAGNETIC SPECTRUM
(in meters)

Visible spectrum

Radio waves    Microwaves    Infrared    Ultraviolet    X-rays    Gamma rays

$10^3$  $10^2$  $10^1$  1  $10^{-1}$  $10^{-2}$  $10^{-3}$  $10^{-4}$  $10^{-5}$  $10^{-6}$  $10^{-7}$  $10^{-8}$  $10^{-9}$  $10^{-10}$  $10^{-11}$  $10^{-12}$

ALMA range

One long baseline can detect fine details; additonal baselines reduce interference.

Expanding from two to three antennas creates three baselines.

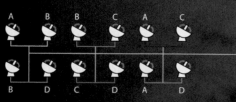
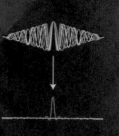

Adding one more antenna doubles the baselines to six. Adding even more antennas further sharpens the signal and reduces the noise.

ALMA's 66 antennas can create 1,291 separate baselines, giving the telescope superb sensitivity and the ability to capture fine details.

SOUTH
AMERICA
ALMA
CHILE

Mt. Everest
Atacama Plateau (ALMA location)
Machu Picchu

🛰 12-meter antenna
△ Antenna pad
— Baseline

Service
roads

Morita Array

Ten-mile diameter

# Early Discoveries

**K** The installation was officially opened in March 2013 and named the Atacama Large Millimeter/submillimeter[5] Array, or ALMA for short. Even before it was completely set up, it had already produced results. The year before, with only 16 antennas **in operation**, researchers led by Caltech's[6] Joaquin Vieira had used ALMA to view 26 distant galaxies. From the images they gathered, they were able to deduce that many stars in those galaxies were a billion years younger than astronomers had previously thought.

**L** Since the official opening of ALMA, there has been a steady stream of other discoveries of great interest to astronomers. In July 2013, the telescope's high-resolution[7] images provided clues that may help answer a question that has long puzzled astronomers: Why are massive galaxies so rare in the universe? ALMA is also helping researchers understand how planets are born, by providing the first-ever images of the planet-forming process.

**M** These observations are just the beginning. In the future, ALMA will show us even finer details of galaxies and star systems. On a dry plateau a few miles from where shepherds[8] once slept, our eyes will open upon an unseen universe.

---

5 **Millimeter/submillimeter** refers to radiation wavelengths that the telescope can detect, from slightly longer than one millimeter (0.001m) to slightly shorter than one submillimeter (0.0001m).

6 **Caltech** is the abbreviation for the California Institute of Technology, located in California, U.S.A.

7 **High-resolution** images or photographs are extremely clear down to the smallest details.

8 A **shepherd** is a person whose job is to look after herds of sheep, goats, llamas, etc.

Four of the giant dishes forming the Atacama Large Millimeter/submillimeter Array (ALMA) stand in the desert. ALMA's gigantic eye is able to see deep into the early universe, when stars and galaxies were first formed billions of years ago. >

# Reading Comprehension

**Multiple Choice.** Choose the best answer for each question.

**Detail**
1. What images can radio telescopes capture that other telescopes cannot?
   a. images of distant hot objects
   b. images of distant cold objects
   c. images of objects that emit light
   d. images of objects that emit high-energy radiation

**Purpose**
2. What is the purpose of paragraph B?
   a. to describe how radio telescopes have changed since the 1960s
   b. to point out the limitation of ground-based dish antennas
   c. to emphasize that radio telescopes can view asteroids, planets, and comets
   d. to give reasons that low-energy radiation is absorbed and distorted by water vapor in the atmosphere

**Detail**
3. What did the group that included Chilean astronomer Hernán Quintana find challenging about the Chajnantor plateau?
   a. It was very difficult to get to.
   b. No one was used to the thin air.
   c. The high elevation made everyone cold.
   d. The best spots were already taken by other astronomers.

**Vocabulary**
4. The phrase *from scratch* (line 114) is closest in meaning to
   _____.
   a. without receiving permission to start
   b. from local materials that anyone can find
   c. from old materials that are difficult to find
   d. from the beginning and without using any work done before

**Cohesion**
5. Where would be the best place to insert this sentence? *"We had to assemble a little city on the mountainside in the middle of nowhere," said Al Wootten, the lead North American scientist on the project.*
   a. before line 100          b. after line 115
   c. before line 103          d. after line 123

**Detail**
6. According to the information on pages 34–35, what is the best way to get a wide-angle shot of a galaxy?
   a. Use a telescope with antennas spaced far apart.
   b. Use several telescopes all aimed at the same place.
   c. Use several telescopes all aimed at different places.
   d. Use a telescope with antennas spaced closely together.

**Sequence**
7. Which of these things happened last?
   a. The installation site was officially opened.
   b. Two transporters were brought to the installation site.
   c. A massive supercomputer was installed at the installation site.
   d. ALMA was used to view 26 distant galaxies.

## Critical Thinking

**Inferring:** The setting up of ALMA was an international project in which several nations were involved. What might be the challenges of this kind of collaboration?

**Discussion:** Where else in the world would be a good location for a project like ALMA? Why?

# Determining the Main Idea of Paragraphs

While it's important to have an overall understanding of a reading, it's equally important to be able to determine the main idea of each paragraph. To get a quick sense of what a paragraph is about, read the first line and then quickly skim the rest. Some paragraphs also have headings; these often indicate what the main idea is. Understanding the main idea of each paragraph is especially useful when you are taking notes, or when you are creating a summary outline or word web of the reading.

**A. Multiple Choice.** Look back at the reading on pages 31–36. What is each paragraph's main idea? Choose the correct answer.

1. Paragraph A    a. the history of telescopes
                      b. different types of telescopes

2. Paragraph C    a. the perfect place to locate antenna arrays
                      b. advantages of using portable arrays of antennas

3. Paragraph E    a. why the Atacama Desert is an ideal spot for observatories
                      b. the challenges of setting up ALMA in the Atacama Desert

**B. Matching.** Match the main ideas to the correct paragraphs.

1. Discoveries made before the observatory was officially opened
    a. paragraph B                    b. paragraph K

2. The arrival in Chile of the first piece of dish antenna
    a. paragraph I                     b. paragraph M

3. How different countries came to cooperate on the observatory project
    a. paragraph D                  b. paragraph G

4. Personal reactions to the trip in the desert
    a. paragraph F                   b. paragraph H

5. The challenges of building an observatory in the remote desert
    a. paragraph B                  b. paragraph H

6. How the work was completed over a five-year period
    a. paragraph H                  b. paragraph J

7. Recent discoveries that are helping astronomers better understand the universe
    a. paragraph B                  b. paragraph L

8. How the discoveries made so far are only the beginning
    a. paragraph C                  b. paragraph M

# Vocabulary Practice

**A. Completion.** Complete the information by circling the appropriate word in each pair.

## Top Discoveries Awaiting Next Big Telescope

Expectations are high for a planned $8 billion telescope. Designed to replace the Hubble Space Telescope, the James Webb Space Telescope will have 18 mirror sections. Once these are **1. (positioned / interrupted)** and assembled in space, they will create the largest orbiting mirror ever seen. Scientists on Earth can expect to see photos about six months after the telescope has been **2. (accompanied / set up)**.

When the telescope is put into **3. (operation / companion)**, it will allow astronomers to look back to when stars began to form in the universe. The first stars in the universe are believed to have been 30 to 300 times larger than our sun and millions of times as bright. They would have burned for only a few million years before dying in tremendous explosions. The Webb will be able to detect the earliest of these explosions.

The Webb sees in infrared light, a wavelength that warm objects **4. (coordinate / emit)** in large amounts, which can be used to see farther and to see through thick cosmic dust. This means the telescope will be able to see into the star-creating centers of galaxies as never before. And because the telescope is in space and not on the ground, light does not have to pass through the atmosphere, which can **5. (interpret / distort)** an image.

∧ Webb Telescope officials describe their goal as learning about the first galaxies when they were just babies. The Hubble Space Telescope (above) has been looking at toddlers.

**B. Words in Context.** Complete each sentence with the correct answer.

1. A **companion** is someone you _____.
   a. avoid talking to      b. spend a lot of time with

2. If you **interrupt** someone, you say something while the other person is _____.
   a. speaking      b. listening

3. It's best to be _____ when you need to **coordinate** something important.
   a. organized      b. fun-loving

4. When you **interpret** something, you _____ of it.
   a. give the origin      b. explain the meaning

5. If you **accompany** someone, you _____ them.
   a. go with      b. move toward

> **Word Link**
> The word root **mit** means "send" or "throw," e.g., *emit, transmit, permit, omit, admit, submit, commit, remit, intermittent.*

Jupiter

Earth

## Before You Read

**A. Discussion.** Read the caption and discuss these questions with a partner.

1. What do astronomers know about CT Cha b? Why is it unusual?

2. What is an exoplanet? Why do you think astronomers are hunting for them? What do you think the main challenges are?

**B. Skimming and Predicting.** Read the title, captions, and section headings and skim the rest of the passage on pages 41–45. Then answer the questions.

1. Which two main questions do you think the passage is going to answer?

☐ How do astronomers locate and identify other Earthlike planets?

☐ Why is finding other Earthlike planets important?

☐ Will other Earthlike planets be similar to our own?

2. What do you think are possible answers to the questions you chose above? Read the article to check your ideas.

⌃ Jupiter and Saturn may be large relative to our home planet, but they're small compared to CT Cha b, one of the 1,500-plus exoplanets—planets circling stars outside our own solar system— that astronomers have so far discovered. With more than twice Jupiter's diameter and 17 times its mass, CT Cha b is, as of 2014, the largest exoplanet for which a diameter has been measured. It orbits a young star more than 500 light-years away.

Saturn

# PLANET HUNTERS:
# ARE WE ALONE?

**A** 1    It took humans thousands of years to explore our own planet, and centuries to comprehend our neighboring planets. Nowadays,
5    new worlds are being discovered every week.

**B**    **To date**, astronomers have identified more than 1,500 "exoplanets"—worlds orbiting stars other than the sun. There's a "hot Saturn" 260
10    light-years from Earth that orbits its parent star so rapidly that a year there lasts less than three days. Circling another star 150 light-years out is a scorched "hot Jupiter," whose upper atmosphere is being blasted off to form a
15    gigantic cometlike tail. Astronomers have found three planets orbiting a pulsar—the remains of a once mighty star shrunk into a spinning atomic **nucleus** the size of a city. Some worlds have evidently fallen into their suns. Others have
20    been thrown out of their systems to become "floaters" that wander in eternal darkness.

**C**    Among all these, scientists are eager to find a hint of the familiar: planets resembling Earth. That is, planets orbiting their stars at just the
25    right distance—neither too hot nor too cold—to support life as we know it. We have not yet found planets that are quite like our own, presumably because they're **inconspicuous**. To see a planet as small and dim as ours
30    amid the glare of its star is like trying to see a firefly in a fireworks display. Yet by pushing technology to the limits, astronomers are rapidly approaching the day when they can find another Earth. And when they do, they
35    can investigate it for signs of life.

# In Search of Other Earths

The most direct approach to finding a planet is to take a picture of it with a telescope. At the time of writing, astronomers had detected about half of the exoplanets this way. All of them are big and bright and conveniently far away from their stars.

A more effective way to detect an exoplanet, though, is to use a method known as the Doppler technique. This involves analyzing starlight for evidence that the star is being pulled by the gravitational pull of its planet. In recent years, astronomers have refined the technique to a fine degree. Now they can tell when a planet is pulling its star by only one

∨ Exoplanets plotted by mass and distance from Earth

EXOPLANET MASS
- 7,000 EARTHS
- 6,000
- 5,000
- 4,000
- 3,000 ◄ BODIES MORE MASSIVE THAN 10 JUPITERS
- 2,000 (3,180 EARTHS) MAY BE FAILED STARS
- 1,000 CALLED BROWN DWARFS.
- LESS THAN 1,000

HD 43848 b
THE MOST MASSIVE
(7,946 EARTHS)

FIRST CONFIRMED
EXOPLANET ORBITING
A SUNLIKE STAR

FOMALHAUT b
PLANETS OF GLIESE 581

SOLAR
SYSTEM

10
LIGHT-YEARS
AWAY

EARTH

SATURN
95 EARTHS

JUPITER
318 EARTHS

## True Giants

Colossal Saturn and Jupiter are tiny compared with the current lineup of exoplanets. The largest for which a diameter has been measured is CT Cha b (artist's conception below). More than twice Jupiter's diameter and 17 times its mass, it orbits a young star, CT Cha, in the constellation Chamaelon.

CT CHA b
5,403 EARTHS
MORE THAN 500 LIGHT-YEARS AWAY

meter a second—about human walking speed. That's sufficient to detect a giant planet in a big orbit, or a small one if it's close to its star. But the Earth tugs the sun around at only one-tenth walking speed, or about the rate that an infant can crawl. So far, astronomers are not able to detect so tiny a signal.

55

To see a planet as small and dim as ours amid the glare of its star is like trying to see a firefly in a fireworks display.

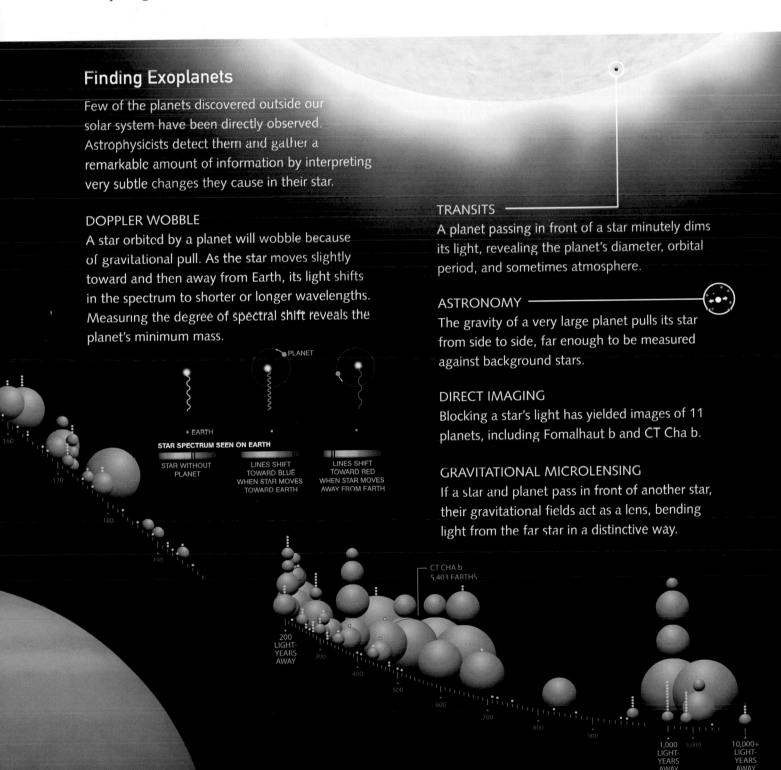

## Finding Exoplanets

Few of the planets discovered outside our solar system have been directly observed. Astrophysicists detect them and gather a remarkable amount of information by interpreting very subtle changes they cause in their star.

### DOPPLER WOBBLE

A star orbited by a planet will wobble because of gravitational pull. As the star moves slightly toward and then away from Earth, its light shifts in the spectrum to shorter or longer wavelengths. Measuring the degree of spectral shift reveals the planet's minimum mass.

PLANET

EARTH

STAR SPECTRUM SEEN ON EARTH

STAR WITHOUT PLANET

LINES SHIFT TOWARD BLUE WHEN STAR MOVES TOWARD EARTH

LINES SHIFT TOWARD RED WHEN STAR MOVES AWAY FROM EARTH

### TRANSITS

A planet passing in front of a star minutely dims its light, revealing the planet's diameter, orbital period, and sometimes atmosphere.

### ASTRONOMY

The gravity of a very large planet pulls its star from side to side, far enough to be measured against background stars.

### DIRECT IMAGING

Blocking a star's light has yielded images of 11 planets, including Fomalhaut b and CT Cha b.

### GRAVITATIONAL MICROLENSING

If a star and planet pass in front of another star, their gravitational fields act as a lens, bending light from the far star in a distinctive way.

CT CHA b
5,403 EARTHS

160

170

180

190

200 LIGHT-YEARS AWAY

300

400

500

600

700

800

900

1,000 LIGHT-YEARS AWAY

5,000

10,000+ LIGHT-YEARS AWAY

**F**

60 Another approach is to watch a star for a slight periodic dip in its brightness. This occurs when an orbiting planet passes in front of it and blocks a fraction of its light. At most, a tenth of all planetary systems are **oriented** so that these mini-eclipses,

65 called transits, are visible from Earth. So astronomers have to monitor a lot of stars to capture just a few transits.

**G**

The dream of astronomers is to discover a rocky planet roughly the size of Earth orbiting

70 in a habitable zone. That is, not so close to a star that the planet's water has been baked away, nor so far out that it has frozen into ice. If they succeed, they will have found what biologists believe could be a promising

75 abode[1] for life.

**H**

The best hunting grounds may be dwarf stars, smaller than the sun. Firstly, dwarf stars are plentiful (seven of the ten stars nearest to Earth are dwarf stars). They also provide a

80 **steady** supply of sunlight to any life-bearing planets within their habitable zone.

**I**

Additionally, dwarf stars are dim, and so the habitable zone lies closer in. (Imagine dwarf stars as small campfires, where campers must

85 sit close to be comfortable.) If the planet is closer to the star, it's easier for astronomers to detect a transit observation. A close-in planet also **exerts** a stronger pull on its star. That makes it easier to detect with the

90 Doppler method. Indeed, the most promising planet yet found—the "super Earth" Gliese 581 d—orbits in the habitable zone of a red dwarf star only a third the mass of the sun.

# Life—But Not as We Know It?

**J**

95 If an Earthlike planet is found within a star's habitable zone, a dedicated space telescope could be used to look for signs of life. Most likely, scientists will examine the light coming from the planet for possible biosignatures such

100 as atmospheric methane and oxygen. They might also look for the "red edge" produced when chlorophyll[2]-containing plants reflect red light.

**K**

Directly detecting and analyzing the planet's

105 own light will not be easy. Its light might be just one ten-billionth the light of the star's. But when a planet transits, starlight shining through the atmosphere could reveal clues to its **composition** that a space telescope might

110 be able to detect.

**L**

The challenge facing scientists is not just having to perform a chemical analysis of planets they cannot see. Scientists must also keep in mind that extraterrestrial life may be

115 very different from life here at home. The lack of the red edge from an exoplanet, for instance, does not exclude the possibility of life. Life thrived on Earth for billions of years before land plants appeared and populated the

120 continents.

**M**

The problem for scientists is that biological evolution is inherently unpredictable. It is possible that life originated on an Earthlike planet at the same time it did here. But life

125 on that planet today would almost certainly be very different from terrestrial[3] life. As the biologist Jacques Monod once **commented**, life evolves not only through necessity—the universal workings of natural law—but also

130 through chance, the unpredictable intervention of countless accidents.

---

1 An **abode** is a home.

2 **Chlorophyll** is the green coloring matter in plants, which enables them to convert sunlight into energy.

3 When we say something is **terrestrial**, we mean it grows or lives on Earth.

**N** Chance has played a role many times in our planet's history. The most dramatic examples are the mass extinctions that wiped out
135 millions of species and created room for new life forms to evolve. Some of these accidents appear to have been caused by comets or asteroids colliding with Earth. An impact 65 million years ago, for instance, helped kill off
140 the dinosaurs and opened up opportunities for the distant ancestors of human beings. **Hence**, scientists look not just for exoplanets identical to the modern Earth, but for planets resembling the Earth as it used to be or might
145 have been.

**O** It was not easy for earlier pioneers to undertake explorations of the ocean floors, map the far side of the moon, or discern evidence of oceans beneath the frozen
150 surfaces of Jupiter's moons. Neither will it be easy to find life on the planets of other stars. But we now have reason to believe that billions of such planets must exist. They hold the promise of expanding not only the **scope**
155 of human knowledge but also the richness of the human imagination.

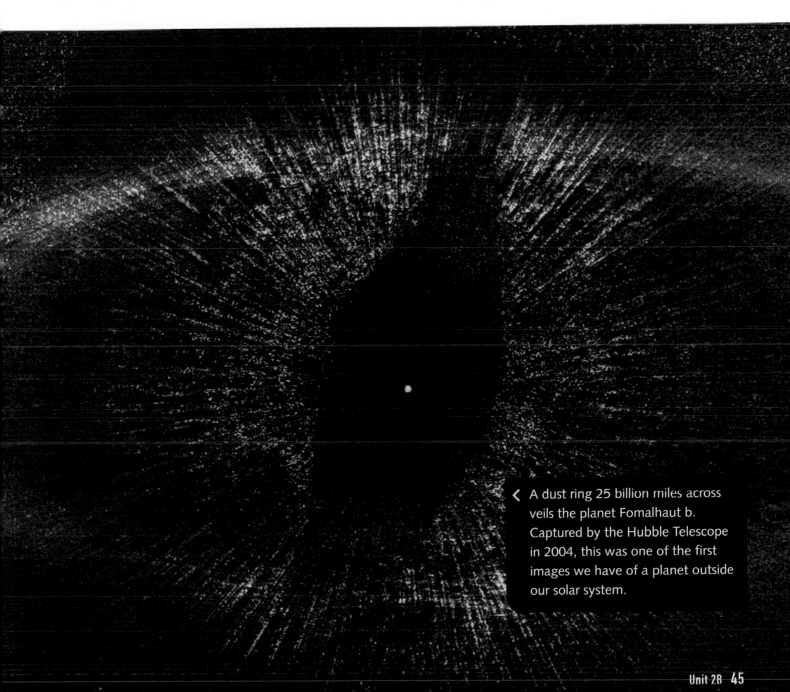

< A dust ring 25 billion miles across veils the planet Fomalhaut b. Captured by the Hubble Telescope in 2004, this was one of the first images we have of a planet outside our solar system.

# Reading Comprehension

**Multiple Choice.** Choose the best answer for each question.

Gist

**1.** The best alternative title for this reading would be _____.
   a. How Exoplanets Were First Discovered
   b. Is There Intelligent Life on Other Planets?
   c. The Search for Earthlike Planets Around Other Stars
   d. The Story of Hot Saturn, Hot Jupiter, and Super Earth

Detail

**3.** When this article was written, how many Earthlike exoplanets had been discovered?
   a. over 1,500      b. billions
   c. about 150       d. none

Detail

**2.** According to the author, a *floater* (line 21) is a planet that

   _____.
   a. is the size of a city
   b. has fallen into its sun
   c. is circling a pulsar star
   d. is no longer circling a star

Vocabulary

**4.** The use of the word *dedicated* (line 96) indicates that the space telescope mentioned in this sentence will _____.
   a. be extremely high-powered
   b. require enthusiastic support
   c. be used primarily for one purpose
   d. involve technology not now available

Detail

**5.** The author indicates in paragraph K that observing and analyzing light from an exoplanet _____.
   a. will probably show signs of life
   b. will be difficult but not impossible
   c. has been accomplished several times
   d. can be done by telescopes on the ground

Inference

**6.** The author implies that on some exoplanets _____.
   a. life may have evolved without chlorophyll-bearing plants
   b. chlorophyll-bearing plants would not produce a "red edge"
   c. methane, ozone, and oxygen may produce a "red edge"
   d. life will be similar to that on Earth if it evolved at the same time

Cohesion

**7.** Where would be the best place in paragraph L to insert this sentence? *"The modern Earth may be the worst model we could use in searching for life elsewhere,"* notes Caleb Scharf, head of Columbia University's Astrobiology Center.
   a. before the first sentence
   b. after the first sentence
   c. after the second sentence
   d. after the third sentence

## Critical Thinking

**Inferring:** Do you think the author believes that Earthlike exoplanets will be found in the near future? Why or why not? Find sentences in the article to support your view.

**Discussion:** Do you believe that life on exoplanets will be found? Why or why not? If yes, what do you think it will be like?

# Understanding Cause and Effect Relationships

In many texts you read—a scientific article, an encyclopedia entry, a business report—authors make use of cause and effect relationships to explain how and why things happen. Sometimes an author may use signal words to indicate this relationship.

**Cause/Effect:**   *therefore, . . .*   *hence, . . .*   *consequently, . . .*   *as a result, . . .*
*so . . .*

**Effect/Cause:**   *. . . because . . .*   *. . . since . . .*   *. . . due to (the fact that) . . .*

Sometimes, however, an author indicates cause and effect in other ways, or the author may not state it directly at all. The reader must then infer the relationship.

**Matching.** Match these effects given in the article (**1–8**) with the causes (**a–h**).

1. \_\_\_\_\_ A year on "hot Saturn" is only about three days long . . .

2. \_\_\_\_\_ So far, astronomers have not been able to locate any Earthlike exoplanets . . .

3. \_\_\_\_\_ Scientists have been able to observe about half of the known exoplanets by photographing them through a telescope . . .

4. \_\_\_\_\_ To observe transits, astronomers will have to observe many stars . . .

5. \_\_\_\_\_ When studying exoplanets, scientists look for oxygen and for the "red edge" . . .

6. \_\_\_\_\_ Scientists know that there can be life on planets without chlorophyll-bearing plants . . .

7. \_\_\_\_\_ If an exoplanet does not show a "red edge," it doesn't necessarily mean it is lifeless . . .

8. \_\_\_\_\_ In the distant past, mass extinctions of plants and animals took place . . .

a. because only about 10 percent of these "mini-eclipses" can be seen from our planet.

b. because life on an exoplanet may be very different from life on present-day Earth.

c. because they are much smaller and less bright than the stars they circle.

d. because the Earth was struck by asteroids and comets.

e. because it orbits its star so quickly.

f. because these may be signs that life exists on these worlds.

g. because life existed on Earth for a very long time before land plants appeared.

h. because their size, brightness, and distance from their stars make them relatively easy to observe.

# Vocabulary Practice

**A. Completion.** Complete the information by circling the appropriate word in each pair.

### Alien Contact More Likely by "Mail" Than Radio, Study Says

A new study suggests it is more energy-efficient to communicate across interstellar space by sending physical material—a sort of message in a bottle—than beams of electromagnetic radiation. Matter made of solid **1. (comment / composition)**, such as organic or genetic material, can hold more information and journey farther than radio waves, which disperse as they travel.

**2. (Hence / To date)**, the main focus among alien-hunters has been on radiation—radio and optical waves. Although much energy has been **3. (oriented / exerted)** on the search for life on other planets, signs of alien life have been **4. (conspicuous / steady)** only by their absence. That does not mean that life is not present somewhere on a distant planet; instead, the lack of signals could be because radio waves are diminished as they travel across space. **5. (Hence / Steadily)**, the great majority of their energy is wasted.

A more energy-efficient way of communicating over great distances is to send a physical object with encoded information. However, the problem with this method is its slow speed. As astronomer Seth Shostak **6. (commented / exerted)**, "It's like the difference between sea post and airmail." Nevertheless, some astronomers argue we should be less concerned about trying to communicate within the **7. (nucleus / scope)** of our own lifetime. It may take tens of thousands of years for a message to reach and return from an alien civilization. Expecting to have a two-way conversation may be a mistake.

︿ Many scientists consider extraterrestrial life to be plausible, but there is no direct evidence of its existence.

**B. Definitions.** Match the correct form of each word or phrase in **red** from **A** with its definition.

1. _____: the central part of an atom or a cell

2. _____: the whole extent or area of something

3. _____: facing a particular direction

4. _____: to give an opinion or explanation

5. _____: to put a lot of effort into something

6. _____: regularly and evenly

7. _____: up until now

8. _____: easy to see

9. _____: the way an item's parts are put together

10. _____: as a result; and so

> **Word Link**
> The word root **com-** means "together" or "with," e.g., *composition, commemorate, compassion, compile, comparison.*

# VIEWING Comet Watchers

## Before You Watch

**Discussion.** Read the information about a famous comet. Then discuss the questions below with a partner.

∧ The Comet Halley can be seen from Earth every 75–76 years. Sightings of the comet go back centuries.

**Comet Halley**

**Age:** 4.5 billion years old (same age as the sun)

**First recorded sighting:** 240 B.C. by Chinese astronomers

**Named after:** English astronomer Edmond Halley

**Time to orbit the sun:** about 200 years

**Composition:** ice, dust, and gas

**Nucleus size:** 14 km (8.3 miles) long and 8 km (5 miles) wide

**Last appearance:** 1986

**Frequency of appearance:** every 75–76 years

1. Could you have seen the comet the last time it was seen from Earth?

2. When will it next be seen from Earth?

3. How easy do you think it is to see the comet from Earth? What could make viewing it easier?

# While You Watch

**A. Sequencing.** Number these topics from 1 to 5 in the order they are first mentioned in the video.

- [ ] viewing the comet with telescopes
- [ ] viewing the comet using spacecraft
- [ ] how early explorers used the stars to navigate
- [ ] advantages of Mauna Kea as a viewing point
- [ ] the comet's age and frequency of appearance

**B. Completion.** Complete the word web about the video. Use words from the box. Two words are extra.

| camera | dust | gases | ice | pollution |
|---|---|---|---|---|
| spacecraft | tail | temperatures | volcano | winds |

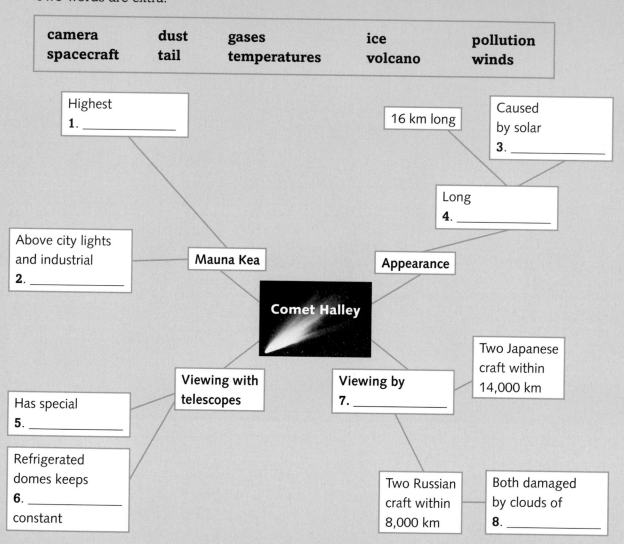

Highest
**1.** _____

Caused by solar
**3.** _____

16 km long

Long
**4.** _____

Above city lights and industrial
**2.** _____

Mauna Kea

Appearance

**Comet Halley**

Has special
**5.** _____

Viewing with telescopes

Viewing by
**7.** _____

Two Japanese craft within 14,000 km

Refrigerated domes keeps
**6.** _____
constant

Two Russian craft within 8,000 km

Both damaged by clouds of
**8.** _____

# After You Watch

**Discussion.** Discuss these questions with a partner.

1. Astronomer Dale Cruikshank says that stars help us "understand more about ourselves as well as the world we live in." What do you think he means? Do you agree?

2. Has the information in this unit changed your view of astronomy in any way? If so, how?

# HEALTH AND GENES

Exercise and a healthy diet are
two main factors in maintaining
good health. However, studies are
revealing that genetics may play
an even bigger part.

## Warm Up

**Discuss these questions with a partner.**

1. What are the most common illnesses affecting people in your country? Why do you think they are common?

2. Do you know anyone who suffers from allergies? What do you think causes them?

3. Do you think a person's health is largely due to his or her lifestyle and environment, or is it decided from the time he or she is born?

51

Tobacco smoking, physical inactivity, and poor diet are the main lifestyle-related factors leading to **cardiovascular** diseases (CVDs), which cause heart attacks and strokes. In the United States and Europe, CVDs have reached epidemic levels and are responsible for nearly half of all deaths. CVD-related **mortality** is also rising in the developing world, as more people become exposed to the risk factors. A diet high in cholesterol, a substance prevalent in many fatty foods, is a leading cause of **coronary** heart disease. High levels of cholesterol can cause plaque to form in **arteries**. This eventually leads to atherosclerosis (arterial blockage), which restricts the flow of blood and causes heart attacks. In addition to lifestyle factors, scientists are looking at how other factors, including genetics, may also contribute to the high incidence of CVDs.

# Before You Read

**A. Discussion.** Read the information above and use the glossary (on the right) to help you understand the words in **bold**. Then answer these questions.

1. What are the main factors affecting the health of the heart?

2. In your own words, explain the process that can lead to heart disease.

**B. Skimming and Predicting.** Read the title and first paragraph, and skim the rest of the passage on pages 53–58. What do you think the passage is going to be mainly about? Then read the passage to check your ideas.

☐ concern about poor eating habits and the effect on heart disease

☐ growing interest in the connection between heart disease and heredity

☐ different methods used over the years to treat heart disease

### Key Terms

**arteries** tubes in the body that carry blood from the heart to other parts of the body

**cardiovascular** relating to the heart and blood vessels

**coronary** belonging or relating to the heart

**mortality (rate)** (the number of) deaths in a particular place

# MENDING BROKEN HEARTS

**A** 1   Cheeseburgers, smoking, **stress**: These are the prime suspects on the list of risk factors for heart disease, a global problem reaching epidemic **proportions**. Now discoveries about genetic triggers may help us spot
5   trouble before it starts.

**B**   Don Steffensen was pulling duck-hunting decoys[1] out on a small lake one fall afternoon in southwestern Iowa when his heart attack hit. The attack was massive and unexpected. It's likely that Steffensen survived only because a friend was carrying nitroglycerin tablets[2] and quickly slipped one
10   under his tongue.

**C**   The Steffensen clan is enormous—more than 200 relatives spread over three generations. Although heart trouble is common in the family, it had never seemed unusual. The Steffensens were raised on the kind of farm food that the state is famous for—ham balls, meatloaf, pie, macaroni and cheese.

^ Danuel Allen lived 54 days with an artificial heart implanted in his chest while waiting for a real human heart.

1   A **decoy** is a person or thing used to lure someone into danger. In hunting, it is an image of a bird or an animal used to lure game.

2   **Nitroglycerin tablets**, or glyceryl trinitrate tablets, can be used as heart medication.

∧ This family from Iowa, U.S.A., has been identified as having the heart attack gene.

**D** 15 But could the high incidence of heart trouble among the Steffensens be related to something else besides high-fat diets? Eleven years after Don's attack, his wife, Barbara, happened to overhear a doctor 20 describing a study about the genetics of heart attacks. Curious, Don and 20 of his relatives each **submitted** a sample of blood to the Cleveland Clinic, where the research was being conducted.

**E** 25 Eric Topol, a cardiologist[3] and genetics researcher at the clinic, spent a year studying their DNA. Each person's genome has millions of individual variations, but Topol was looking for something distinctive. The **mutation** he 30 and his team finally spotted—in a gene called *MEF2A*—produced a faulty protein. "We knew we had something," Topol says. "But the question was: How does this sick protein, present at birth, lead to heart attacks 50 years 35 later in life?"

---

3 A **cardiologist** is a doctor who specializes in dealing with the heart and its diseases.

As one doctor commented, any person's heart attack risk is "50 percent genetic and 50 percent cheeseburger."

**F** Topol himself is lean and weathered in a cowboyish way. He talks slowly and eats minimally: salads for dinner and high-fiber cereal for breakfast. He doesn't eat lunch at all. "People have looked at the cadavers[4] of men in their 20s who died in car accidents or as casualties of war, and nearly all had arterial cholesterol deposits," Topol says. "This disease starts much earlier than people realize."

**G** Topol's study did find that although dysfunctional[5] *MEF2A* is very rare, the chance of heart disease in those carrying it may approach 100 percent. Most other genetic variations identified thus far increase the risk by much less.

**H** "Heart disease is not a one- or two-gene problem," says Steven Ellis, a Cleveland Clinic cardiologist. Ellis oversees a genetic study that collects DNA samples from patients who enter hospitals with atherosclerosis. Ellis, like most cardiac researchers, suspects that dozens of genes contribute to a predisposition[6] to heart disease. Of the several dozen genes, each may contribute just one percent to a person's total risk—an amount that may be **compounded** or offset by outside factors like diet. As one doctor commented, any person's heart attack risk is "50 percent genetic and 50 percent cheeseburger."

**I** The point of tracking down all these small mutations, Ellis explains, is to create a comprehensive blood test—one that could calculate a person's genetic **susceptibility** by adding up the number of risky (and, eventually, beneficial) variables. Combined with other important factors, such as smoking, weight, blood pressure, and cholesterol levels, doctors could decide which patients need aggressive treatment, such as high-dose statins,[7] and which ones are likely to benefit from exercise or other lifestyle changes. Some genes can already predict whose cholesterol level will respond strongly to dietary changes, and whose won't. Assessing risk is crucial, Ellis says, because heart disease is often invisible. Fifty percent of men and 64 percent of women who die of heart disease die suddenly, without experiencing any previous symptoms.

**J** Although standard tests can detect atherosclerosis, they aren't foolproof.[8] They may reveal plaques, but give no indication whether or not they are life-threatening.

---

4 A **cadaver** is a dead body, especially one intended for dissection.

5 Something (in medical situations, an organ or a body part) that is **dysfunctional** is not working or functioning normally.

6 If something or someone has a **predisposition** to a disease or condition, they are more likely to get that disease, or suffer from that condition.

7 **Statins** are a class of drug used to lower cholesterol levels.

8 If something is **foolproof**, it is incapable of going wrong or failing to succeed.

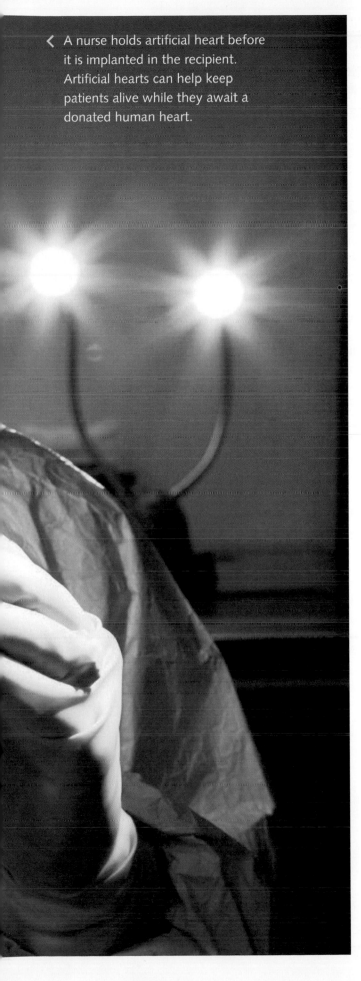

<A nurse holds artificial heart before it is implanted in the recipient. Artificial hearts can help keep patients alive while they await a donated human heart.

**K** Tests like angiography, for example, in which doctors inject a dye into the bloodstream and
90 track it with X-rays, can show how much blood is flowing through an artery, but cannot discern the plaques embedded inside the artery wall—often the **principal** cause in a heart attack.

**L** 95 Until there are tests, genetic or otherwise, that give a clearer measure of risk, everyone would be advised to exercise, watch their diet, and take statins for elevated cholesterol—the same advice doctors gave when the clogged-pipes
100 model of heart disease was unchallenged (see page 58).

**M** But statins, like any drug, carry the risk of side effects: Muscle aches are a well-known effect, and periodic blood tests to check liver function
105 are recommended. The fact is, many of us just like to eat cheeseburgers, lie back and watch TV, and get around in cars. And it's hard, says Leslie Cho, a director at the Cleveland Clinic, for a person to worry about a disease that hits
110 ten years down the road—particularly since heart patients, unlike cancer patients, can't easily observe the progress of their disease. "You've done damage over years, and it will take years to undo that damage. That's a very
115 hard thing to sell," she says. "We do what we can, but then people go home."

**N** The good news is that genetic research continues to thrive. Should we want to, we will soon be able to know the state of our
120 hearts—and our genes—in ever-growing detail. That knowledge, and what we do with it, could make the difference between dying at 65 and living until 80. The choice, increasingly, will be ours.

# Clogged Pipes and Ruptured Walls

Worldwide, coronary heart disease kills 17 million people every year. **Exacerbated** by the export of Western lifestyle—motorized transportation, abundant meat and cheese, workdays conducted from the comfort of a well-padded chair—incidence of the disease is soaring.

Until recently, cardiologists approached heart disease as a plumbing problem. Just as mineral deposits restrict the flow of water through a pipe, a buildup of plaque **impedes** the flow of blood through an arterial channel. Doctors now dismiss this "clogged-pipes model" as an idea whose time has passed. It's just not that simple.

Most heart attacks are caused by plaque embedded within the artery wall that ruptures,[9] cracking the wall and triggering the formation of a blood clot. The clot reduces the **volume** of blood flowing to the heart muscle, which can die from lack of oxygen and nutrients. Suddenly, the pump stops pumping.

Contrary to the clogged-pipes model, heart attacks generally occur in arteries that have minimal or moderate blockage, and their occurrence depends more on the kind of plaque than on the quantity. Findings suggest that softer plaques rich in cholesterol are more unstable and likely to rupture than the hard, dense plaques that extensively narrow the artery channel. But understanding the root cause of the disease will require much more research.

---

**9** If something **ruptures**, it is breaks or is broken apart.

## Buildup to a heart attack

**(1)** Cholesterol in the blood enters the arterial wall. **(2)** The body's immune system sends white blood cells (macrophages) to consume the cholesterol; **(3)** these grow to form foam cells, a component of plaque. **(4)** Muscle cells on the wall create a cap, **(5)** which may be weakened by the foam cells. **(6)** If the cap cracks, plaque moves into the bloodstream. A clot may form, restricting the volume of blood, causing a heart attack.

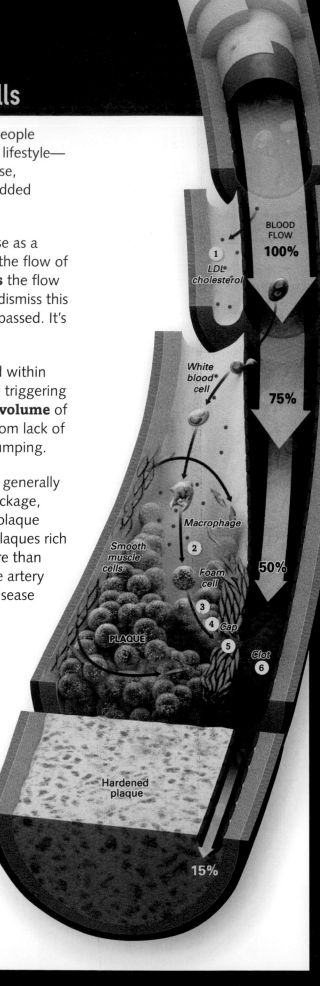

BLOOD FLOW
100%

1 LDL cholesterol

White blood cell

75%

Macrophage

Smooth muscle cells

2

Foam cell

50%

3

4 Cap

PLAQUE

5

Clot 6

Hardened plaque

15%

# Reading Comprehension

**Multiple Choice.** Choose the best answer for each question.

**Detail**

1. According to the information in paragraph F, most people do not realize that heart disease _____.
   a. begins quite early in life
   b. can be predicted in most cases
   c. kills more people than wars or car accidents
   d. can be prevented by eating salad and high-fiber cereal

**Detail**

2. What does the author say about dysfunctional *MEF2A*?
   a. It is not common, but it is very dangerous.
   b. It cannot be detected with current technology.
   c. It can cause problems other than heart disease.
   d. It is less dangerous than most genetic mutations.

**Vocabulary**

3. The phrase *tracking down* in line 65 is closest in meaning to _____.
   a. taking apart
   b. classifying
   c. searching for
   d. isolating

**Reference**

4. The word *ones* in line 75 refers to _____.
   a. doctors
   b. genes
   c. statins
   d. patients

**Rhetorical Purpose**

5. The purpose of the statistics in paragraph I is to _____.
   a. warn readers not to ignore the signs of heart disease
   b. explain how it is possible to misinterpret certain symptoms
   c. show why risk assessment is vital for preventing heart disease
   d. prove that heart disease is more dangerous to women than to men

**Inference**

6. The author implies that the drugs known as statins _____.
   a. may cause liver damage
   b. will help patients lose weight
   c. are used to treat muscle pains
   d. produce results that are easily measured

**Main Idea**

7. The main idea of the section on page 58 is that _____.
   a. doctors are unsure exactly why plaque builds up inside artery walls
   b. the "clogged-pipes model" does not fully explain why heart attacks occur
   c. the export of Western lifestyle has caused a sudden increase in heart disease
   d. a diet high in cholesterol is the biggest single factor contributing to heart disease

## Critical Thinking

**Analyzing:** The author indicates that genetic factors can contribute to the possibility of heart disease. What evidence is given to show that this is true?

_____

**Discussion:** Imagine that, in the future, there will be a medical test that can accurately predict your life expectancy. Would you want to know that information? Why or why not?

# Scanning for Details (I)

We scan to find specific information that we need from an article, for example, key details like dates, names, amounts, or places. To scan, you must have a clear idea of the kind of information you are looking for. If possible, have one or two key words in mind. Then read through the material quickly, looking for these words or related words. Don't try to read every word and don't worry about understanding every word that you read. When you find the relevant word(s), read the surrounding context to check how the information relates to the rest of the text.

**Scanning.** Quickly scan the article to find answers to these questions. Write each answer and note the line number(s) where you found it.

1. A single gene might contribute what percentage to a person's total risk of heart disease?

_____ line(s) _____

2. What would a comprehensive blood test for coronary risks show?

_____ line(s) _____

3. How did Don Steffensen first know about the genetics research?

_____ line(s) _____

4. What can an angiography test show?

_____ line(s) _____

5. What is Stephen Ellis collecting from his patients?

_____ line(s) _____

6. Where does Eric Topol work?

_____ line(s) _____

7. How did Don Steffensen survive his heart attack?

_____ line(s) _____

8. People with what condition would be advised to take statins?

_____ line(s) _____

# Vocabulary Practice

**A. Completion.** Complete the information by circling the correct word in each pair.

Gloria Stevens is lying on her back, staring at an image of her own beating heart. At this moment, she is **1. (exacerbating / submitting)** herself to a life-saving procedure. Her doctor is inserting a thin tube that will pass through a series of arteries to Gloria's heart. It eventually arrives at a spot where plaque has narrowed the arterial channel by 90 percent, severely **2. (compounding / impeding)** the blood passing through it. As Gloria watches on the monitor, the narrowing in her artery disappears, and suddenly a large **3. (stress / volume)** of blood starts flowing, like a river in a flood.

The procedure is over. It has lasted only half an hour. In all likelihood, Gloria will be able to go home the next day. So will a few thousand other patients in the United States undergoing such routine procedures today—more than a million of them a year with a disease that has reached epidemic **4. (mutations / proportions)**. Genetic factors may account for some patients' heart disease, but in most cases it is **5. (compounded / submitted)** by a high-fat diet and low levels of activity. Additionally, the **6. (proportion / stress)** of busy modern lifestyles is likely to **7. (exacerbate / impede)** cardiac symptoms.

The procedure has not fully cured Gloria of her coronary atherosclerosis, and she is still **8. (principal / susceptible)** to future blockages and coronary heart disease. But her quality of life will likely improve as a result of treatment. She'll breathe more easily, and maybe she'll live longer, too.

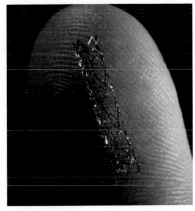

⌃ A stent is a tiny tube placed into an artery, blood vessel, or other hollow structure in the body to hold it open.

**B. Definitions.** Match the correct form of words in **red** from above with their correct definition.

1. to make movement or development difficult _____

2. a feeling of worry and tenseness _____

3. to develop different characteristics _____

4. amount of space something contains _____

5. a partial number compared to a total number _____

6. likely to be affected by something _____

7. first in order of importance _____

8. to allow something to be done _____

> **Usage**
> As verbs, **exacerbate** and **compound** have similar meanings. If something *exacerbates* a problem, it makes it worse. To *compound* a problem means to make it worse by adding to it.
>
> As a noun, **compound** has several usages: A *compound* is an enclosed area of land used for a particular purpose. In chemistry, a *compound* is a substance that consists of two or more elements. If something is a *compound* of different things, it is made of those things.

A single grain of pollen may be only one-quarter the width of a human hair, but to a person with hay fever allergies, it's a dangerous invader. Particles of pollen enter the body through the nose, mouth, or skin and trigger an overactive response from the body's immune system—an allergic reaction. The result: People who are allergic to pollen will suffer from repeated sneezing and watery, red eyes; often they will also have difficulty breathing.

# Before You Read

**A. Discussion.** Read the information in the caption. Then answer these questions.

1. What causes a hay fever allergy? What symptoms do people with hay fever usually suffer from?

2. Do you know of other things, aside from plant pollen, that people can be allergic to? What happens if they eat, breathe, or touch these things?

**B. Scanning and Predicting.** The passage on pages 63–67 has four main sections. Scan for where each section starts (look for words that are all capitalized), and write the line numbers below. Match each section with the topic you think it will be about (**a–e**). One topic is extra. Then read the article to check your ideas.

1. (from line 1) _____      **a.** how an allergy starts
2. (from line ___) _____    **b.** allergy symptoms and statistics
3. (from line ___) _____    **c.** allergy prevention and treatment
4. (from line ___) _____    **d.** how allergies were first detected
                              **e.** possible causes of rising allergy rates

# THE WAR ON ALLERGIES

**A** 1  **SUPPOSE THAT 54.3 PERCENT** of your country's population had cancer. That figure might **set off** a nationwide panic—a search for something wrong with people's diet, the environment, activity levels. In fact, that's the percentage of Americans who show a positive skin response
5  to one or more allergens.

**B**  The manifestations[1] of allergy—sneezing, itching, rashes—are signs of an immune system running amok,[2] attacking foreign invaders—allergens— that mean no harm. Allergens include pollen, dust mites, mold, food, drugs, stinging insects, or any other substance to which the body can
10  choose to react, or overreact. Allergies rarely kill. They just make the sufferer **miserable**—sometimes for brief periods, and sometimes for life.

**C**  Allergies are essentially an epidemic of modernity. As countries become more industrialized, the percentage of population affected by them tends to grow higher. There are remote areas of South America and Africa where
15  allergies are virtually nonexistent.

**D**  In contrast, six percent of young children in the U.S. today have food allergies. **Federal legislation** requires manufacturers to clearly label whether major allergens—peanuts, soy, shellfish, eggs, wheat, milk, fish,

---

1 **Manifestations** are clear and observable appearances, e.g., symptoms of a medical condition.

2 If something is **running amok,** it has gone into a frenzy, acting in a wild or dangerous manner.

# Mechanisms of an asthma[3] attack

The diagram illustrates how the airways constrict during an asthma attack.

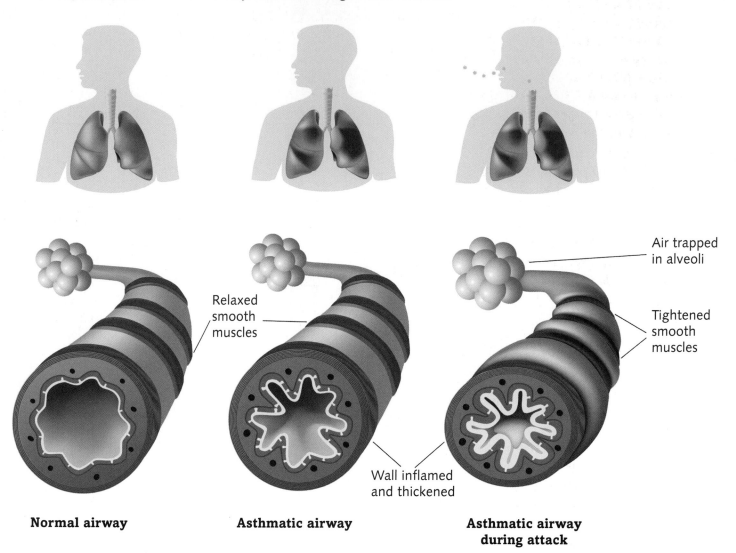

Relaxed smooth muscles

Air trapped in alveoli

Tightened smooth muscles

Wall inflamed and thickened

**Normal airway**          **Asthmatic airway**          **Asthmatic airway during attack**

and tree nuts—are ingredients in any product.
20 Children who cannot **tolerate** these foods sit at special tables at lunchtime; there are websites and support groups for parents who homeschool their severely allergic children.

**E** **HERE'S HOW AN ALLERGY DEVELOPS:**
25 One day, a body is exposed to a protein in something that seems perfectly harmless—the wheat flour, say, in a home-baked muffin. But for some unclear reason, the body looks at the protein and sees trouble. There will
30 be no symptoms at first, but the body is remembering—and planning.

**F** That first exposure causes the immune system to produce an antibody called IgE (immunoglobulin E). Then IgE antibodies
35 attach to certain cells, called mast cells, in tissue throughout the body. There they stay like wary soldiers waiting for war. With a second exposure, even months later, some of the allergen binds with the IgE on the mast
40 cell. This time, the mast cell releases a flood of irritating chemicals, which cause inflammation and itching.

---

3 **Asthma**, is a lung condition that causes difficulty in breathing.

**G** A minor or isolated reaction can become more serious with repeated exposure to an allergen, or when other cells involved in the immune system, the T cells, come into play. Certain T cells remember the "insult" of the allergen and ensure that some part of the body keeps becoming inflamed. Often the allergen and the immune system become increasingly antagonistic,[4] and the reaction worsens.

**H** **THERE IS, UNQUESTIONABLY,** a hereditary **component** to allergies. In some cases, people with allergies show signs of asthma. A child with one asthmatic parent has a good chance of developing the condition. If both parents have asthma, the chance of occurrence increases.

**I** Still, the rise in allergies is too rapid to be explained solely by genetics. "The genetic pool can't change that much in such a short time," says Donald Leung, director of an allergy-immunology program in the U.S. "There have to be environmental and behavioral factors as well." Dozens of theories have blamed everyone from urban landscapers for favoring male plants (the ones that produce pollen), to women who don't breastfeed. Breastfeeding, the theory goes, **confers** greater protection against allergies.

**J** Another probable factor: diet. "Reduced fresh fruit and vegetable intake, more processed food, fewer antioxidants,[5] and low intake of some minerals—these are all shown to be a risk," says professor of medicine Harold Nelson, considered one of the foremost experts on allergies in the U.S.

**K** The use of antibiotics may also be an underlying cause of rising allergy rates. Certain bacteria in the intestine are associated with greater or lesser chances of having allergies. Researchers believe, as Donald Leung says, "Overuse of antibiotics may be disrupting certain gut flora that **suppress** allergy."

**L** Another prime **culprit**: environmental pollutants. Exactly what pollutants and in what quantities are a source of heated debate. One of dozens of examples: Children who are raised near major highways and are exposed to diesel fumes from trucks **register** an increased sensitivity to allergens they already react to.

**M** Ironically, it's not just the pollutants that are affecting us. It may be too much cleanliness. A prevalent theory among allergists is known as the hygiene hypothesis. While it's true that industrialization brings with it better health care and fewer serious childhood infections, it also brings an obsession with cleanliness. We are not exposed to dirt at a young enough age to give our immune systems a good workout. Also, because of the high cost of energy, more homes are built with better insulation—insulation that seals in mold and dust.

**N** "The hygiene hypothesis has been on the scene since people first started looking at allergies," says associate professor Andrew Liu. "John Bostock, the guy who first identified hay fever in 1819, noted that it was a condition of the educated. He couldn't report any cases among poor people."

**O** But if dirt is a good thing, why are allergies and asthma so prevalent today in poor, inner-city neighborhoods? "It's not just a question of exposure to dirt that reduces allergies—it has to be the right kind of dirt," says Liu. "We're talking about exposure to endotoxin and good microbes in soil and animal waste." Research supports the hygiene hypothesis. "There was a famous study," says Harold Nelson, "where one of the protective factors for asthma was having a pig in the house."

---

4 If things or people are **antagonistic** toward each other, they oppose each other, behaving like enemies.

5 **Antioxidants** are molecules, often found in plants, that are known to prevent cell damage.

**P**  **SINCE MOST OF US ARE UNABLE** to room with a pig, we have to come up with a plan. Can we avoid allergies altogether? Can
125  we get rid of allergies we already have? Can we desensitize our immune systems? "We still don't know exactly how to prevent allergies," says Andrew Liu. "We know the immune response is supposed to be a helpful one, that
130  it's not supposed to be the cause of disease. We know that the immune system of someone with allergies needs to be reeducated. But how? It's not always clear." Leung agrees, adding, "If you are exposed to . . . microbial
135  products early in life, it may prevent allergies. But later in life, the early exposure may actually make things worse."

**Q**  There are those who argue that to prevent allergies, we should reduce exposure to
140  harmful allergens early on. Others believe allergens should be administered in large quantities at a young age. Many believe it depends on the specific allergen. And food allergies may work on an altogether different
145  principle. Confused? So are the allergists.

**R**  But there is hope that allergy sufferers may one day live in a world that's far more comfortable. Suddenly there's a booming market for products and services that were
150  unimaginable 30 years ago. Hotels offer allergy sufferers rooms with special ventilation systems and linens washed with nontoxic products. Scientists are finding ways to get rid of the allergenic proteins in common
155  offenders. Researchers at the University of Melbourne in Australia also claim to have developed the first hypoallergenic rye grass: It doesn't cause hay fever.

**S**  But the questions remain: Are allergies truly
160  preventable? How much genetic engineering is feasible? And even if we can eliminate the allergens we fight today, what will our immune systems decide are the enemies tomorrow?

Skin allergy testing is a method for medical diagnosis of allergies by triggering small and controlled allergic responses.

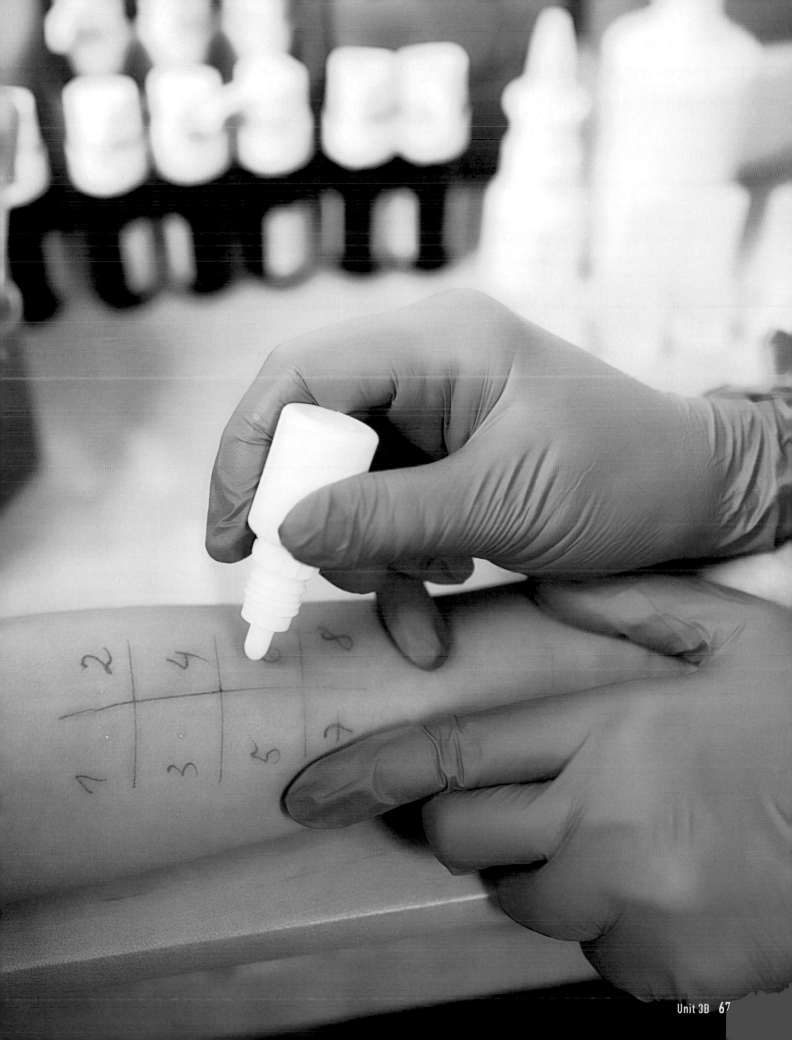

# Reading Comprehension

**Multiple Choice.** Choose the best answer for each question.

Gist

**1.** The best alternative title for the article would be _____.
   a. A New Theory on How Allergies Develop
   b. How Can We Prevent Allergies in Our Children?
   c. Medical Science's Latest Victory over Allergies
   d. What's Causing the Allergy Epidemic?

Inference

**2.** In paragraph A, the author implies that _____.
   a. more than half of all Americans will suffer from some form of cancer
   b. because more people are now affected by allergies, the nation has begun to panic
   c. a surprisingly high percentage of people have positive skin responses to allergens
   d. scientists are trying to find something wrong in our lifestyles

Detail

**3.** Which of the following actually produce the chemicals that cause allergic reactions?
   a. T cells    b. allergens    c. mast cells    d. IgE antibodies

Vocabulary

**4.** The phrase *come into play* in line 46 is closest in meaning to _____.
   a. begin to have an effect          b. form suddenly
   c. start to weaken                  d. move to another place

Detail

**5.** According to the author, scientists do not believe allergies are solely caused by heredity because _____.
   a. so many people have developed allergies so quickly
   b. there are so many new types of allergies today
   c. allergies can only be transmitted by one parent
   d. the symptoms of allergies are so much more severe today

## Critical Thinking

**Analyzing:** The author indicates that allergies are more common in developed countries than in developing countries. Give reasons from the article and your own ideas to explain why this is true.

Detail

**6.** According to the information in paragraph L, what is the effect of diesel fumes on children?
   a. They cause children to develop new allergies.
   b. They make existing allergies worse.
   c. They may help prevent further allergies.
   d. They can cause allergies when the children grow up.

Paraphrase

**7.** Which of the following is closest in meaning to this sentence (lines 131–132): *We know that the immune system of someone with allergies needs to be reeducated.*
   a. Certainly, people with allergies must be taught new ways of thinking about their problem.
   b. Scientists know that they must develop new ways of thinking about the immune system.
   c. Clearly, the immune systems of people with allergic responses must somehow be altered.
   d. As we know, people around the world must learn more about their own immune systems.

**Discussion:** In the last paragraph of the article, the author asks a series of "rhetorical questions" (questions that he does not expect an answer to). What is the purpose of these questions? How might you answer these questions?

# Using Concept Maps

A major part of this article is a discussion of known causes and possible causes of allergies. One way to present visually the relationships in an article or part of an article—for example, the factors that contribute to something—is to create a concept map. The concept map below illustrates the causes and possible causes of allergies.

**Completion.** Look back at pages 63–67, paying attention to factors that cause or may cause people to develop allergies. Complete the concept map using words from the article. Use up to three words for each blank.

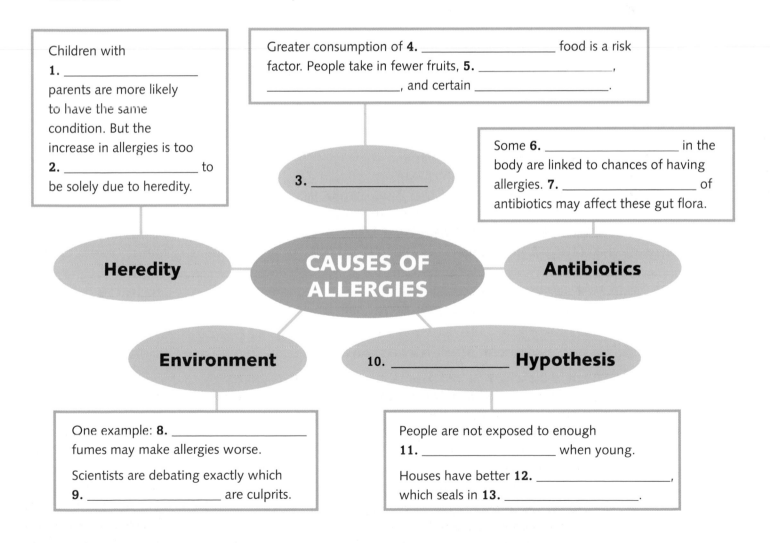

Children with

**1.** _____

parents are more likely to have the same condition. But the increase in allergies is too

**2.** _____ to be solely due to heredity.

Greater consumption of **4.** _____ food is a risk factor. People take in fewer fruits, **5.** _____,

_____, and certain _____.

Some **6.** _____ in the body are linked to chances of having allergies. **7.** _____ of antibiotics may affect these gut flora.

**3.** _____

**Heredity**

**CAUSES OF ALLERGIES**

**Antibiotics**

**Environment**

**10.** _____ **Hypothesis**

One example: **8.** _____ fumes may make allergies worse.

Scientists are debating exactly which **9.** _____ are culprits.

People are not exposed to enough **11.** _____ when young.

Houses have better **12.** _____, which seals in **13.** _____.

## Vocabulary Practice

**A. Completion.** Complete the information using the correct form of words from the box. Two words are extra.

| | | | | |
|---|---|---|---|---|
| component | confer | culprit | federal | legislation |
| miserable | register | set off | suppress | tolerate |

Seven-year-old Cameron Liflander is feeling **1.** _____.
He is suffering from watery, swollen eyes and a scratchy throat. The likely
**2.** _____? Like 50 million other Americans, Cameron suffers
from allergies. But his problem is not just the watery eyes and scratchy
throat we associate with allergies. Cameron's body is at war with his
environment. And his mother fears that one day the environment could
win.

Cameron was a sickly baby, but his growth rate was relatively normal.
For almost a year, he drank breast milk, which is supposed to
**3.** _____ some protection against allergies. One day,
his mother gave him a bite of tuna. Cameron turned red and started
choking. Benadryl, a medicine given to **4.** _____ allergy
symptoms, helped him recover, but the next severe reaction sent him to
the emergency room. It would be the first of many visits.

Cameron still requires a daily supply of drugs and skin creams to
help counter his asthma and allergic skin conditions. Nevertheless,
life is looking more positive now for Cameron. For instance, his
reaction to certain substances is decreasing with age. He now
**5.** _____ soy—a huge relief because soy is an ingredient
in a vast range of products. In addition, recent **6.** _____ by
the U.S. **7.** _____ government on labeling major allergens
in food products has allowed him and countless other allergy sufferers to
avoid foods that **8.** _____ allergic reactions.

⌃ Symptoms of an
allergic reaction
include watery eyes
and a scratchy throat.

**B. Definitions.** Use the correct form of words in the box in **A** to complete
the definitions.

**1.** If you feel _____, you feel extremely unhappy or uncomfortable.

**2.** The _____ of something are the parts that it is made of.

**3.** If a natural function of your body is _____, it is stopped or
prevented.

**4.** When something _____ on a scale of measurement, it shows on
the scale.

**5.** To _____ something on someone (e.g., power) means to give it
to them.

**Thesaurus tolerate**
Also look up: (v.) *stand,
bear, stomach, endure,
take, put up with*

# VIEWING Fighting Malaria

## Before You Watch

**A. Discussion.** What flowers (**a–j**) are typically used in your country for the purposes listed (**1–8**)? Use the flowers from the box and other flowers you know.

1. _____ : to eliminate bad odors
2. _____ : to decorate a home
3. _____ : to adorn your body
4. _____ : to use in perfume
5. _____ : to express affection
6. _____ : to express sympathy
7. _____ : to consume as food or drink
8. _____ : to use as medicine

| Common flowers | |
|---|---|
| **a.** chrysanthemum | **f.** lily |
| **b.** daisy | **g.** lotus |
| **c.** jasmine | **h.** orchid |
| **d.** lavender | **i.** rose |
| **e.** lilac | **j.** violet |

❮ Flowers have many uses. Some flowers have symbolic meanings, while others are valued for their pleasing smell or medicinal value.

**B. Discussion.** Do you know what malaria is? What are the symptoms of malaria? What causes it? How serious is it? Is it common in your home country?

**C. Predict.** A type of chrysanthemum called pyrethrum is being used more and more to help fight malaria. How do you think it might be used?

# While You Watch

**A. Sequencing.** The video discusses the advantages of using the pyrethrum flower to fight malaria in Kenya. Number them from **1** to **6** in the order they are discussed in the video.

☐ Farmers can grow hundreds of kilos of pyrethrum from a relatively small area.

☐ Pyrethrum is environmentally friendly because it's natural.

☐ Kenya's semi-arid climate is ideal for growing pyrethrum.

☐ There is a growing demand for insecticides worldwide that use pyrethrum.

☐ Pyrethrum is able to kill very quickly.

☐ Mosquitoes are not able to build up resistance to pyrethrum.

**B. Multiple Choice.** Choose the best answer for each question.

1. According to the video, the world's most dangerous animal is _____.
   a. bacteria
   b. the mosquito
   c. a type of fly

2. How many children in Africa die from malaria?
   a. between 300 and 400 a day
   b. between one and two million a year
   c. 40 percent of those under 5 years old

3. Why don't mosquitoes build up a resistance to pyrethrum?
   a. Because pyrethrum was only recently introduced to Kenya.
   b. Because the pyrethrum is quickly dried where mosquitoes can't find it.
   c. Because pyrethrum kills the mosquitoes so quickly.

4. What is true about pyrethrum?
   a. It grows best at sea level.
   b. It grows well in Kenya.
   c. It is deadly if eaten by humans.

5. What does Joshua Kiptoon mean when he says, "It fights his enemies."
   a. Malaria fights against people who are trying to eliminate it.
   b. Mosquitoes fight against natural insecticides like pyrethrum.
   c. Pyrethrum kills insects that carry the deadly disease.

# After You Watch

**Discussion.** Discuss these questions with a partner.

1. How exactly does pyrethrum fight malaria? In your own words, describe what happens.

2. Can you think of other benefits to using pyrethrum? For example, how is the production of the flower helping Kenya's economy?

# 4

# VANISHING CITIES

If all the ice on Earth melts, scientists estimate that the seas could rise up by more than 60 meters (200 feet), covering much of the Statue of Liberty.

## Warm Up

**Discuss these questions with a partner.**

1. Which are the most crowded cities or regions in your country? Why are they crowded?

2. What places in the world do you think are most at risk from a rise in sea levels?

3. Can you think of any places that have recently experienced floods? What was the result?

## Before You Read

**A. Quiz.** How much do you know about Venice? Answer the questions. Then check your answers at the bottom of the page.

1. Approximately how many people visit Venice each year?

   a. 200,000          b. 2,000,000          c. 20,000,000

2. Venice is regularly threatened by *acqua alta* (high tides) and has been sinking into the water for years. Over the last century, how much has the city sunk?

   a. 13 cm (5 inches)     b. 25 cm (10 inches)   c. 38 cm (15 inches)

3. What did Venice recently prohibit people from doing in the Piazza San Marco (the city's main square)?

   a. feeding birds          b. selling T-shirts        c. riding skateboards

**B. Skimming.** Look quickly at the passage on pages 75–79. Which problem facing Venice do you think the article is mainly about? Circle one option below. Then read through the passage to check your ideas.

   a. dangers caused by rising tides        b. problems caused by tourism

   c. the city's declining birthrate        d. rising levels of pollution

∧ Every year, crowds of tourists travel to Venice, Italy. Highlights for many visitors are the chance to ride in a gondola along the famous Grand Canal (**above**) and to attend Carnevale, an elaborate costume party that is one of the city's biggest celebrations (**above right**).

Quiz Answers: 1. c, 2. c, 3. a

# CITY UNDER SIEGE

A 1 The city Thomas Mann[1] called "half fairy tale and half tourist trap" finds itself threatened by more than just the rising tide. Cathy Newman investigates the trouble with Venice.

B 5 Nowhere in Italy is there a crisis more beautifully **framed** than in Venice. Neither land nor water, the city lifts like a mirage from a lagoon[2] at the head of the Adriatic Sea. For centuries it has threatened to vanish beneath the waves of the *acqua alta*, the relentlessly regular flooding caused by rising tides and sinking foundations. But that is the least of its problems.

C 10 Just ask Massimo Cacciari, former mayor of Venice and professor of philosophy, fluent in German, Latin, ancient Greek; a man who raises the level of political intellect to just short of the stratosphere.[3] Ask about the acqua alta and Venice sinking, and he says, "So go get boots."

D 15 Boots are fine for water, but useless against the flood that causes more concern for Venetians than any lagoon spillover: the flood of tourism. Number of Venetian residents in 2012: 60,000. Number of visitors in 2012: 21 million.

1 **Thomas Mann** (1875–1955) was the author of the 1912 novella *Death in Venice*.

2 A **lagoon** is a body of water cut off from the open sea by coral reefs or sand bars.

3 The **stratosphere** is the atmospheric layer between about 15 and 50 km (10 and 30 miles) above the Earth.

Carnevale masks for sale in Venice. Each year the Carnevale draws thousands of tourists.

**E** In May 2008, for example, on a holiday weekend, 80,000 tourists descended on the city. Public parking lots in Mestre, where people board a bus or train to the historic center, filled with floodwater and were closed. Those who managed to get to Venice surged through the streets like schools of bluefish, snapping up pizza and gelato, leaving paper and plastic bottles in their wake.[4]

> "Now, Venice gets giant cruise ships. You can't understand Venice from ten stories up. You might as well be in a helicopter."

**F** "Beauty is difficult," says Cacciari, sounding as if he were addressing a graduate seminar in aesthetics[5] rather than answering a question about municipal[6] regulation. The black of Cacciari's dark hair and luxuriant beard **complement** his current mood. The preceding day, heavy rains had flooded Mestre again. Rain caused the flood, not acqua alta, Cacciari says. "High tide is not a problem for me. It's a problem for you foreigners." End of discussion on flooding.

**G** No, he stresses, the problems lie elsewhere. The cost of maintaining Venice: "There is not enough money from the state to cover it all— the cleaning of canals, restoration of buildings, raising of foundations. Very expensive." The cost of living: "It's three times as costly to live here as in Mogliano, 20 kilometers away. It's affordable only for the rich or elderly who already own houses because they have been passed down. The young? They can't afford it."

**H** Finally, there is tourism. Of that, Cacciari says: "Venice is not a **sentimental** place of honeymoon. It's a strong, contradictory, overpowering place. It is not a city for tourists. It cannot be reduced to a postcard."

**I** If you are a Venetian who lives in a fifth-floor walk-up apartment—someone who gets up, goes to work, goes home—Venice is a different place altogether. The abnormal is normal. A flood is routine. The alarm sounds, protective steel doors come down. Boots, essential to any Venetian wardrobe, are pulled on. The four kilometers (two and a half miles) of *passerelle*—an **elevated** boardwalk[7] supported on metal legs—are set up. Life goes on.

**J** When Silvia Zanon goes to Campo San Provolo, where she teaches middle school, she knows it will take 23 minutes to walk there from her apartment on the Calle delle Carrozze. On the way she crosses the Piazza San Marco, blissfully[8] empty in early morning. "I step on the paving stones and fall in love with the city all over again," she says.

**K** Gherardo Ortalli, a professor of medieval history, finds his path less poetic. "When I go out in the *campo* with my friends, I have to stop because someone is taking a photograph of us as if we are aboriginals,"[9] he says. "Perhaps one day we will be. You will go and see a sign on a cage: 'Feed the Venetians.' When I arrived 30 years ago, the population was 120,000. Now it is less than 60,000."

**L** The decline seems inexorable.[10] Ortalli thinks Venice will end up as simply a theme park for the rich, who will jet in to spend a day or two in their palazzo, then leave. It is 10 a.m., and he is headed toward a kiosk to buy a newspaper before going to his office, though you can hardly find the papers for all the

---

4 Something that is left in someone's **wake** remains behind after the person has left.

5 **Aesthetics** is a branch of philosophy dealing with the nature of beauty.

6 Something that is **municipal** is controlled or owned by the government of a city or town.

7 A **boardwalk** is a footpath made of wooden boards.

8 Somewhere that is **blissfully** empty is a place that is happy and peaceful because it is empty.

9 **Aboriginals** are the original and native people of a country or region.

10 Something that is **inexorable** cannot be prevented from continuing or progressing.

tourist kitsch: miniature masks, gondola pins, jester[11] caps. "Everything is for sale," he sighs. "Even Venice."

90 In 2008, the official in charge of managing the impact of tourism in Venice was Augusto Salvadori. *Love* is an **inadequate** word to describe how Salvadori feels about Venice. He was not just the city's director
95 of tourism and promoter of tradition; he was its defender. "The city is consumed by tourism," says Salvadori. "What do Venetians get in exchange? During part of the year, Venetians cannot elbow their way onto public
100 transportation. The cost of garbage collection increases; so does the price of living."

"Perhaps to help," Salvadori says, "we put a city tax on hotels and restaurants. [Then] they said tourists would not come—but I say,
105 tourists won't come for a few euros?" He glares. "I could not worry about hotels. I had to think of the Venetians. My battle was for the city. Because Venice is my heart."

110 Tourism has been part of the Venetian landscape since the 14th century, when pilgrims stopped en route to the Holy Land. So, what's so different about tourism now? I ask Ortalli. "Now, Venice gets giant cruise
115 ships. The ship is ten stories high. You can't understand Venice from ten stories up. You might as well be in a helicopter. But it's not important. You arrive in Venice, write a postcard, and remember what a wonderful evening you had."

120 "There goes another piece of Venice," Silvia Zanon, the teacher, said sadly when La Camiceria San Marco, a 60-year-old clothing store, had to move to a smaller, less prime spot because the rent had tripled. Susanna Cestari
125 worked there for 32 years. "It's like leaving the house where you were born," she said, while packing boxes for the move. Since December

---

11 A **jester** was a professional clown employed by the nobility during the Middle Ages. Jesters' hats are known for being colorful with pointed tips.

Elevated boardwalks known as *passerelle* allow visitors to appreciate Venice's beauty without getting their feet wet.

2007, at least ten hardware stores have gone out of business. In the Rialto market, souvenir
130 sellers have replaced vendors who sold sausages, bread, or vegetables. Tourists will not notice. They do not visit Venice to buy an eggplant.

Tourism in Venice generates $2 billion a year in
135 revenue, probably an underestimate because so much business is done off the books. It is, reports the University of Venice's International Center of Studies on the Tourist Economy, "the heart and soul of the Venetian economy—
140 good and bad." Some people suggest that Venice's wounds are self-**inflicted**. "They don't want tourists," observes a former resident, "but they want their money." There is talk about **implementing** new policies
145 to limit the number of tourists, **imposing** additional taxes, and urging visitors to avoid the high seasons of Easter and Carnevale. But tourism—together with the loss of resident population, and combined with the

150 interests of hotel owners, gondoliers, and water taxi drivers who all have an interest in **maximizing** the influx of visitors—defies simple solutions.

"Let me remind you, the loss of population
155 . . . is not only a problem in Venice but in all historical towns, not only Italy," cautions former Mayor Cacciari. "The **so-called** exodus, which dates back very far in time, is deep-rooted with the lodging[12] issue." For
160 some, a solution to Venice's troubles already seems out of reach. "It is too late," Gherardo Ortalli, the historian, says. "The stones will remain. The people won't."

But for now there is still life as well as death
165 in Venice. Silvia Zanon, on her way to school, still crosses San Marco only to fall in love with the city again. And, assuming it is in season, you can still manage to buy an eggplant. The city's beauty, difficult and bruised, somehow
170 survives.

---

**12 Lodging** is temporary, often rented, accommodation.

# Reading Comprehension

**Multiple Choice.** Choose the best answer for each question.

**Main Idea**

1. What is the main idea of this article?
   a. Besides flooding, Venice faces several other serious environmental problems.
   b. The flooding problem in Venice is caused mainly by rain, not by the *acqua alta*.
   c. The most difficult problem facing Venice is the large number of tourists it receives.
   d. Because tides are rising and foundations are sinking, Venice is disappearing into the sea.

**Rhetorical Purpose**

2. Why does the author present the statistics in paragraph D?
   a. to indicate that more tourists are coming to Venice than before
   b. to emphasize the population decline in Venice
   c. to contrast the number of tourists with the number of residents
   d. to point out the dangers of serious flooding

**Inference**

3. What can be inferred about the holiday weekend in May 2008, mentioned in the article?
   a. There were more tourists than residents in the city.
   b. Many residents left the city because of the floods.
   c. All of the city center's parking lots were full of cars.
   d. Vendors ran out of snacks for tourists such as pizza and gelato.

**Detail**

4. What does Massimo Cacciari say about the young people of Venice in paragraph G?
   a. Most of them have moved to the nearby town of Mogliano.
   b. They find it is too expensive to live in Venice these days.
   c. They are involved in cleaning canals, restoring buildings, and raising foundations.
   d. Many of them live in houses that have been passed down from their parents.

**Detail**

5. Which of the following is given as an example of an ordinary resident of Venice?
   a. Massimo Cacciari
   b. Silvia Zanon
   c. Thomas Mann
   d. Augusto Salvadori

**Vocabulary**

6. The phrase *off the books* (line 136) indicates that much of the tourist business in Venice is done _____.
   a. unofficially
   b. carelessly
   c. unwillingly
   d. rapidly

**Reference**

7. The word *they* in line 141 refers to the _____.
   a. people who live in Venice
   b. International Center of Studies on the Tourist Economy
   c. people who say that Venice's wounds are self-inflicted
   d. tourists who visit Venice

**Critical Thinking**

**Evaluating:** Do you think that the author offers enough evidence to support her main idea? Why or why not?

_____

**Analyzing:** "[Tourism] is the heart and soul of the Venetian economy—good and bad" (lines 137–139). What effects (good and bad) does the author mention in the passage? What other positive and negative effects can tourism have on a city or a region?

# Recognizing Literal vs. Figurative Language

Some words and phrases in the reading passage have a literal meaning, while others have a figurative meaning. When you read, it is important to be able to recognize when figurative language is being used instead of literal language. Literal language means exactly what it says. Figurative language, such as similes, metaphors, and personification, uses words with a meaning that is different from the literal interpretation.

Read these two sentences.

*The farmers plowed their fields.* (literal)

*The ship plowed through the sea.* (figurative)

In the first sentence, farmers use real plows (agricultural tools) to prepare their land for planting. In the second sentence, a metaphor, the ship moves through the sea *like* a plow. There is no real plow.

∧ A plow is a tool used by farmers to loosen or turn the soil. The word *plow* can also be used to describe a ship cutting through the water like a plow.

**A. Classification.** Find these words or phrases in the article. Mark them **L** if used literally and **F** if they are used figuratively.

1. flooding (line 8) _____

2. stratosphere (line 12) _____

3. flood (line 14) _____

4. foundations (line 42) _____

5. elevated (line 61) _____

6. poetic (line 72) _____

7. theme park (line 81) _____

8. consumed (line 96) _____

9. garbage collection (line 100) _____

10. pilgrims (line 111) _____

11. wounds (line 141) _____

12. bruised (line 169) _____

**B. Applying.** Write a sentence about your own city or region using figurative language.

# Vocabulary Practice

**A. Completion.** Complete the information by circling the correct word in each pair.

A popular image of the European Alps consists of cowbells, cheese-making, and quiet villages **1. (framed / imposed)** against a background of snow-capped mountains. But a less **2. (sentimental / complementary)** picture must also include the 12 million trucks and about 50 million cars that cross the mountains each year.

The movement of 77 million tons of goods annually through the mountains **3. (frames / inflicts)** significant environmental damage on the Alpine environment. Carbon dioxide ($CO_2$) from vehicle fumes becomes trapped in the narrow valleys beneath an upper layer of warmer air. The steep valley walls also **4. (maximize / implement)** the sounds generated by the traffic. The **5. (inadequate / elevated)** levels of noise and pollution **6. (impose / complement)** serious problems on the health of Alpine residents.

Laws have been **7. (elevated / implemented)** to reduce the number of vehicles in residential areas, but they have so far proved largely **8. (inadequate / maximized)** for reducing the overall volume of traffic. There are hopeful signs, however: October 2010 saw the completion of the first of two single-track tunnels comprising the Gotthard Base Tunnel—the **9. (sentimental / so-called)** GBT—which at 57 kilometers (35 miles) is the world's longest rail tunnel. It is hoped that the rail tunnel will help reduce the environmental strain on one of the world's most famous landscapes.

⌃ The purpose of the Gotthard Base Tunnel is to reduce traffic on roads and shift the focus to rail transport.

**B. Definitions.** Match the correct form of words in **red** from above with their correct definition.

1. _____: cause something undesirable
2. _____: to increase as much as possible
3. _____: not enough
4. _____: surrounded or outlined
5. _____: nostalgic for things in the past
6. _____: differ, but go well together
7. _____: raised up higher
8. _____: carry out, fulfill
9. _____: generally named or known as
10. _____: force something on someone

> **Usage**
> **Complement** and **compliment** sound alike but have different meanings.
>
> **Complement** means "things may be different, but they combine well together," e.g., (*v.*) The tie **complemented** his suit. (*n.*) The tie is a good **complement** to his suit.
>
> **Compliment** means "to say something nice to or about someone," e.g., (*v.*) My daughter **complimented** me on my new dress. (*n.*) My daughter gave me a nice **compliment** about my new dress.

# RISING SEAS

As the planet warms, the sea rises and coastlines flood. How will we face the danger of rising seas?

## Before You Read

**A. Discussion.** Discuss these questions with a partner.

1. Why do you think many people are concerned about global warming?

2. If you could make one new law to reduce the dangers of global warming, what would it be?

**B. Skimming and Predicting.** The passage on pages 84–89 discusses some of the challenges of rising sea levels. Read the headings and captions, and skim the passage. In your own words, write what you think these sections are mainly about. Then read the article to check your ideas.

1. Storm of the Century _____

2. Coastlines at Risk _____

3. Dutch Lessons _____

4. Retreat from the Coast _____

∧ A parking lot full of yellow cabs is flooded as a result of superstorm Sandy that hit New York City on October 29, 2012.

# Storm of the Century

**A** By the time Hurricane Sandy veered toward the northeast coast of the United States on October 29, 2012, it had mauled[1] several
5  countries in the Caribbean and left dozens dead. Faced with the largest storm the Atlantic had ever produced, New York and other cities ordered mandatory evacuations[2] of low-lying areas. Not everyone **complied**. Those who
10  chose to ride out Sandy got a preview of the future, in which a warmer world will lead to rising seas.

**B** Brandon d'Leo, a sculptor and surfer, rented a second-floor apartment across the street
15  from the beach on New York City's Rockaway Peninsula. At about 3:30 in the afternoon, he went outside. Waves were crashing against the nine-kilometer- (5.5-mile-) long boardwalk. A short time later, d'Leo and a
20  neighbor watched the sea through the glass door of his living room. As it was getting dark, his neighbor saw something alarming. "I think the boardwalk just moved," she said. Within minutes, another **surge** of water lifted the
25  boardwalk again. It began to break apart.

**C** Three large sections of the boardwalk smashed against two pine trees in front of d'Leo's apartment. The street had become a 1.2-meter- (four-foot-) deep river. Cars began
30  to float, their alarms adding to the sound of rushing water and cracking wood. After the storm, d'Leo said, "I have six surfboards in my apartment, and I was thinking, if anything comes through that wall, I'll try to get
35  everyone on those boards and try to get up the block."

**D** After a difficult night's sleep, d'Leo went outside. The water had **retreated**, but thigh-deep pools still filled parts of some streets.
40  "Everything was covered with sand," he said. "It looked like another planet."

# Coastlines at Risk

**E** By the end of the century, a hundred-year storm surge like Sandy's might occur every
45  decade or less. Coastal cities like New York now face a double threat: rising oceans and more severe storm surges. Experts estimate that by 2070, 150 million people in the world's large port cities will be at risk from
50  coastal flooding, along with 35 trillion dollars in property. How will they cope?

**F** Malcolm Bowman, a researcher at the State University of New York, believes that storm-surge **barriers** must be built across New
55  York City's harbor. Compared with some other leading ports, New York is essentially defenseless in the face of hurricanes and floods. London, Rotterdam, St. Petersburg, New Orleans, and Shanghai have all built
60  levees[3] and storm barriers in the past few decades. When Hurricane Sandy struck, New York paid a high price for not having such protection. The storm left 43 dead and cost the city about 19 billion dollars. According
65  to Bowman, storm-surge barriers could have prevented it. He says, "It might take five years of study and another ten years to get the political will to do it. By then, there might have been another disaster. We need to start
70  planning immediately."

**G** Mayor Michael Bloomberg outlined a 19.5-billion-dollar plan to defend New York City against rising seas. His proposal called for the construction of levees, local storm-
75  surge barriers, sand dunes, and more than 200 other measures. It went far beyond anything planned by any other U.S. city. But the mayor dismissed the idea of a harbor barrier. "A giant barrier across our harbor is neither practical
80  nor affordable," Bloomberg said. The plan notes that since a barrier would remain open most of the time, it would not protect the city from inch-by-inch creep of sea-level rise.

---

1 If someone is **mauled** (e.g., by a wild animal), they are attacked fiercely and aggressively.

2 During an **evacuation**, people are removed from a dangerous place.

3 A **levee** is a raised structure of earth or other material built to hold back water.

Hurricane Sandy narrowed New Jersey's beaches by more than 9 meters (30 feet). In Seaside Heights, it swept away the pier under the roller coaster.

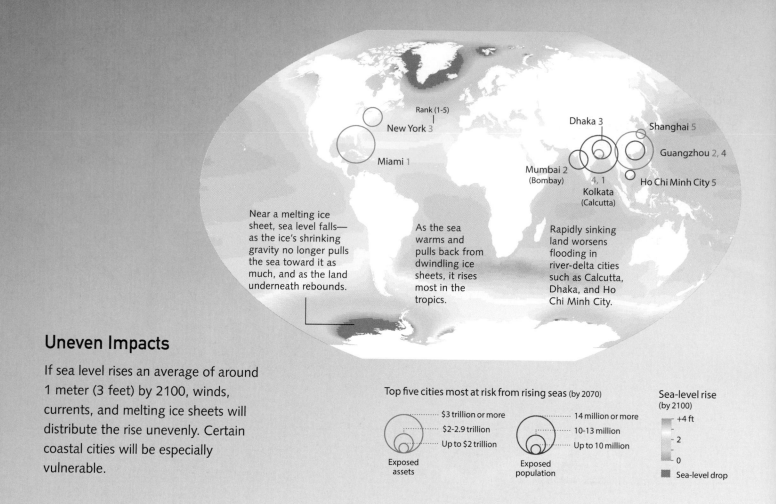

Rank (1-5)

New York 3

Dhaka 3

Shanghai 5

Miami 1

Guangzhou 2, 4

Mumbai 2
(Bombay)

4, 1
Kolkata
(Calcutta)

Ho Chi Minh City 5

Near a melting ice sheet, sea level falls— as the ice's shrinking gravity no longer pulls the sea toward it as much, and as the land underneath rebounds.

As the sea warms and pulls back from dwindling ice sheets, it rises most in the tropics.

Rapidly sinking land worsens flooding in river-delta cities such as Calcutta, Dhaka, and Ho Chi Minh City.

## Uneven Impacts

If sea level rises an average of around 1 meter (3 feet) by 2100, winds, currents, and melting ice sheets will distribute the rise unevenly. Certain coastal cities will be especially vulnerable.

Top five cities most at risk from rising seas (by 2070)

$3 trillion or more

$2-2.9 trillion

Up to $2 trillion

Exposed assets

14 million or more

10-13 million

Up to 10 million

Exposed population

Sea-level rise (by 2100)

+4 ft

2

0

Sea-level drop

# Retreat from the Coast

**H** 85 With the threat of sea-level rise everywhere, cities around the world have turned to the Netherlands for guidance—a country that has faced and overcome the problem of rising seas. One Dutch firm, Arcadis, has prepared 90 a design for a storm-surge barrier to protect New York City. The same company helped design a 3.2-kilometer- (two-mile-) long barrier that protected New Orleans from Hurricane Isaac's four-meter (13.6-foot) storm 95 surge in 2012. "Isaac was a tremendous victory for New Orleans," said Piet Dircke, an Arcadis executive. "All the barriers were closed; all the levees held; all the pumps worked. You didn't hear about it? No, because 100 nothing happened."

**I** New Orleans may be safe for a few decades, but the long-term prospects for it and other low-lying cities look **dire**. Even if we begin reducing our emissions of heat-trapping 105 gases tomorrow, oceans will likely rise several feet, and perhaps several dozens of feet, as Earth slowly adjusts to the amount already in the atmosphere. Among the most vulnerable cities is Miami. "I cannot 110 **envision** southeastern Florida having many people at the end of this century," says Hal Wanless, chair[4] of the University of Miami's Department of Geological Science. "We think Miami has always been here and will always 115 be here. How do you get people to realize that Miami—or London—will not always be there?"

---

4 The **chair** of a committee, organization, or company is the head of it.

## Rising Seas

Sea level didn't change much for nearly 2,000 years, judging from sediment cores. It began to rise in the late 19th century, as the Earth started to warm. If sea levels continue to track temperature, it could rise 1 meter (3 feet) or more by 2100. The great unknown: the future of the ice sheets. The four scenarios shown here span the range of possibilities for 2100. The sea will keep rising after that.

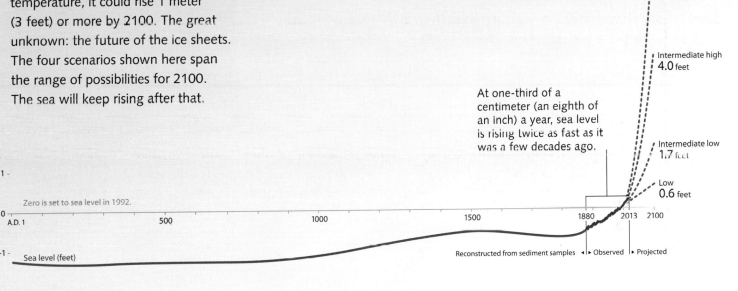

SEA-LEVEL SCENARIOS, 2100

High
6.6 feet

Intermediate high
4.0 feet

At one-third of a centimeter (an eighth of an inch) a year, sea level is rising twice as fast as it was a few decades ago.

Intermediate low
1.7 feet

Low
0.6 feet

Zero is set to sea level in 1992.

A.D. 1      500      1000      1500      1880   2013   2100

Sea level (feet)

Reconstructed from sediment samples    Observed    Projected

Experts estimate that by 2070, 150 million people in the world's large port cities will be at risk from coastal flooding, along with 35 trillion dollars in property. How will they cope?

J

120 Unless we change course dramatically, our carbon emissions will drastically change the geography of many shorelines by the next century, if not sooner, and large numbers of people will have to abandon coastal areas in Florida and other parts of the world. "From the Bahamas to Bangladesh and a major

125 amount of Florida, we'll have to move, and we may have to move at the same time," says Wanless. Columbia University geophysicist Klaus Jacob sees most of Manhattan's population fleeing to higher ground and the

130 island becoming a kind of Venice, subject to periodic flooding, perhaps with canals and yellow water cabs. At different times in different countries, engineering solutions will no longer be enough. Then the retreat from

135 the coast will begin.

# Dutch Lessons

Can a single storm change not just a city's but a nation's **policy**? It has happened before. The Netherlands experienced its own coastal catastrophe 60 years ago, and it transformed the country.

The storm roared in from the North Sea on the night of January 31, 1953. Ria Geluk was six years old at the time and living on an island in the southern Dutch province of Zeeland. She remembers a neighbor knocking on her family's door in the middle of the night to tell them that the dike had failed. Later that day, the whole family climbed to the roof, where they huddled[5] in blankets and heavy coats. Geluk's grandparents lived just across the road, but water poured into the village with such force that they were trapped in their home. They died when it collapsed. The disaster killed 1,836 in all, including a baby born on the night of the storm.

Afterward the Dutch began an **ambitious** program of dike and barrier construction called the Delta Works, which lasted more than four decades and cost more than six billion dollars. One crucial project was the eight-kilometer- (five-mile-) long barrier built to defend Zeeland from the sea. The final component of the Delta Works—a movable barrier protecting Rotterdam Harbor and some 1.5 million people—was finished in 1997. Like other primary sea barriers in the Netherlands, it's built to **withstand** a 1-in-10,000-year storm—the strictest standard in the world.

The transparent domes of Rotterdam's Floating Pavilion represent an even more innovative approach to taming[6] the sea. The three domes—each about three stories tall—are made of a plastic that is a hundred times as light as glass. Though the domes are used for meetings and exhibitions, their main purpose is to demonstrate the potential of floating urban architecture. The city anticipates that as many as 1,200 homes will float in the harbor by 2040. "We think these structures will be important not just for Rotterdam but for many cities around the world," says Bart Roeffen, the architect who designed the pavilion.

An inscription[7] on the side of a storm-surge barrier in Zeeland says *Hier gaan over het tij, de maan, de wind, en wij*—Here the tide is ruled by the moon, the wind, and us. It reflects the confidence of a generation that **took for granted**—as we no longer can—a reasonably stable world. "We have to understand that we are not ruling the world," says Jan Mulder of Deltares, a Dutch coastal management firm. "We need to adapt."

---

5 If people **huddle** together, they stand, sit, or lie close to each other, usually because they are cold or frightened.

6 If you **tame** something dangerous, you bring it under control.

7 An **inscription** is writing carved into something made of stone or metal.

The Oosterschelde Flood Barrier is the largest of 13 ambitious Delta Works, designed to protect a large part of the Netherlands from flooding.

Rotterdam's Floating Pavilion is an innovative approach to addressing the challenges of climate change and rising seas. >

# Reading Comprehension

**Multiple Choice.** Choose the best answer for each question.

Gist
**1.** What would be another good title for this reading?
   a. Can Our Coasts Be Saved?
   b. The Devastation of Hurricane Sandy
   c. How the Netherlands Beat Back the Sea
   d. How to Slow Global Warming

Inference
**2.** What helped save lives when Hurricane Sandy struck New York?
   a. Levees and storm barriers held most of the water back.
   b. Boardwalks helped slow the surge of water.
   c. The storm had weakened after leaving the Caribbean.
   d. Low-lying areas had already been evacuated.

Figurative Language
**3.** Which of these sentences does NOT include an example of figurative language?
   a. By the time Hurricane Sandy . . . left dozens dead. (lines 2–6)
   b. "Everything was covered . . . like another planet." (lines 40–41)
   c. Columbia University . . . yellow water cabs. (lines 127–132)
   d. Then the retreat from the coast will begin. (lines 134–135)

Reading Maps
**4.** Which city is at risk of losing up to $3 trillion in assets due to rising sea levels?
   a. Miami    b. Dhaka    c. Ho Chi Minh City    d. Shanghai

Inference
**5.** How does the author choose to end the article?
   a. Optimistically. We have the capacity to fix the problem.
   b. Pessimistically. Unless we change course, we will have to move inland.
   c. Neutrally. We don't know how the author feels.
   d. With humor. Mentioning that New York will be like Venice with water cabs takes away the seriousness of the issue.

Detail
**6.** What is Rotterdam's Floating Pavilion?
   a. temporary shelters for flood victims
   b. an example of possible future living spaces
   c. domes that convert wave energy into power
   d. meeting spaces that also act as surge barriers

Purpose
**7.** What is the main purpose of the section on page 88?
   a. to describe the event that caused the Netherlands to begin their dike- and barrier-building program
   b. to show how dangerous coastal communities like Zeeland can be, even when they are well protected
   c. to make a case for expanding the Dutch success story in Zeeland to other parts of the country
   d. to illustrate that storms 60 years ago were just as dangerous as the storms of today

## Critical Thinking

**Analyzing:** Why does Piet Dircke say that "Isaac was a tremendous victory for New Orleans"? What do you think he means by that?

**Discussion:** How do you feel when you look at the map on page 86? Do you think we could cope with such a scenario? What would be the effect of such a retreat away from the coasts?

# Reading a Text Critically

Critical reading is a process of reading that goes beyond simply understanding what a text says. It involves analyzing, interpreting, and evaluating the text as you read through it, and reflecting on it afterward. Being a successful critical reader allows you to see how a text fits into a greater academic context.

When you read a text critically, you identify the text's overall strengths and weaknesses, and evaluate the writer's arguments. A useful technique is to read a text twice. The first time, read it with as much generosity as possible. Look for what makes the writer's argument compelling. Find claims that are persuasive. Assume the arguments are well supported, balanced, and reasonable. The second time, read the text from the opposite viewpoint. Scrutinize each argument. Look for poorly supported or exaggerated claims. See if you can find bias, faulty reasoning, or other weaknesses. Then reflect on what you have read and decide where you stand.

A. **Reading Critically.** Read this excerpt from *Rising Seas* using the technique described above.

Unless we change course dramatically, our carbon emissions will drastically change the geography of many shorelines by the next century, if not sooner, and large numbers of people will have to abandon coastal areas in Florida and other parts of the world. "From the Bahamas to Bangladesh and a major amount of Florida, we'll have to move, and we may have to move at the same time," says Wanless. Columbia University geophysicist Klaus Jacob sees most of Manhattan's population fleeing to higher ground and the island becoming a kind of Venice, subject to periodic flooding, perhaps with canals and yellow water cabs. At different times in different countries, engineering solutions will no longer be enough. Then the retreat from the coast will begin.

B. **Discussion.** Discuss the questions below with a partner.

1. How important does the author think the issue is? What persuasive language does the author use to convey this?

2. Look at the numbers and dates the author uses in the first sentence. How reliable and accurate do you think this information is? Do we know the source of the data?

3. The author's view is supported by the opinions of two other people. Who are they? How valid are their opinions?

4. Do you think the author might be biased? Give reasons for your answer.

# Vocabulary Practice

**A. Completion.** Complete the information using the correct form of the words and phrases in the box. One word is extra.

| | | | | |
|---|---|---|---|---|
| ambitious | barrier | comply | dire | envision |
| policy | retreat | surge | take for granted | withstand |

Imagine Boston's Faneuil Hall, the U.S. Naval Academy, and Jamestown—site of the first English colony in North America—lost forever due to the effects of rising seas. It's a future many Americans cannot **1.** _____, but according to a report from the Union of Concerned Scientists (UCS), their future looks bleak.

Amid all the concern and **2.** _____ warnings regarding climate change, little attention has been paid to how it could affect cultural resources, and what the country's **3.** _____ should be to protect them. "It's an ignored issue in the world of climate change assessment," says Adam Markham, director of climate impacts for the UCS.

In North Carolina, north of Cape Hatteras, sea levels have risen by four times the national average. Residents and vacationers in the resort area may **4.** _____ that the low-lying area will always be as they remember it. But the delicate seashore would not be able to **5.** _____ the rising sea levels and increase in storm activity. Residents will undoubtedly have to **6.** _____ from the coast and move inland.

Even sites from recent history will require drastic changes to last into the next generation. NASA is dealing with rising seas at many of its locations. According to the report, "More than two-thirds of NASA facilities [are] within 16 feet of sea level," including the Kennedy Space Center launch pads. NASA has embarked on a(n) **7.** _____ program to rebuild and strengthen nearby dunes that acted as natural **8.** _____ several times, but storm **9.** _____ still broke through.

∧ According to a recent report, several cultural landmarks such as Boston's Faneuil Hall could be at risk due to the effects of rising seas.

**B. Definitions.** Match the definitions to words from the box in **A**. Three words are extra.

**1.** _____: to do what you are asked to do

**2.** _____: to move back to get away from danger

**3.** _____: a sudden, large increase

**4.** _____: a set of rules about how something should be done

**5.** _____: to not be harmed or affected by something

**6.** _____: not easily done or achieved

**7.** _____: to picture something in your mind

> **Word Link**
> The word root **poli** means "city," e.g., *police, policy, politics, metropolis, Acropolis.*

# VIEWING Time and Tide

## Before You Watch

**A. Definitions.** Read the information and then circle the correct definition for each word.

Smith Island is a lonely **outpost**, 12 miles out in the Lower Chesapeake Bay. The shallow grassy waters around the **cluster** of islands that comprise Smith Island are ideal blue crab **habitat**. For more than 300 years, the people here have survived on this remote island, but increasingly they sense that a more **precarious** future lies ahead.

1. An **outpost** is a town that is _____.
   a. far from other towns          b. close to a large city

2. A **cluster** of islands is _____.
   a. a long line of islands          b. a group of islands that are close together

3. A **habitat** is a place where a plant or an animal _____.
   a. naturally grows or lives     b. is displayed to the public

4. Something that is **precarious** is _____.
   a. unsafe or unsteady          b. safe or steady

**B. Discussion.** Discuss these questions with a partner.

1. What do you think is the main occupation of residents on Smith Island?

2. What kind of problems do you think they face?

‹ Smith Island has no land bridges, so people traveling there can only access it by boat.

# While You Watch

**A. Main idea.** Watch the video and check (✓) the main idea.

- [ ] Smith Island is dependent on seafood. There are fewer fish and crabs these days, and no one is sure why. Some scientists think the area has been overfished.

- [ ] Smith Island has lost half of its population. People can no longer make a living on Smith Island and are moving to the mainland where there are more jobs.

- [ ] Smith Island is vulnerable to the ocean. Its land is being eroded, and this is difficult for its inhabitants. Rising seas may one day make the island unfit to live on.

- [ ] Smith Island was hit by a Category 4 hurricane. This caused severe erosion of its land and made much of the island impossible to live on.

**B. Completion.** Circle the correct words to make the sentences true.

1. In the past 100 years, the population of Smith Island has dropped by (**500 / 800**).

2. Most of Smith Island is (**one foot / two feet**) above sea level.

3. Chesapeake Bay has risen by more than a half foot over the past (**decade / century**).

4. The people of Smith Island are (**building barriers to slow erosion / in denial about the effects of the rising seas**).

5. If a Category 4 hurricane hits Smith Island, (**the island will completely disappear / there will only be a few high spots left**).

# After You Watch

**Discussion.** Discuss these questions with a partner.

1. What else could be done to help the people of Smith Island?

2. Why do you think crab catches are so small? Is the rising sea to blame for this?

3. What other places do you know that are threatened by rising seas?

❮ Smith Island faces an uncertain future due to rising sea levels.

# ECO-LIVING

Urban agriculture reduces the carbon footprint of a city by cutting down the transportation needed to deliver goods to the consumer.

## Warm Up

**Discuss these questions with a partner.**

1. What are the world's main sources of energy? Which are the most important in your country?

2. What are some advantages and disadvantages of each type of energy discussed above?

3. In what ways could people in your country reduce their energy consumption?

The New York skyline viewed via thermal imaging. Red and yellow patches indicate escaping heat. Heating, cooling, and powering of these buildings account for almost three-quarters of New York City's emissions.

# Before You Read

**A. True or False.** Use the information on page 99, and circle **T** (True) or **F** (False) for each of the sentences below.

1. A carbon footprint is the total amount of greenhouse gases emitted by a country, product, or person in a year.     **T**    **F**

2. Brazilian households have relatively low levels of per capita (per person) carbon dioxide ($CO_2$) emissions.     **T**    **F**

3. The country with the world's highest per capita household $CO_2$ emissions is the United States.     **T**    **F**

4. The European country with the highest per capita household $CO_2$ emissions is Luxembourg.     **T**    **F**

**B. Skim and Predict.** Skim the passage on pages 97–101, looking especially at the title, section headings, captions, and the first sentence of each paragraph. Try to answer the questions below. Then read the passage to check your ideas.

1. What kind of experiment is the author participating in?

2. What do you think he found out?

# CARBON FOOTPRINT

With a little effort, and not much money, most of us could reduce our energy diets by 25 percent or more. So what's holding us back? Writer Peter Miller goes on a strict low-carbon diet to find out.

**A** 1 Not long ago, my wife and I tried a new diet—not to lose weight but to answer a question about climate change. Scientists have reported that the world is heating up even faster than they predicted just a few years ago. The consequences, they say, could be severe if we don't keep reducing emissions
5 of carbon dioxide and other greenhouse gases that are trapping heat in our atmosphere. But what can we do about it as individuals? And will our efforts really make any difference?

## The Experiment

**B** We decided to try an experiment. For one month we tracked our personal
10 emissions of $CO_2$ as if we were counting calories. We wanted to see how much we could cut back.

**C** The average U.S. household produces about 70 kilograms (150 pounds) of $CO_2$ a day by doing **commonplace** things like turning on air conditioning or driving cars. That's more than twice the European average and almost five
15 times the global average. But how much should we try to reduce?

> A study . . . found that "vampire" power sucked up by electronics . . . can add up to 8 percent of a house's electric bill.

**D** I checked with Tim Flannery, author of *The Weather Makers: How Man Is Changing the Climate and What It Means for Life on Earth*. In his book, he challenged readers
20 to make deep cuts in personal emissions to keep the world from reaching critical tipping points,[1] such as the melting of the ice sheets in Greenland or West Antarctica. "To stay below that **threshold**, we need to reduce
25 $CO_2$ emissions by 80 percent," he said. "That sounds like a lot," my wife said. "Can we really do that?"

**E** It seemed unlikely to me, too. Still, the point was to answer a simple question: How close
30 could we come to a lifestyle the planet could handle? Finally, we agreed to aim for 80 percent less than the U.S. average: a daily diet of about 13 kilograms (30 pounds) of $CO_2$. Our first challenge was to find ways to convert
35 our daily activities into pounds of $CO_2$. We wanted to track our progress as we went so that we could change our habits if necessary.

**F** To get a rough idea of our current carbon footprint, I put numbers from recent **utility**
40 bills into several calculators on websites. None was flattering.[2] The Environmental Protection Agency (EPA) website figured our annual $CO_2$ emissions at 54,273 pounds, 30 percent higher than the average U.S. family with two people.
45 The main culprit was the energy we were using to heat and cool our house. Clearly we had further to go than I thought.

## The Diagnosis

**G**
50 We got some help in Week Two from a professional "house doctor," Ed Minch of Energy Services Group in Wilmington, Delaware. We asked Minch to do an energy **audit** of our house. The first thing he did was to walk around the outside of the house.
55 Had the architect and builder created any opportunities for air to seep[3] in or out, such as overhanging floors? Next he went inside and used an infrared scanner to look at our interior walls. Finally, his assistants set up a
60 powerful fan in our front door to lower air pressure inside the house and force air through whatever leaks there might be in the shell of the house.

**H** Our house, his instruments showed, was 50
65 percent leakier than it should be. Addressing this became a priority, as heating represents up to half of a house's energy costs, and cooling can account for a tenth. Minch also gave us tips about lighting and **appliances**. "A typical
70 kitchen these days has ten 75-watt spots[4] on all day," he said. "That's a huge waste of money." Replacing them with **compact** fluorescents could save a homeowner $200 a year. Refrigerators, washing machines,
75 dishwashers, and other appliances, in fact, may represent half of a household's electric bill.

**I** Everywhere I looked, I saw things sucking up energy. One night I sat up in bed and counted ten little lights in the darkness: cell phone
80 charger, desktop calculator, laptop computer, printer, clock radio, cable TV box, camera battery recharger, carbon monoxide detector, cordless phone base, smoke detector. What were they all doing? A study by the Lawrence

---

1 A **tipping point** is a stage of a process when a significant change takes place, after which the process cannot be turned back.
2 Something that is **flattering** makes us look or seem better than we really are.
3 If something **seeps** in or through, it leaks in slowly.
4 The word **spots** is short for spotlights, or strong, focused lights.

# CO₂ emisions by country

A **carbon footprint** is the amount of greenhouse gases, such as carbon dioxide ($CO_2$), emitted by a country or a person in a year. Emissions from human activities—such as the burning of fossil fuels to produce energy—are the main cause of high levels of greenhouse gases in the atmosphere. The production of these gases results in a warming of the lower atmosphere, particularly in the polar regions, leading to melting of polar ice and rising sea levels.

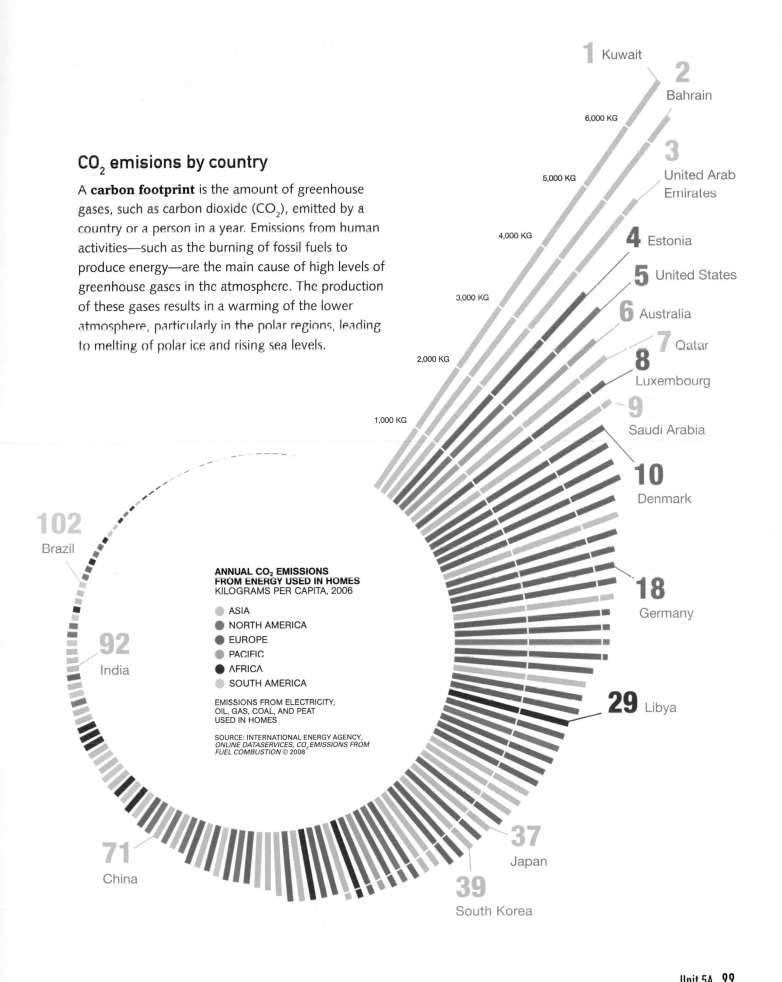

1 Kuwait
2 Bahrain
3 United Arab Emirates
4 Estonia
5 United States
6 Australia
7 Qatar
8 Luxembourg
9 Saudi Arabia
10 Denmark
18 Germany
29 Libya
37 Japan
39 South Korea
71 China
92 India
102 Brazil

6,000 KG
5,000 KG
4,000 KG
3,000 KG
2,000 KG
1,000 KG

**ANNUAL CO₂ EMISSIONS FROM ENERGY USED IN HOMES**
KILOGRAMS PER CAPITA, 2006

● ASIA
● NORTH AMERICA
● EUROPE
● PACIFIC
● AFRICA
● SOUTH AMERICA

EMISSIONS FROM ELECTRICITY, OIL, GAS, COAL, AND PEAT USED IN HOMES

SOURCE: INTERNATIONAL ENERGY AGENCY, ONLINE DATASERVICES, CO₂ EMISSIONS FROM FUEL COMBUSTION © 2008

85 Berkeley National Laboratory found that "vampire" power sucked up by electronics in standby **mode** can add up to 8 percent of a house's electric bill. What else had I missed?

J
90 "You can go nuts[5] thinking about everything in your house that uses power," said Jennifer Thorne Amann, author of *Consumer Guide to Home Energy Savings*. "You have to use common sense and prioritize. Don't agonize[6] too much. Think about what you'll be able
95 to sustain after the experiment is over. If you have trouble reaching your goal in one area, remember there's always something else you can do."

## The Results

K 100 By the last week in July, we were finally getting into the flow of the reduced carbon lifestyle. We walked to the neighborhood pool instead of driving, biked to the local farmers market on Saturday morning, and sat out on
105 the deck until dark, chatting over the sound of the crickets. Whenever possible I worked from home, and when I **commuted**, I took the bus and subway.

L
110 Our numbers were looking pretty good, in fact, when we crossed the finish line on August 1. Compared with the previous July, we cut electricity use by 70 percent, natural gas by 40 percent, and reduced our driving to half the national average. In terms of $CO_2$,
115 we trimmed our emissions to an average of 32 kilograms (70.5 pounds) a day, which, though twice as much as we'd targeted as our goal, was still half the national average.

M
120 We can do more, of course. We can sign up with our utility company for power from regional wind farms. We can purchase locally grown foods instead of winter raspberries from Chile and bottled water from Fiji. We can join a carbon-reduction club, or set up one of
125 our own.

Cyclists commute to work through Hyde Park, London, on a warm, sunny morning.

## The Future

N Will it make any difference? That's what we really wanted to know. Our low-carbon diet had shown us that, with little or no hardship
130 and no major cash outlays,[7] we could cut day-to-day emissions of $CO_2$ in half—mainly by wasting less energy at home and on the highway. Similar efforts in office buildings, shopping malls, and factories throughout
135 the nation, combined with incentives and efficiency standards, could halt further increases in U.S. emissions.

O Yet efficiency, in the end, can only take us so far. To get the deeper reductions we need, as
140 Tim Flannery advised, we must replace fossil

---

5 If someone goes **nuts**, he or she goes crazy.
6 When people **agonize** about something, they are very worried about it.

7 A **cash outlay** is the amount of money that has to be spent, often at the beginning of a project, for the project or business to get started.

fuels faster with renewable energy from wind farms, solar plants, geothermal facilities, and biofuels. We must slow deforestation, which is an additional source of greenhouse gases. And we must develop technologies to capture and bury carbon dioxide from existing power plants. Efficiency can buy us time—perhaps as much as two decades—to figure out how to remove carbon from the world's diet.

**P** 150 Not that there won't still be **obstacles**. Every sector of our economy faces challenges, says energy-efficiency guru[8] Amory Lovins of the Rocky Mountain Institute. "But they all have huge potential. I don't know anyone who has failed to make money at energy efficiency. There's so much low-hanging fruit, it's falling off the trees and mushing up[9] around our ankles."

**Q** 160 The rest of the world isn't waiting for the United States to show the way. Sweden has **pioneered** carbon-neutral houses, Germany affordable solar power, Japan fuel-efficient cars, the Netherlands prosperous cities filled with bicycles. Does the U.S. have the will to match such efforts?

**R** Change starts at home with the replacement of a light bulb, the opening of a window, a walk to the bus, or a bike ride to the post office. My wife and I did it for only a month, but I can see the low-carbon diet becoming a habit. As my wife said, "What do we have to lose?"

---

8 A **guru** is a religious teacher or leader, or an expert in a particular field.

9 If a fruit is **mushing up**, it is becoming a soft pulpy mass, a process caused by rotting.

# Reading Comprehension

**Multiple Choice.** Choose the best answer for each question.

Gist

**1.** The best alternative title for this reading would be _____.
  a. Replacing Fossil Fuels
  b. One Family's Energy Diet
  c. Our Current Carbon Footprint
  d. How People Are Changing the Climate

Reference

**2.** The word *it* in line 6 refers to _____.
  a. a new diet        b. an effort
  c. climate change    d. the world

Detail

**3.** How much $CO_2$ does the average family in Europe produce a day?
  a. 30 pounds         b. 70 pounds
  c. 150 pounds        d. 300 pounds

Inference

**4.** The author is initially _____ reducing his family's $CO_2$ production by 80 percent.
  a. fairly agreeable to    b. enthusiastic about
  c. not very interested in  d. not confident about

Detail

**5.** What does the author say in paragraph I about the standby mode on electronic devices?
  a. Using it is an efficient way to save energy and money.
  b. It uses as much energy as leaving the device turned on.
  c. It uses less energy than turning a device off and then on again.
  d. Using it can account for up to 8 percent of a household's electricity.

Paraphrase

**6.** Which of the following is closest in meaning to this sentence (lines 114–118)? *In terms of $CO_2$, we trimmed our emissions to an average of 32 kilograms (70.5 pounds) a day, which, though twice as much as we'd targeted as our goal, was still half the national average.*
  a. The author's family reduced their $CO_2$ emissions to half the national average, but only reached half their targeted goal.
  b. The author and his wife were not able to cut their $CO_2$ output to the national average, but they still met their goal.
  c. The author's family reduced their $CO_2$ output to 70.5 percent of the national average, but not as much as they had targeted.
  d. The author's family planned to reduce their $CO_2$ emissions to half the national average, but they were able to reduce emissions by twice that much.

Detail

**7.** According to the information in paragraph Q, which of these countries are known for using "green" modes of transportation?
  a. the Netherlands and Sweden     b. Germany and Japan
  c. Sweden and Germany             d. Japan and the Netherlands

## Critical Thinking

**Analyzing:** Is the author's attitude toward the experiment mainly positive or negative? How do you know?

_____

**Discussion:** Would you be willing to do a $CO_2$-cutting experiment similar to the author's? Why or why not? What do you think would be the most difficult challenges?

## Reading Skill

# Distinguishing Main Ideas and Supporting Information

Most articles have a single, unifying idea (also called the thesis). In addition, each section of an article will normally have its own main idea, and so may individual paragraphs. The author develops these main ideas by supplying details, reasons, and explanations that strengthen the most important points. To clearly understand an article, it's important to identify main ideas and to distinguish between them and supporting information.

**A. Matching.** Read the sentences below (**a–h**). Find four sentences that summarize the main ideas of the sections in the table below. Write a letter to complete each main idea.

**a.** According to the EPA website, the author's annual household $CO_2$ emissions totaled 54,273 pounds.

**b.** Increasing household energy efficiency is a first step, but other measures are needed to tackle global warming.

**c.** With some outside advice, the author learned his house was losing a lot of energy through heat leakage and household appliances.

**d.** Although there was more he could do, the author was pleased that he was able to significantly lower his carbon footprint.

**e.** To help reduce his carbon emissions, the author walked and cycled whenever possible.

**f.** The author investigated his household carbon footprint and found it was surprisingly high.

**g.** The author learned that compact fluorescents can save house owners about $200 a year.

**h.** Countries such as Germany and Japan have developed some innovative ways to reduce carbon emissions.

**B. Matching.** Choose four more sentences from the list above to complete the supporting information column.

**Main idea of the article:** *The author and his wife performed an experiment to see if they could significantly reduce their carbon footprint on the planet.*

|  | Main idea | Supporting information |
|---|---|---|
| Section 1: The Experiment |  |  |
| Section 2: The Diagnosis |  |  |
| Section 3: The Results |  |  |
| Section 4: The Future |  |  |

**A. Completion.** Complete the information with the correct form of words from the box. One word is extra.

| | | |
|---|---|---|
| **audit** | **commonplace** | **mode** |
| **obstacle** | **pioneer** | **threshold** |

Marathon Monday is an official state holiday in Massachusetts, a day when citizens crowd the streets to watch some of the world's top long-distance runners compete in the Boston Marathon. Over 30,000 runners compete each year to win this famous race, or at the very least, to reach their personal **1.** _____ of endurance.

The 2009 race was the 113th marathon in Boston's history, and it was the start of the "green" era. For the first time, electric scooters rather than motorcycles followed the runners. A "green team" was employed to ensure that thousands of items discarded along the marathon route—including **2.** _____ items like plastic cups and bottles—found their way into recycling containers. It was the first step toward making the race more sustainable.

While the Boston Marathon has **3.** _____ green thinking for large-scale events, an energy **4.** _____ shows that it still has many **5.** _____ to overcome before it can claim to be truly sustainable. For example, only about two percent of the runners are from the surrounding area, so there is a considerable carbon footprint from airplane and car emissions as the runners travel long distances to get to the event.

In recent years, other races in the U.S. have also made efforts to improve their efficiency in energy consumption. The race to become the nation's greenest marathon has just begun.

∧ Up to 30,000 people run the Boston Marathon every year, but they leave more than just their footprints. Each year, discarded drinking cups litter Boston's roads.

**B. Completion.** Complete the sentences using the correct word from each pair.

1. There are things everyone can do to save money on their (**utility / compact**) bills.

2. Driving cars and using computers are examples of (**pioneering / commonplace**) activities that consume energy.

3. Household (**obstacles / appliances**) are a major source of electricity consumption.

4. Putting your computer on standby (**audit / mode**) can be a waste of energy.

5. In the past, there were many (**obstacles / thresholds**) to implementing solar- and wind-powered projects.

6. Most (**mode / compact**) cars are a more energy-efficient way to (**commute / audit**) to work.

> **Word Partnership**
> Use *obstacle* with:
> (*n.*) obstacle **course**, obstacle to **peace**;
> (*v.*) **be** an obstacle, **overcome** an obstacle, **hit** an obstacle; (*adj.*) **major** obstacle, **serious** obstacle.

# PLUGGING INTO THE SUN

## Before You Read

A. **Understanding Maps.** Look at the map on page 110, and answer the questions below.

1. Which countries are world leaders in renewable energy?
2. Which country has the highest capacity for solar PV energy?
3. Which country is top for solar thermal energy?

B. **Scan.** The passage on pages 106–111 discusses solar power. Scan the passage and then answer the questions below.

1. Which countries does the article focus on?

_____

_____

2. What kinds of sites in those countries does it mention?

_____

_____

In Albuquerque, New Mexico, U.S., mirror arrays concentrate solar rays to make electricity.

Nevada Solar One at sunrise in the Mojave desert, California, U.S. >

**A** 1 Early on a clear November morning in the Mojave Desert, a full moon is sinking over the gigawatt[1] glare of Las Vegas. 5 Nevada Solar One is sleeping. But the day's work is about to begin.

**B** It is hard to imagine that a power plant could be so beautiful: 100 hectares (247 acres) of gently curved mirrors lined up like canals of 10 light. Parked facing the ground overnight, they are starting to awaken—more than 182,000 of them—and follow the sun.

**C** "Looks like this will be a 700-degree day," says one of the operators in the control room. His 15 job is to monitor the rows of mirrors as they concentrate sunlight on long steel pipes filled with **circulating** oil, heating it as high as 400 degrees Celsius (750°F). The heat produces steam, driving a turbine and dynamo, pushing 20 as much as 64 megawatts onto the grid— enough to electrify 14,000 households, or a few Las Vegas casinos.

**D** When Nevada Solar One came online in 2007, it was the first large solar plant to be built 25 in the United States in more than 17 years. During that time, solar technology blossomed[2] elsewhere. The owner of Nevada Solar One is a Spanish company, Acciona; the mirrors were made in Germany. Putting on hard hats 30 and dark glasses, plant manager Robert Cable and I drive out to take a closer look at the mirrors. Men with a water truck are hosing some down. "Any kind of dust affects them," Cable says. On a clear summer day with the 35 sun directly overhead, Nevada Solar One can convert about 20 percent of the sun's rays into electricity. Gas plants are more efficient, but this fuel is free. And it doesn't emit planet-warming carbon dioxide.

**E** 40 "If we talk about geothermal or wind, all these other sources of **renewable** energy are limited in their quantity," said Eicke Weber,

---

1 One **gigawatt** is a billion ($10^9$) watts.
2 If something has **blossomed**, it has grown and developed well.

On a clear summer day with the sun directly overhead, Nevada Solar One can convert about 20 percent of the sun's rays into electricity.

director of the Fraunhofer Institute for Solar Energy Systems, in Freiburg, Germany. "The
45  total power needs of the humans on Earth is approximately 16 terawatts," he said. (A terawatt is a trillion—1,000,000,000,000—watts.) "In the year 2020, it is expected to grow to 20 terawatts. The sunshine on the
50  solid part of the Earth is 120,000 terawatts. From this perspective, energy from the sun is virtually unlimited."

## Tapping the Sun

**F**
55  Solar energy may be unlimited, but its potential is barely tapped. "Right now solar is such a small fraction of U.S. electricity production that it's measured in tenths of a percent," said Robert Hawsey, an associate director of the National Renewable Energy
60  Laboratory (NREL) in Golden, Colorado. "But that's expected to grow. Ten to 20 percent of the nation's peak electricity demand could be provided by solar energy by 2030."

**G**
65  Achieving that level will require government help. Nevada Solar One was built because the state had set a **deadline** requiring utilities to generate 20 percent of their power from renewable sources by 2015. During peak demand, the solar plant's electricity is almost
70  as cheap as that of its gas-fired neighbor—but that's only because a 30-percent federal tax credit helped **offset** its construction costs.

**H**
75  The aim now is to bring down costs and reduce the need for subsidies and incentives. To achieve this, NREL's engineers are studying mirrors made from lightweight polymers instead of glass, and tubes that will absorb more sunlight and lose less heat. They're also working on solar power's biggest problem:
80  how to store some of the heat produced during daylight hours for release later on.

**I**
Power plants such as Nevada Solar One use solar thermal energy (STE) technology, in other words, collecting the sun's rays via
85  mirrors to produce thermal energy (heat).

**J** Another method is to convert sunlight directly into electricity with photovoltaic (PV) **panels** made of semiconductors such as silicon. Back in the 1980s, an engineer named Roland Hulstrom calculated
90 that if PV panels covered just three-tenths of a percent of the United States, they could electrify the entire country.

**K** Twenty years later, PV panels still contribute only a tiny amount to the nation's electricity supply.
95 But on rooftops in California, Nevada, and other states with good sunshine and tax incentives, they are increasingly common—almost as familiar as air conditioners. Though not yet as developed as solar thermal, they may have a brighter future.
100 Two U.S. companies, First Solar and Nanosolar, say they can now **manufacture** thin-film solar cells at a cost of around a dollar a watt—close to what's needed to compete with fossil fuels.

## Germany's Solar Solution

**L** 105 On a cold December morning west of Frankfurt, Germany, fog hangs frozen in the trees, and clouds block the sun. In the town of Morbach, the blades of a 100-meter- (330-foot-) high wind turbine appear and disappear in the gloom.[3]
110 Down below, a field of photovoltaic panels struggle for light. Considering its unpredictable weather, who would have thought that Germany would transform itself into the largest producer of photovoltaic power in the world?

**M** 115 A fraction of Germany's five-gigawatt photovoltaic power comes from centralized plants like the one at Morbach. With land at a **premium** in Germany, solar panels can be found mounted on rooftops, farmhouses, even on soccer stadiums and along
120 the autobahn.[4] The panels, dispersed across the German countryside, are all connected to the national grid.

---

3 Something that is in the **gloom** is in partial or total darkness.

4 **Autobahn** is a word used to describe super highways in Austria, Germany, and Switzerland, on which vehicles travel very fast.

▼ In Bavaria, Germany, solar panels are installed on rooftops of farmhouses. These facilities are not only eco-friendly, but they also absorb more energy than is needed—earning a profit for the owners and residents.

"In the year 2020, [the total power needs of the humans on Earth] is expected to grow to 20 terawatts. The sunshine on the solid part of the Earth is 120,000 terawatts. From this perspective, energy from the sun is virtually unlimited."

— Eicke Weber

# RENEWABLE ENERGY: WORLD LEADERS

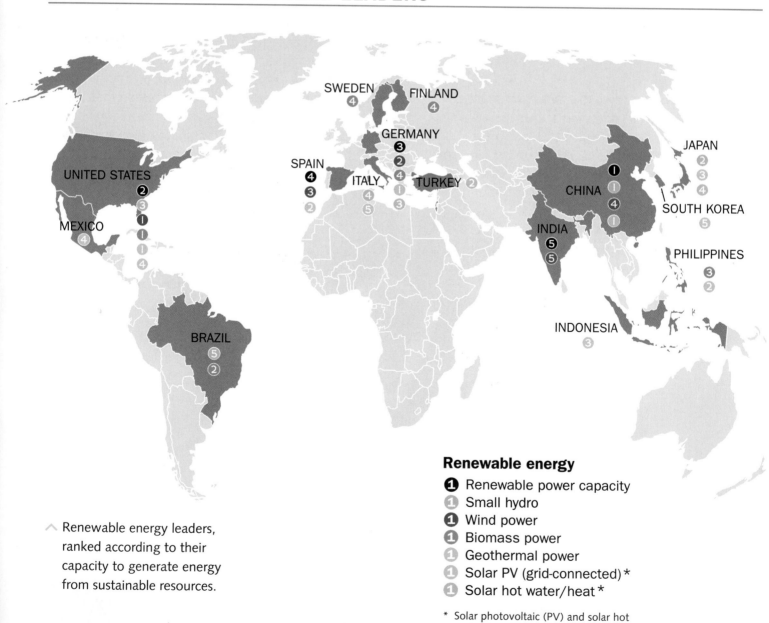

Renewable energy leaders, ranked according to their capacity to generate energy from sustainable resources.

**Renewable energy**
- ❶ Renewable power capacity
- ① Small hydro
- ❶ Wind power
- ❶ Biomass power
- ① Geothermal power
- ① Solar PV (grid-connected) *
- ① Solar hot water/heat *

\* Solar photovoltaic (PV) and solar hot water/heat (thermal) are two methods for generating electricity using solar energy.

**N** The solar boom has completely transformed towns like "sunny Freiburg," as the tourist
125 brochures call it, which sits at the edge of the Black Forest in the southern part of the country. Towering walls of photovoltaics greet visitors as they arrive at Freiburg's train station. Across the street from a
130 school covered with photovoltaic panels is Solarsiedlung ("solar settlement"), one of the town's condominium complexes.[5]

**O** "We are being paid for living in this house," said Wolfgang Schnürer, one of Solarsiedlung's
135 residents. The day before, when snow covered the roof, Schnürer's system produced only 5.8 kilowatt-hours, not enough power for a German household. But on a sunny day in May, it **yielded** more than seven times that
140 much.

**P** In Germany, regulations require utility companies to pay even the smallest PV producers a premium of about 50 euro cents a kilowatt-hour. In 2008, Schnürer's personal
145 power plant yielded over 6,000 kilowatt-hours, more than double the amount the family consumed. When they **subtracted** their usage from the amount they produced, the family found they were more than 2,500
150 euros (nearly $3,400) in profit.

**Q** Anybody who installs a PV system is guaranteed above-market rates for 20 years—the equivalent of an 8 percent annual return on the initial investment. "It is an **ingenious**
155 mechanism," Eicke Weber said. "I always say the United States addresses the idealists, those who want to save the planet. In Germany, the law addresses anyone who wants to get 8 percent return on his investment for
160 20 years."

**R** In total, Germany now generates more than 2,000 gigawatt-hours of electricity annually from solar energy, whereas the U.S. generates less than half this amount. The
165 largest photovoltaic installation in the United States—at Nellis Air Force Base just outside Las Vegas—is only about the 25th largest in the world. Nearly all the bigger ones are located in either Germany or Spain. But in the
170 U.S., too, there is a gathering sense that the time for solar energy has arrived—if there is a commitment to jump-start[6] the technology. "Originally it seemed like a pie-in-the-sky idea," said Michelle Price, the energy manager
175 at Nellis. "It didn't seem possible." Many things seem possible now.

---

5 **Condominium complexes** are apartment compounds, or living areas.

6 To **jump-start** something means to cause it to start quickly

# Reading Comprehension

**Multiple Choice.** Choose the best answer for each question.

Inference **1.** The author seems surprised by Nevada Solar One because it _____.
   a. heats oil to very high temperatures
   b. can provide electricity for many households
   c. is more attractive than a typical power plant
   d. is more efficient than other solar power plants

Detail **2.** What is the job of the men with the water truck in paragraph D?
   a. to cool the solar plant
   b. to pump water that will then be heated
   c. to provide the workers with drinking water
   d. to clean the surface of some of the mirrors

Inference **3.** The phrase *barely tapped* (line 55) indicates that _____.
   a. the use of solar energy has been growing rapidly
   b. someday, much more solar energy can be utilized
   c. the supply of solar power will never meet the demand
   d. no one knows how much solar energy can be generated

Detail **4.** Which of these is NOT mentioned in paragraph H as a way to cut prices for solar energy production?
   a. making mirrors from different materials
   b. finding a way to store heat for use at night
   c. obtaining more subsidies from the government
   d. designing tubes that take in more sunlight and hold heat better

Inference **5.** What does the author imply in paragraph N about the town of Freiburg, Germany?
   a. It is sunny there throughout the year.
   b. It does not really get that much sunshine.
   c. Its solar industry helps to attract tourists.
   d. It was the first town with a large-scale solar plant.

Paraphrase **6.** What does Wolfgang Schnürer mean when he says, "We are being paid for living in this house" (line 133)?
   a. "The money we get for producing electricity is greater than our total living costs."
   b. "The government pays us a salary for maintaining a personal solar power plant."
   c. "The income from our personal power plant is greater than our energy costs."
   d. "We receive free housing in exchange for our work for the utility company."

Vocabulary **7.** The phrase *pie-in-the-sky* in paragraph R is closest in meaning to _____.
   a. unrealistic
   b. brilliant
   c. believable
   d. unwelcome

## Critical Thinking

**Analyzing:** Do you think the author of this article is generally optimistic or pessimistic about this topic? Find places in the article that support your opinion.

_____

**Discussion:** Is your country or region a good place for solar power production? Are there incentives for people to try solar power or other renewable sources of energy?

# Identifying Similarities and Differences

To understand a comparison between two things, you first need to identify which ideas relate to each category. We can organize this information by classifying it into different categories based on ways that they are similar or different.

**Classification.** Look back at the reading on pages 106–111. Write which country the sentence refers to: Germany (**G**), the United States (**U**), both (**B**), or neither (**N**).

**a.** _____ Despite unpredictable weather, it has the world's largest PV solar industry.

**b.** _____ The mirrors for Nevada Solar One were made here.

**c.** _____ It is the second largest producer of photovoltaic power.

**d.** _____ Solar power produces less than one percent of the country's electricity.

**e.** _____ The company that owns Nevada Solar One is from this country.

**f.** _____ Manufacturers here have recently developed very cheap, thin solar cells.

**g.** _____ According to one expert, the government policies here regarding solar energy appeal to people who want to make money on their investment.

**h.** _____ Even the smallest solar providers here are connected to the national electrical grid.

**i.** _____ According to one expert, the government policies here regarding solar energy appeal to idealists.

**j.** _____ The government here has given incentives for the increased use of solar power.

**k.** _____ It generates less than 1,000 gigawatt-hours of electricity every year from solar power.

**l.** _____ There is optimism that solar electricity production here will be more significant in the future.

# Vocabulary Practice

**A. Completion.** Complete the information by circling the correct word in each pair.

Germany needs a place to store its wind power. And in the small town of Cuxhaven on the windy North Sea coast, they think they've found a(n) **1. (ingenious / manufacturing)** answer—in frozen fish.

One of **2. (renewable / panel)** energy's most problematic issues is the uncertainty of wind and solar power. Customers need a steady, predictable stream of electricity. But how do you produce a steady **3. (yield / offset)** of electricity from wind power, when winds are so unpredictable? This is particularly an issue in Germany, where seven percent of electricity comes from wind energy.

One possible solution is cold storage. When fish from the North Sea are stored in a warehouse, such as Erwin GOOSS warehouse in Cuxhaven, they need to be kept cold. Ordinarily, air **4. (deadlines / circulation)** inside the warehouse is controlled so temperatures remain at about –20°C (–4°F). But during peak hours of wind production, the temperature can be pushed as low as –30°C (–22°F). The frozen fish absorb and "store" this extra energy. When winds die down, the cooling is switched off, but the warehouse remains cold enough for fish to stay frozen. This keeps cooling costs to a minimum, especially during the summer when electricity is at a **5. (subtraction / premium)**.

"It's not that we're using less power, it's just that we're using it when it's cheaper," says Gunter Krins, technical director of Erwin GOOSS. By investing in storage methods such as Cuxhaven's, it is hoped that wind power could become an efficient long-term solution to Germany's energy needs—no matter how hard the wind is blowing.

∧ Globally, wind supplies less than one percent of electric power. But its share is growing, particularly in European countries such as Germany.

**B. Definitions.** Match the correct form of words in **red** from above with their correct definition.

1. _____ : make something on a large scale

2. _____ : specific time for completion

3. _____ : take away, deduct

4. _____ : higher price, usually due to short supply

5. _____ : flat, rectangular piece of material

6. _____ : counteract by having an equal and opposite effect

7. _____ : movement of something (e.g., air or water) from place to place

> **Word Partnership**
> Use ***premium*** with:
> (*n.*) premium **rate**, premium **brand**, premium **product**, premium **service**; (*v.*) **pay** a premium; (*prep.*) **at** a premium.

# VIEWING Eco-Detectives

## Before You Watch

**A. Matching.** You will hear these words and phrases in the video. What do you think they mean in these contexts? Match each word or phrase to its meaning.

1. ... **lurking** beneath this innocent façade
2. ... lurking beneath this innocent **façade**
3. ... an energy-eating **monster**
4. ... political resistance is going to **melt**
5. ... about 60 **bucks** a year just sitting there
6. ... high technology and good ol' **common sense**
7. ... there is energy **to spare**

a. _____ left over
b. _____ dollars
c. _____ hiding
d. _____ gradually become less, or disappear
e. _____ ability to use good judgement and make sensible decisions
f. _____ something unusually large and frightening
g. _____ a deceptive outward appearance

∧ Eco-detectives checking a house for possible energy leaks

**B. Discuss.** In the video, eco-detectives discuss ways in which people can save money on home energy. What are some ways that a home can become more energy-efficient? Brainstorm ideas with a partner.

## While You Watch

**A. Inference.** Watch the video and check (✓) the statements that the eco-detectives would probably agree with.

a. ☐ There are many simple things that people can do at home to save money.
b. ☐ Most people are not interested in trying to find ways to save money around the house.
c. ☐ We will not solve our energy problems until we start to give up some of our conveniences.
d. ☐ The main way to save money on energy is to use energy more efficiently.

**B. Multiple Choice.** Choose the correct answer to each question.

1. How much energy consumption in the United States do homes and buildings account for?
   a. about a quarter
   b. less than half
   c. more than half

2. Which claim does the video make?
   a. Many homes waste more energy than they actually use.
   b. Home owners can cut their energy bill in half by using more insulation.
   c. Few people care about saving money on home efficiency.

3. What is a *vampire load*?
   a. a simple switch that lets you turn off appliances
   b. energy that you can save by buying more energy-efficient appliances
   c. the power used by an electrical appliance when it is not in use

4. Where does Amory Lovins get his home energy from?
   a. a wood furnace
   b. solar panels
   c. heat-retaining windows

5. How much electricity does Lovins' house run on?
   a. 120,000 watts
   b. slightly more energy than a single light bulb uses
   c. His home doesn't use electricity.

## After You Watch

**Discussion.** Discuss these questions in a group.

1. How efficient is your home? Do you think it is more or less efficient than the average home? Why?

2. How could you make your home more efficient?

3. Amory Lovins says, "Climate change is a problem we don't need to have, and it's cheaper not to." What does he mean by this? Do you agree?

# 6

# WILDLIFE IN TROUBLE

Lonesome George was the last surviving Pinta Island tortoise, native to the Galapagos. When he died in 2012, the species disappeared from the face of the Earth.

## Warm Up

**Discuss these questions with a partner.**

1. What are some animals that are endangered? Why are they endangered?

2. Should some animals be protected over others? Why or why not?

3. Do you know any success stories about endangered animals?

117

## Before You Read

**A. Discussion.** Discuss these questions with a partner.

1. Do you eat a lot of fish? Do you know where it comes from? Is it farmed or caught wild?

2. What are some of the challenges facing the fishing industry today?

3. What measures are being or could be taken to protect and increase low fish populations?

**B. Skim and Predict.** The passage on pages 119–123 is about bluefin tuna and the fishing industry that depend on them. Skim the first paragraph and each of the four sections. In your own words, write what you might learn about in each section. Then read the article to check your ideas.

1. The Super Fish _____

2. Tagging a Giant _____

3. Bluefin Migration _____

4. Uncertain Future _____

Bluefin tuna are fattened in an undersea pen. These fish were taken from the wild, reducing the potential breeding population.

# QUICKSILVER

Prized for sushi, the fast and powerful Atlantic bluefin tuna is being relentlessly overfished. Kenneth Brower goes in search of the story behind the king of all fish.

**A** 1   One moment the undersea scenery is an empty blue cathedral, the sun an undulating[1] hot spot in the waves overhead. Its beams shine down as if from stained glass.[2] The next moment the ocean is full of giant, bomb-shaped bluefin tuna, the largest measuring
5   over four meters (14 feet) and weighing three-quarters of a ton. In the sea's refracted[3] sunlight, their pale sides flash and sparkle like polished **shields**. Their long, curved fins cut the water like swords. Quick-moving tail fins drive them forward at ten knots,[4] with bursts of speed to 25. And just as suddenly, they are gone. The ocean
10   is empty again. Here and there, a small galaxy of scales marks where a bluefin swallowed a herring. The victim's scales swirl in the **turbulence** of the departed tuna, now heading off at high speed.

---

1 Something that **undulates** moves up and down or back and forth in a smooth, gentle motion.
2 **Stained glass** is colored glass used to create designs and pictures in windows.
3 When a beam of light is **refracted**, it changes direction (e.g., when it enters the water).
4 A **knot** is a unit of speed measurement for boats equivalent to 1.85 kilometers per hour.

# The Super Fish

A bluefin swims with its mouth open, forcing water past the gills in a process called ram ventilation. Its gills have up to 30 times more surface area than those of other fish, and they extract nearly half the oxygen dissolved in the water. If the tuna ever stops swimming, it dies.

## BODY HEAT

Tunas are unique among bony fish in their ability to keep key parts of their body warm. Rather than lose heat to cold water in the gills like most fish, tunas have heat-exchange systems that retain heat produced in the tissue. These systems are present in three areas (orange outline, below).

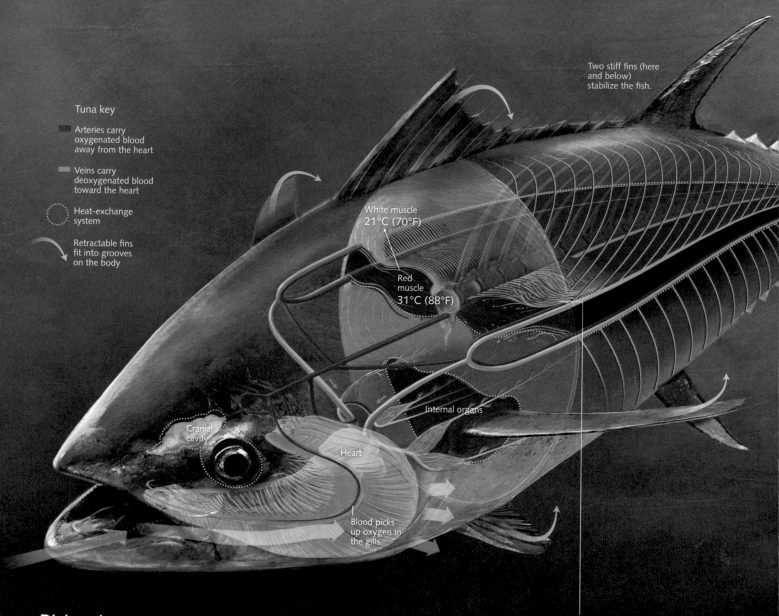

Tuna key

- Arteries carry oxygenated blood away from the heart
- Veins carry deoxygenated blood toward the heart
- Heat-exchange system
- Retractable fins fit into grooves on the body

Two stiff fins (here and below) stabilize the fish.

White muscle
21°C (70°F)

Red muscle
31°C (88°F)

Internal organs

Cranial cavity

Heart

Blood picks up oxygen in the gills.

## Diving deep

Tunas spend much of their lives in the sun-warmed water near the surface. Juveniles and smaller species always hover and feed there, but large adult bluefin dive to deep, cold waters, where their heat-exchange systems keep the brain and eyes alert for prey—and predators.

## Heat-exchange system

Tunas rely on a network of tightly packed, parallel blood vessels that allow the transfer of heat between warm and cool blood moving in opposite directions. As a result, heat is retained in the tissues of the body that produced it rather than being lost through the gills.

The bluefin is one of the fastest fish in the ocean, thanks to a combination of physical characteristics. Its large tail maximizes thrust, while the tapered shape of its body minimizes drag. For superior streamlining, some fins can be pulled into the body when not in use.

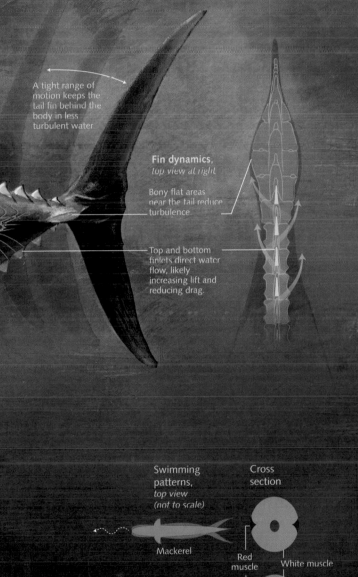

A tight range of motion keeps the tail fin behind the body in less turbulent water.

Fin dynamics, *top view at right*

Bony flat areas near the tail reduce turbulence.

Top and bottom finlets direct water flow, likely increasing lift and reducing drag.

Swimming patterns, *top view (not to scale)*

Cross section

Mackerel

Tuna

Red muscle    White muscle

## Muscles and motion

Tunas have a greater proportion of red muscle fiber than do other fish, favoring long-distance swimming over short bursts. And while most fish swim by undulating along their entire length, a tuna's body remains relatively rigid while only its tail whips back and forth, reducing drag.

# The Super Fish

B
15 Bluefin tuna are streamlined[5] to perfection and equipped with cutting-edge biological **gear**. The characteristics that distinguish them include great size, great range, efficient swimming, warm bodies, large gills, excellent regulation of heat, rapid oxygen uptake, and a
20 cleverly adapted heart. All of these reach their zenith in the bluefin, "the king of all fish," as Ernest Hemingway described them after seeing Atlantic bluefin off the coast of Spain.

C The three species of bluefin—the Atlantic,
25 Pacific, and southern—are found in all the oceans except around the North and South Poles. The bluefin is a modern fish, yet its relationship with humanity is ancient. Japanese fishermen and the Haida people of the Pacific
30 Northwest have caught Pacific bluefin for more than 5,000 years. Stone Age artists painted Atlantic bluefin tuna on the walls of Sicilian caves. Iron Age[6] fishermen watched and waited for the arrival of bluefin schools
35 at their Mediterranean spawning[7] grounds. Ancient coins of that region have images of giant bluefin on them.

D But this relationship with humans has lately been **detrimental** to the bluefin. They are
40 today among the most overfished species on Earth, largely because people are prepared to pay a high price for them. One medium-size bluefin in Tokyo brings in between $10,000 and $20,000, depending on quality. It is a
45 **startling** measure of what the bluefin tuna is up against if more than a handful are to see the 22nd century.

---

5 A **streamlined** animal has a shape that allows it to move smoothly through air or water.
6 The **Iron Age** in Europe took place from around 1200 B.C.E to 1 B.C.E.
7 When fish **spawn**, they lay their eggs.

# Tagging a Giant

**E**

50 The day dawned red-orange over Cape Breton, Nova Scotia, as Captain Dennis Cameron and his crew left port in his fishing boat, *Bay Queen IV*. Along the back wall of the boat's cabin, fishing rods were racked and ready. In the open ocean ahead, fishermen catch the biggest

55 bluefin tuna in the world.

**F**

Cameron knows the history of the local fishing industry well. "We didn't fish tuna," he says of his father's generation. "Tuna fishing was more of a sport. Years ago they used to call it

60 'horse mackerel.' It was cat food back then, or fertilizer."

**G**

To the right, we passed the big island of Cape Breton. To the left, a small island with a scattering of white houses, including

65 the one in which Cameron grew up. The waterfront—crowded with fishing boats in the 1920s—is now **deserted**. So it goes in fishing communities worldwide. The ocean is dying, and overfishing is the primary cause.

**H** 70 That day, however, we were on a different kind of fishing trip. We had come to tag and measure bluefin, not to kill them. While Cameron steered toward deep water, Steve Wilson, a Stanford University researcher who

75 works with the Tuna Research and Conservation Center (TRCC), checked the satellite tags he hoped to attach to bluefin that day.

**I**

Nine kilometers (six miles) offshore, drifting with three fishing lines in the water, we had

80 a strike. Sheldon Gillis—Captain Cameron's assistant—fought the fish. Twenty minutes later, a good distance from the boat, the fish made its first appearance. Gillis reeled in furiously each time the tuna gave him the chance—sweating

85 despite the cool of the morning. After another 20 minutes came the loud, slapping bang of tail fin against the boat. The tuna was **hauled** aboard through a specially designed "tuna door," then laid on its side on a padded mat,

90 perfectly still and enormous. Out of water, it looked like some kind of wonderful machine, biologically inspired and poured of living metal.

**J**

Wilson and his tagging team worked quickly and efficiently. A wet black cloth went over

95 the eyes. A green hose went in the mouth and began pumping seawater past the gills. The fish measured three meters long—almost ten feet. A tuna of that length is around 550 kilograms (1,220 pounds). In nearly 20 years of work,

100 it was the third biggest bluefin ever tagged by the team.

**K**

Wilson then stuck a harmless dart into the fish to hold a satellite tag, and his assistant cut a thin piece of a fin for DNA analysis. Then the

105 two men at the tail lifted their end of the mat, and the tuna plunged back into the gulf, raising a splash like a horse diving off a pier. Two flicks of its tail fin and it was gone. On his laptop the night before, Wilson had programmed

110 the satellite tag to release in a little over nine months. The tag will rise to the ocean's surface and send information about the tuna's movements to TRCC's home base in California.

# Bluefin Migration

**L** 115 Stanford University professor Barbara Block, a preeminent[8] **scholar** of the bluefin, runs TRCC out of Hopkins Marine Station in **collaboration** with the Monterey Bay Aquarium next door. The walls and cabinets of

120 Block's lab are covered with charts, maps, and illustrations from scientific journals. One poster shows a graph of the spawning population of Gulf of Mexico bluefin above a similar graph for Mediterranean bluefin. Both populations

125 are represented by lines that are diving toward the bottom of their graphs. They have plunged past the dotted line representing sustainable yield and are headed for zero.

**M**

The locations of bluefin, as reported by

130 the many satellite tags over the years, are represented by small circles in different colors. The western bluefin—represented as reddish-orange circles—pack the Gulf of Mexico, their

---

**8** Someone who is **preeminent** in a group is the most important, capable, or distinguished person in that group.

spawning grounds. From there they spread
135 eastward into the western Atlantic and cross
over to the eastern Atlantic, reaching all
the way to Portugal and Spain. The eastern
bluefin—represented as white circles—fill their
Mediterranean spawning grounds, and from
140 there spread westward, crossing over to the
western Atlantic, covering the coastal waters of
the United States and Canada.

**N** The fact of this mixing has been firmly
established by Block, other taggers, and DNA
145 researchers. The best estimates today are
that around half of the bluefin caught off the
eastern shores of North America were spawned
in the Mediterranean. However, until recently
these tuna—if caught in the west—have been
150 mistakenly counted as fish of western origin.
The discovery of the **mingling** of the two
populations is making more accurate fisheries
management possible.

## Uncertain Future

**O** 155 But an alarming lesson lies hidden at Hopkins
Marine Station. Established by Stanford
University in 1892, it was the first marine lab
on the west coast of the United States. Its
old buildings, like the abandoned canneries[9]
160 immediately to the east, were built during
the age of sardines, which ended 60 years
ago due to overfishing. By the 1980s sardine
populations had started to come back a little,
but now they are falling again.

**P** 165 In a building near Hopkins are three large,
waist-deep tanks, where a number of Pacific
bluefin tuna are swimming. Block and her
colleagues practice their tagging techniques
here on fish like these. To maintain healthy
170 populations, the bluefin tuna will need wise
management assisted by good science. Here in
Monterey, the consequences of the opposite
are clear. Directly below the tanks of bluefin are
the ruins of cannery piers that reach out into
175 the bay for sardines that are no longer there.

9 A **cannery** is a factory where food is canned.

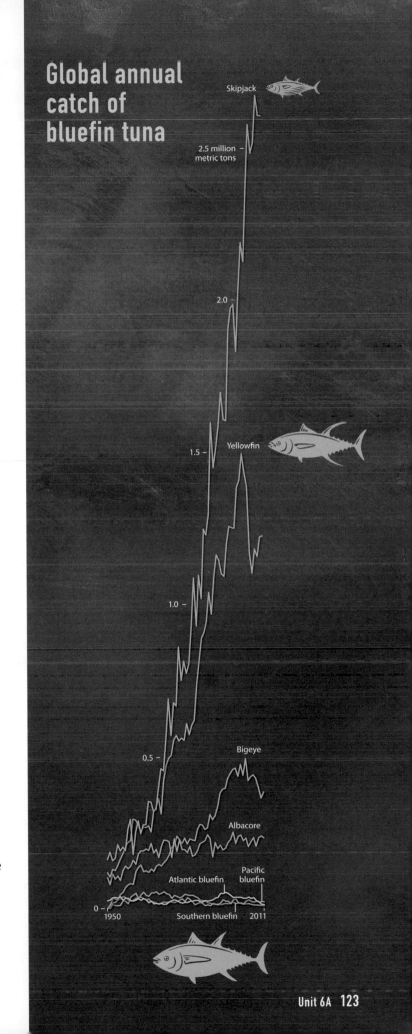

Global annual catch of bluefin tuna

Skipjack

2.5 million – metric tons

2.0 –

1.5 – Yellowfin

1.0 –

0.5 – Bigeye

Albacore

Atlantic bluefin

Pacific bluefin

0 –
1950          Southern bluefin     2011

# Reading Comprehension

**Multiple Choice.** Choose the best answer for each question.

Figurative Language

**1.** Which sentence from paragraph A does NOT contain figurative language?
   a. One moment the undersea scenery is an empty blue cathedral.
   b. Its beams shine down as if from stained glass.
   c. Quick-moving tail fins drive them forward at ten knots.
   d. Their long, curved fins cut the water like swords.

Purpose

**2.** What is the purpose of the paragraph C?
   a. to give reasons for the bluefin's decline
   b. to explain why the bluefin is a modern fish
   c. to show that ancient Sicilians worshipped the bluefin
   d. to explain our long history with the bluefin

Vocabulary

**3.** If you are *up against* something challenging (line 46), you are _____ it.
   a. denying            b. facing
   c. afraid of          d. comforted by

Understanding Infographics

**4.** According to the infographic on pages 120–121, which of these is NOT true about bluefin tuna?
   a. Its entire body moves from side to side as it swims.
   b. Juvenile tunas feed near the water surface.
   c. Tunas are able to retain heat produced in their tissues.
   d. A bluefin's gills have 30 times more surface area than other fish.

Detail

**5.** Why did Steve Wilson and his team want to tag the bluefin?
   a. so they could later identify people who fish bluefin illegally
   b. so paying tourists who enjoy fishing could help pay for their research
   c. so they could determine the depths to which bluefin can dive
   d. so they could track its movements

Detail

**6.** Where are western bluefin NOT found?
   a. in the Mediterranean Sea
   b. in the middle of the Atlantic Ocean
   c. off the coast of the eastern United States
   d. off the coast of Spain and Portugal

Inference

**7.** Why does the author discuss sardines in paragraph O?
   a. to warn that bluefin could face a similar fate
   b. to explain that the cause of their decline remains unknown
   c. to show that research done 60 years ago is no longer relevant
   d. to give hope of bringing back fish populations after overfishing

## Critical Thinking

**Evaluating:** What evidence does the author give when he says that the bluefin has an ancient history of interaction with humanity?

**Discussion:** What do you feel is the greatest threat to the bluefin? How optimistic are you of its future?

# Identifying Homonyms

Many words in English, called homonyms, have more than one meaning. By using the context, you can generally determine its meaning. Sometimes one definition is a literal meaning and the other a figurative one. (See Unit 4A for more information about literal vs. figurative meanings of words.) At other times, the words are similar in meaning but are not used in the same way.

**Definitions.** Find these words in the passage. Then decide which definition is correct according to how the word is used in the article.

1. beams (line 2)
   a. (*pl. n.*) lines of light
   b. (*pl. n.*) heavy pieces of wood

2. range (line 17)
   a. (*n.*) the area an animal lives in
   b. (*n.*) a group of things that are similar

3. yet (line 27)
   a. (*conj.*) but
   b. (*adv.*) until now

4. measure (line 45)
   a. (*n.*) a planned action
   b. (*n.*) a basis for comparison

5. left (line 51)
   a. (*v.*) departed
   b. (*adj.*) opposite of *right*

6. back (line 52)
   a. (*n.*) rear; opposite of *front*
   b. (*adv.*) into the past

7. primary (line 69)
   a. (*adj.*) coming first
   b. (*adj.*) main

8. lines (line 79)
   a. (*pl. n.*) people or things in a row
   b. (*pl. n.*) long ropes or strings for fishing

9. perfectly (line 90)
   a. (*adv.*) completely
   b. (*adv.*) without errors

10. dart (line 102)
    a. (*v.*) to move quickly in a particular direction
    b. (*n.*) a small object with a sharp point

11. past (line 127)
    a. (*n.*) a time before now
    b. (*prep.*) up to and beyond

12. pack (line 133)
    a. (*v.*) to fill a place
    b. (*pl. n.*) a group of similar things

13. age (line 161)
    a. (*n.*) the time something has existed
    b. (*n.*) a period of time

14. like (line 169)
    a. (*v.*) to enjoy
    b. (*prep.*) such as

15. clear (line 173)
    a. (*adj.*) obvious and apparent
    b. (*adj.*) easily seen through

# Vocabulary Practice

**A. Completion.** Complete the information by circling the correct word in each pair.

Kiribati President, Anote Tong, recently made a **1. (mingling / startling)** announcement: Commercial fishing will end in the country's Phoenix Islands Protected Area. These islands represent some of the most pristine coral reefs in the Pacific Ocean. For years, foreign fishermen have caught and **2. (collaborated / hauled)** away large quantities of fish from the area.

In 2006, Kiribati, an island nation halfway between Hawaii and Fiji, established the Phoenix Islands Protected Area. The park was expanded in 2008, becoming the largest marine protected area in the world at that time, about as large as California.

The president cautioned that declarations of marine protected areas "have no meaning unless they are enforced." He said technology, such as aircraft and satellite-based tracking **3. (turbulence / gear)**, will be needed to help monitor the vast area. Tong called on other nations to **4. (mingle / collaborate)**. "Let us pool our resources to protect this gift, our mother ocean," he said.

National Geographic researcher and **5. (shield / scholar)** Dr. Enric Sala looks to Spain as an example. Overfishing was **6. (detrimental / deserted)** to Spain's fishing grounds decades ago. He explains that once fishing was banned in a marine reserve, the number of fish increased so much that they spread outside of the reserve, reviving the fishing industry and creating jobs. He calls the president's declaration a "great first step."

A scorpionfish passes over regrown coral in the Phoenix Islands Protected Area.

**B. Words in Context.** Complete each sentence with the correct answer.

1. A **shield** is a large piece of metal or wood carried for _____.
   a. protection                     b. farming

2. **Turbulence** is the _____ movement of air or water.
   a. soft and gentle           b. sudden and violent

3. If an area is **deserted**, _____ there.
   a. no one lives               b. large groups live

4. When two groups **mingle**, they _____.
   a. stay separate              b. mix

5. Something that is **detrimental** to your health _____ it.
   a. is a positive influence on     b. causes damage to

> **Word Link**
> The word root **turb** means "to spin, drive, or throw into disorder," e.g., *disturb, perturb, turbulence, turbine, turbojet.*

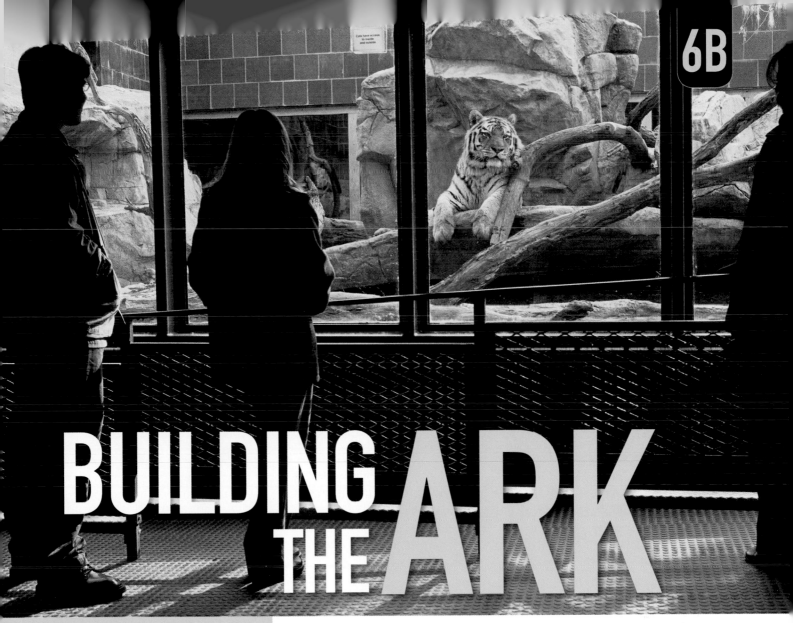

# BUILDING THE ARK

## Before You Read

**A. Discussion.** Look at the photo and caption. Discuss the questions with a partner.

1. What role can zoos play in protecting threatened species?

2. Which criteria do you think zoos consider when deciding which animals to keep?

**B. Scan.** Scan the reading on pages 128–133 to find the following animals. Write the names of the zoos that were involved in breeding programs for these animals.

1. Sumatran rhinoceros _____

2. American bison _____

3. red wolf _____

4. Kihansi spray toad _____

5. Amur leopard _____

6. northern white rhino _____

△ Visitors observing Khuntami, a Siberian tiger in his enclosure at the Henry Doorly Zoo in Nebraska, U.S. The zoo is famous for its pioneering work with breeding endangered species.

Zoos may have to choose between keeping the animals we most want to see and saving the ones we may never see again.

**A** 1 When the Cincinnati Zoo opened its gates in 1875, there were perhaps as many as a million Sumatran rhinos foraging[1] in forests from Bhutan to Borneo. Today, there may be
5 fewer than a hundred left in the world. Three of these were born in Cincinnati—a female named Suci and her brothers, Harapan and Andalas. In 2007, the zoo sent Andalas to Sumatra, where he has since sired[2] a calf at
10 Way Kambas National Park. If the species escapes **extinction**, it will in no small part be thanks to the work done at the zoo. And what goes for the Sumatran rhino goes for a growing list of species saved from **oblivion**.
15 As the wild **shrinks**, zoos are increasingly being looked to as modern-day arks:[3] the last **refuge** against a rising **tide** of extinction.

---

1 When animals **forage**, they search for food.

2 The verb **sired** means to become the father of (an animal).

3 In the Bible, the **ark** was a large boat that Noah built in order to save his family and two of every kind of animal from the Great Flood.

A newborn Sumatran rhino calf (right) with his mother at the Way Kambas National Park, Indonesia. The father, Andalas, was born at the Cincinnati Zoo and sent to the national park as part of a captive-breeding program.

## Who to Save?

B 20 From the early 19th century, American zoos were involved in animal conservation. At the end of the century, the Cincinnati Zoo tried—unsuccessfully—to breed passenger pigeons, whose numbers were in rapid decline. (The bird thought to be the very last 25 passenger pigeon, named Martha, died at the zoo in 1914; the building where she lived is now a memorial.) And in the early 20th century, when one count showed just 325 wild American bison left in North America, 30 the Bronx Zoo started a **captive**-breeding program that helped save the species. Other animals that owe their existence to captive-breeding efforts are the Arabian oryx, the 35 black-footed ferret, the red wolf, the Guam rail, and the California condor.

C Because such programs tend to be expensive—the condor program costs participating institutions up to $2 million a year—they're usually led by large, big-city 40 zoos. But smaller zoos are increasingly joining in. The Miller Park Zoo in Bloomington, Illinois, is one of the smallest zoos in the United States—just four acres—but it has bred red wolves and is hoping to breed the 45 endangered Mount Graham red squirrel. "It's a small animal that doesn't require a huge amount of space," said zoo official Jay Tetzloff.

**D** But zoos also have to financially support themselves, and small animals like squirrels just don't attract the crowds necessary to keep business in the black.[4] Robert Lacy, a conservation biologist at the Chicago Zoological Society, says that zoos are going to have to make some really difficult decisions. "Do you save a small number of large animals—the crowd favorites—or do you focus on saving a whole lot more little, unpopular creatures for the same amount of money?" he asks.

**E** Right now, the world's most threatened group of animals is probably amphibians. According to the International Union for Conservation of Nature (IUCN)—which maintains what's known as the Red List—more than a third of the world's frog, toad, and salamander species are at risk of extinction. Unfortunately for them, amphibians are far less popular than zoo species such as pandas or lions, which are not yet facing **imminent** extinction in the wild. But there are advantages to being small. For one thing, a whole population of amphibians can be kept in less space than that required by a single rhinoceros.

**F** Others question whether zoos should devote resources to species, large or small, that are doing fine on their own. "I think it's a bit of a cop-out[5] to say the public wants to see x, y, or z," says Onnie Byers, chair of the Conservation Breeding Specialist Group, part of the IUCN Species Survival Commission. "Plenty of species need exactly the expertise that zoos can provide. I would love to see a trend toward zoos phasing out species that don't need that care and using the spaces for species that do."

## Small Victories

**G** "It's an amazing responsibility to have half the remaining members of a species in your care," says Jim Breheny, the director of the Wildlife Conservation Society's Bronx Zoo. He's standing in a **state-of-the-art** breeding facility filled with tanks of Kihansi spray toads—small, yellow amphibians about 2.5 centimeters (one inch) long.

**H** Depending on how you look at things, the Kihansi spray toad is either one of the most unfortunate or one of the luckiest species around. Until the late 1990s, the Kihansi spray toad was unknown to science. It was not actually identified until a hydroelectric[6] project was already destroying its tiny habitat—five acres of mist-soaked land in the Kihansi River Gorge, in eastern Tanzania. In 2000, recognizing that the project would probably harm the newly discovered species, the Tanzanian government invited the Bronx Zoo to collect some of the toads. Exactly 499 spray toads were captured and kept in the Bronx and Toledo Zoos in the United States. Just nine years later, as a result of disease and habitat destruction, the Kihansi spray toad was declared extinct in the wild.

**I** In the meantime, the zoos were **struggling** to figure out how to recreate the habitat that gives the spray toad its name. In the Kihansi River Gorge, a series of waterfalls had provided the toads with constant spray, so the tanks in the Bronx were provided with spray in the same way. Among amphibians, Kihansi toads are unusual in that the young are born live: At birth, they are no bigger than a match head. For the tiny young, the zoo had to find even tinier prey; eventually, they settled on tiny insectlike animals called springtails, which the researchers also had to figure out how to raise. But then keepers noticed that the toads seemed to be suffering from a nutritional deficiency,[7] so a special vitamin **supplement** had to be designed.

---

4 If a business is **in the black**, it is making money and not losing it.

5 **Cop-out** means taking the easy way out of a difficult situation.

6 **Hydroelectric** means relating to electricity made from the energy of running water.

7 If you have a **nutritional deficiency**, you are not getting the vitamins, minerals and other substances your body needs from what you eat and drink.

**J** After some initial losses, the toads began to thrive and reproduce. By 2010, there were several thousand of them in New York and Toledo. That year a hundred toads were sent
135 back to the Kihansi River Gorge, but there was a problem. By diverting water from the falls, the hydroelectric project had eliminated the mist that the toads depend on. So the Tanzanians set up a system to restore the spray
140 to the gorge. In 2012, the first toads bred in the Bronx Zoo were released back into the wild.

## The Frozen Zoo

**K** But for every success story like the Kihansi toad, there are dozens of other species on
145 the edge of extinction. Many of these—the Sumatran orangutan, the Amur leopard, a songbird from the island of Kauai, and a thousand other species—can be found in a single room at the San Diego Zoo Institute
150 for Conservation Research. Vials containing cells from each of these animals are being kept in a bath of liquid nitrogen[8] where the temperature is minus 200°C (minus 320°F). These thousands of identical-looking frozen
155 vials represent what might be described as a beyond-the-last-ditch[9] conservation effort: the Frozen Zoo.

**L** For now, at least, only one of the animals in the Frozen Zoo is actually extinct: the po'ouli,
160 a fat bird with a sweet black face and a light-colored chest that lived on the Hawaiian island of Maui until 2004. But it seems safe to predict that in the coming years, more and more will become extinct.

**M** 165 "I think there are going to be more and more species where the only living material left is going to be cells in the Frozen Zoo," says Oliver Ryder, the institute's director of genetics. By chance, one such species—the
170 northern white rhino—can be found just a few hundred meters from Ryder's office. Native to central Africa, the northern white rhino is down to its last seven individuals, and its extinction is, at this point, considered
175 inevitable. Two of the seven—Nola, a female, and Angalifu, a male—live at the San Diego Zoo Safari Park. The animals are both nearing 40 and are too old to breed. But after they die, they will, in a way, live on—one last hope,
180 suspended in a frozen cloud.

---

8 **Nitrogen** is a colorless element with no smell; it is usually found as a gas and is a liquid below −196°C (-320°F).

9 A **last-ditch** effort is a final attempt to achieve something after all else has failed.

# The Photo Ark

The Photo Ark, a 20-year-long documentary project founded by National Geographic photographer and fellow Joel Sartore, is an extensive online archive of studio-quality photographs of animals around the world, from the largest carnivores to the smallest insects, all to showcase biodiversity. "We stand to lose half of all the planet's species by the turn of the next century," says Sartore. "The Photo Ark seeks to document as many of these as possible, using captive animals as ambassadors." More than 4,200 species have already been documented since his project began in 2006, and Sartore plans to continue until all of the roughly 12,000 species currently inhabiting zoos, aquariums, and breeding centers around the world take their place on board the Ark. Sadly, several of the animals he photographed have already become extinct. The goal of the project is to bring amazing images of animals to the public eye in order to inspire people everywhere to care about these species, and to do something to help save them, before it's too late. "People won't work to save something if they don't know it exists," Sartore said. "That's where these photos come in." See more of Sartore's work at either www.joelsartore.com or www.photoark.com.

Fulvous whistling duck

Chimpanzee

Hawk-headed parrot

Malayan tiger

Giant panda

Florida panther

Mountain tapir

Northern white-faced owls

Ring-tailed lemur

Yellow and blue poison dart frog

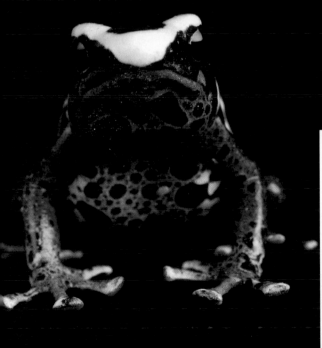

Reimann's snake-necked turtle

# Reading Comprehension

**Multiple Choice.** Choose the best answer for each question.

**Main Idea**

**1.** According to the article, what is the main ethical question that zoos are facing?
   a. Do we return zoo animals back to the wild?
   b. Should we try and bring back extinct animals?
   c. Which of the many threatened animals do we save?
   d. Is it right to put animals like pandas and lions in zoos?

**Detail**

**2.** Why are so many amphibians at risk of extinction?
   a. Not enough scientists study amphibians.
   b. They have little value for medical researchers.
   c. It's hard for conservationists to differentiate species.
   d. They are small, so they don't get much support from zoos.

**Vocabulary**

**3.** In line 84, *phasing out* can be replaced with _____.
   a. slowing increasing        b. gradually removing
   c. humanely sending back   d. partially using

**Cause and Effect**

**4.** What prompted the Tanzanian government to invite the Bronx Zoo to collect some Kihansi spray toads?
   a. They realized a hydroelectric dam was destroying their habitat.
   b. Scientists said the toads could no longer reproduce in the gorge.
   c. Disease had begun to spread through the toad population.
   d. The toads started to suffer from a nutritional deficiency.

**Cohesion**

**5.** This sentence would best be placed at the end of which paragraph? *It is estimated that a third of all reef-forming corals, a quarter of all mammals, a fifth of all reptiles, and a sixth of all birds are headed toward oblivion.*
   a. paragraph C
   b. paragraph F
   c. paragraph G
   d. paragraph L

**Detail**

**6.** What is the Frozen Zoo?
   a. a place to see frozen but now extinct animals
   b. the frozen DNA of thousands of extinct animals
   c. a place to keep frozen cells of threatened animal species
   d. a part of the San Diego Zoo where people see endangered animals

**Inference**

**7.** Which animal is probably the most in danger of becoming extinct?
   a. the panda
   b. the northern white rhino
   c. the po'ouli
   d. the Kihansi spray toad

## Critical Thinking

**Evaluating:** The author describes the Kihansi spray toad as a success story. Do you agree?

_____

**Discussion:** The passage asks, "Do you save a small number of large animals—the crowd favorites—or do you focus on saving a whole lot more little, unpopular creatures for the same amount of money?" What's your opinion?

# Understanding Root Words of Greek and Latin Origin

Many words in English are composed of a root word and one or more affixes (prefixes or suffixes). By having an understanding of root words of Greek or Latin origin, learners can build and greatly increase their vocabulary. If you come across an unknown word, having knowledge of its root can help you make an educated guess at its meaning.

**A. Identifying.** Work with a partner. Look at these words from the reading. Choose the correct meaning of the underlined root. (Think of other words with the root to help you.)

1. <u>nutri</u>tional     a. feed     b. water     c. old

2. <u>bio</u>logist     a. many     b. life     c. death

3. centi<u>meter</u>     a. small     b. measure     c. weight

4. <u>zoo</u>logical     a. animal     b. inside     c. true

5. <u>hydro</u>electric     a. slow     b. planet     c. water

**B. Completion.** Work with a partner. Complete the charts with the correct words.

| carry | distant | earth | earth | feel | hear | see |
|-------|---------|-------|-------|------|------|-----|
| see | self | sound | speak | study of | write | write |

| Greek Root | Definition | Examples |
|------------|------------|----------|
| **1.** auto | _____ | autograph, autobiography, automobile |
| **2.** geo | _____ | geography, geology, geopolitics |
| **3.** graph | _____ | phonograph, autograph, graphic |
| **4.** ology | _____ | biology, zoology, archeology |
| **5.** phon | _____ | phonetics, telephone, phonograph |
| **6.** scope | _____ | telescope, microscope, stethoscope |
| **7.** tele | _____ | television, teleport, televise |

| Latin Root | Definition | Examples |
|------------|------------|----------|
| **1.** audi | _____ | audience, auditory, auditorium |
| **2.** dict | _____ | dictate, predict, contradict |
| **3.** port | _____ | import, export, transport |
| **4.** sens/t | _____ | sensitive, sensation, resent |
| **5.** scrip | _____ | script, transcript, inscription |
| **6.** terr | _____ | terrain, territory, terrestrial |
| **7.** vis | _____ | visible, vision, supervise |

# Vocabulary Practice

**A. Completion.** Complete the information using the words in the box. Three words are extra.

| | | | | |
|---|---|---|---|---|
| captive | extinct | imminent | oblivion | refuge |
| shrinking | state-of-the-art | struggle | supplement | tide |

The International Union for Conservation of Nature (IUCN) recently added a number of new species to its Red List and reassessed the status of many species placed there years ago.

The **Japanese eel** was added to the IUCN's list with an endangered classification, meaning it has a high risk of becoming **1.** _____. It has been hit by overfishing, habitat loss, and pollution.

The **Brazilian three-banded armadillo**, Brazil's 2014 World Cup mascot, remains vulnerable. The species has declined by an estimated 30 percent in the past 10 to 15 years, primarily because of its **2.** _____ habitat. It is **3.** _____ to survive.

The **Chinese crocodile lizard**, found only in China and Vietnam, was classified as endangered because the species is thought to have declined by 84 percent in the past 35 years. Extinction in the wild is likely to be **4.** _____. Zoos may be the lizard's last **5.** _____.

Once on the edge of **6.** _____, the **Yarkon bream** stands out as a success story. The fish, found in the Middle East, disappeared from the wild in 1999 after the last hundred were saved from a drying riverbed. After a successful **7.** _____-breeding program, 9,000 fish were released into their native habitat.

^ The Brazilian three-banded armadillo, which rolls into a ball when threatened, is classified as vulnerable.

**B. Definitions.** Use the correct form of words in the box in **A** to complete the definitions. Three words are extra.

1. If an event is _____, it is likely or certain to happen very soon.

2. When you _____ something, you add something extra in order to improve it.

3. A(n) _____ animal is one that lives in a zoo or park, not in the wild.

4. Something that is _____ has the newest and most advanced ideas and features.

5. A(n) _____ is a place where people or animals can go to be safe from danger.

6. _____ refers to a state of being destroyed completely.

7. The _____ of something (e.g., history) refers to the way it is changing or developing.

**Thesaurus**
**imminent**
Also look up:
(*adj.*) *likely, looming, immediate, forthcoming, inevitable, approaching, impending*

# VIEWING Life on Ice

## Before You Watch

**A. Definitions.** You are going to watch a video about a frozen zoo. Here are some words you will hear in the video. Match the words with their definitions.

1. ___ archive
2. ___ genome
3. ___ ecology
4. ___ plunge
5. ___ instantaneous
6. ___ elaborate
7. ___ mechanism
8. ___ gold standard

**a.** happening very quickly

**b.** a process or system used to produce a result

**c.** detailed and complicated in design

**d.** a complete set of genetic material in an organism

**e.** a place where public or historical records are kept

**f.** to thrust or throw forcefully into a substance

**g.** something that is the best, and used to judge other things with

**h.** the study of the relationships between organisms and their environment

**B. Discuss.** Read the information below. Then discuss the questions with a partner.

The Smithsonian Institution's Museum of Natural History has started the largest bio-repository in the world. It stores frozen specimens from hundreds of thousands of plant and animal species, primarily for genomic research.

1. Why exactly do you think researchers are interested in storing frozen specimens?
2. How do you think they store the specimens?

## While You Watch

**A. True or False.** As you watch the video, mark each statement True (**T**) or False (**F**).

1. Biologists will be able to sequence the genomes of all of Earth's life forms in ten years.                    **T**    **F**

2. The main reasons Jonathan Coddington is involved in the project is he wants to understand the history and diversity of life on Earth.                    **T**    **F**

3. Coddington is interested in spider poison because they are one of the least understood and most threatened animals.                    **T**    **F**

4. According to the researchers, liquid nitrogen is the best way to preserve specimens for a long time.                    **T**    **F**

5. Coddington feels that a library of frozen tissue will concentrate life into a centralized collection that will support research on genomics.                    **T**    **F**

**B. Completion.** Complete these quotations with the missing words.

**Jonathan Coddington, Associate Director of Science**
**Smithsonian Museum of Natural History**

"Museums are really the archives of **1.** _____ knowledge. We think that the future of meeting the needs of 21st-century biology will be about **2.** _____ tissue—life on ice. The Smithsonian has just built the largest natural history biorepository in the world. Biologists are going to be spending a lot of the next few decades **3.** _____ the genomes of many kinds of life on Earth."

**Amy Driskell, Researcher**
**Smithsonian Museum of Natural History**

"Museums are repositories of all sorts of **4.** _____ that people have used in the past and haven't used yet. So we're adding to it . . . to a museum **5.** _____ in a different way than has been traditional. And basically, you know, museums will have specimens in ethanol, they'll have specimens that are dried and pinned, they'll have specimens that are in drawers, and they'll have specimens that are in the biorepository in **6.** _____ nitrogen."

**Chris Huddleston, Coordinator**
**Smithsonian Repository**

"Now we're starting to **7.** _____ our frozen tissue collections. So we're somewhere between 200,000 and a half a million samples. The reason we do this is people like to do genomic work, they do biogenetics, they do toxicology work with our samples. So researchers **8.** _____ samples and we actually go in and we pull samples out, we cut a small **9.** _____ of it, and send them out to the researchers."

## After You Watch

**Discussion.** Discuss these questions with a partner.

1. How might the genome project shown in the video help humans?
2. Can you think of any possible problems or disadvantages to the project?

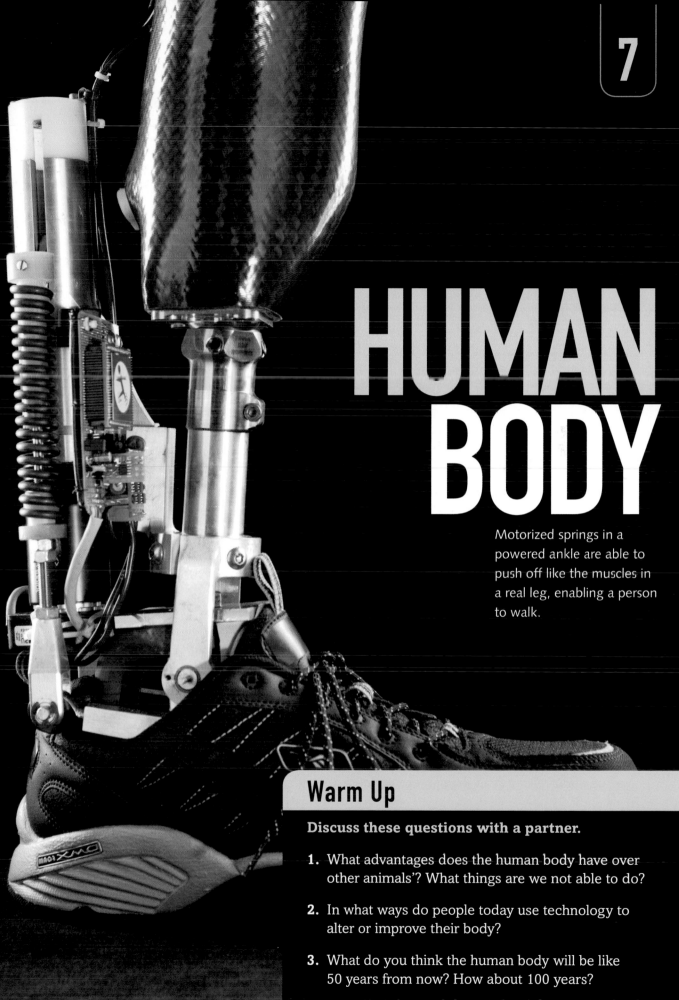

# 7

# HUMAN BODY

Motorized springs in a powered ankle are able to push off like the muscles in a real leg, enabling a person to walk.

## Warm Up

**Discuss these questions with a partner.**

1. What advantages does the human body have over other animals'? What things are we not able to do?

2. In what ways do people today use technology to alter or improve their body?

3. What do you think the human body will be like 50 years from now? How about 100 years?

139

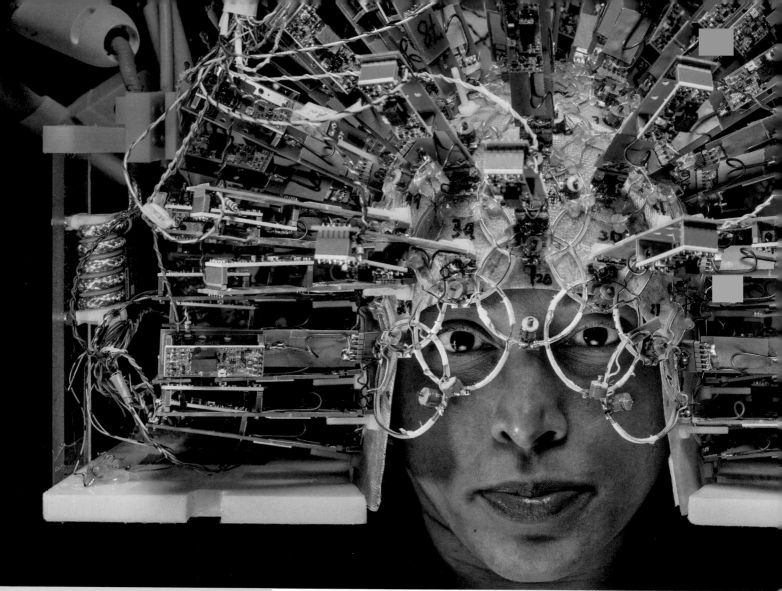

# Before You Read

**A. Discussion.** Answer the questions below with a partner.

1. What kinds of things might brain researchers hope to learn about the brain?

2. In what ways could a greater knowledge of the brain help individuals or society?

**B. Skim.** Skim the passage on pages 141–146. What do you think each section will be about? Then read the passage to check your ideas.

1. My Contribution to Science

_____

2. Mapping the Brain

_____

3. Connecting Brain with Machine

_____

An engineer wears a helmet of sensors—part of a brain scanner that requires almost as much power as a nuclear submarine. Antennae pick up signals produced in the brain. Computers convert this data into maps of the brain.

# SECRETS OF THE BRAIN

New technologies are helping researchers solve a great biological mystery: how the brain really works. Carl Zimmer takes a journey into his own head, to see what it's all about.

## 1 My Contribution to Science

**A** In a scanning room at the Martinos Center for Biomedical Imaging in Boston, Massachusetts, I lay on my back on a slab,[1] my head resting in an open plastic box. I had offered myself as a guinea pig[2] to neuroscientist Van
5 Wedeen and his colleagues who were now going to scan my brain. A white plastic helmet was lowered over my face, and the slab slowly glided into the scanner tube.

**B** The magnets that surrounded me began to rumble[3] and beep. For an hour I lay still, eyes closed, and tried to remain calm in the narrow scanner.
10 It wasn't easy. To suppress feelings of panic, I breathed smoothly and transported myself to places in my memory. At one point I recalled walking my nine-year-old daughter to school through the snow. And as I lay there,

---

1 A **slab** is a thick, flat piece of a hard material.
2 If someone is used as a **guinea pig,** they are used in an experiment or a test.
3 Something that **rumbles** makes a deep, vibrating sound.

I reflected on the fact that all my thoughts and emotions were the creation of the three-pound loaf of flesh that was under **scrutiny**: my brain.

15

C Submitting to this uncomfortable scanning procedure was part of reporting on the stunning advances in understanding the
20 human brain. Wedeen, who is at the **forefront** of brain imaging, creates in **unprecedented** detail representations of the brain's wiring. My brain scan was the first step in creating an image of my own brain, but I would have to
25 make a second appointment to see the final product.

D On my return trip to his lab, Wedeen opened up the image on a computer screen. His technique—called diffusion spectrum
30 imaging—translates radio signals given off by the brain. What I saw was a map of the nerve fibers that form hundreds of thousands of pathways, carrying information from one part of my brain to another. Wedeen had painted
35 each path a rainbow of colors, so that my brain appeared as an explosion of colorful fur, like a psychedelic[4] Persian cat.

## Mapping the Brain

E Cutting-edge techniques for mapping the
40 brain are giving researchers greater access to that **organ** than ever before. Some neuroscientists focus in on the structure of individual nerve cells, or neurons. Others chart genes that interact with those neurons.
45 Still others—Wedeen among them—work on revealing as much of the brain's vast **neural** network as they can.

F Jeff Lichtman and his colleagues at Harvard University are creating extremely detailed
50 three-dimensional images of neurons, revealing every bump and stalk branching from them. They begin by slicing preserved mouse brains into thin layers of tissue, each less than a thousandth the thickness of a
55 human hair. An electron microscope[5] is then used to take a picture of each layer, and the

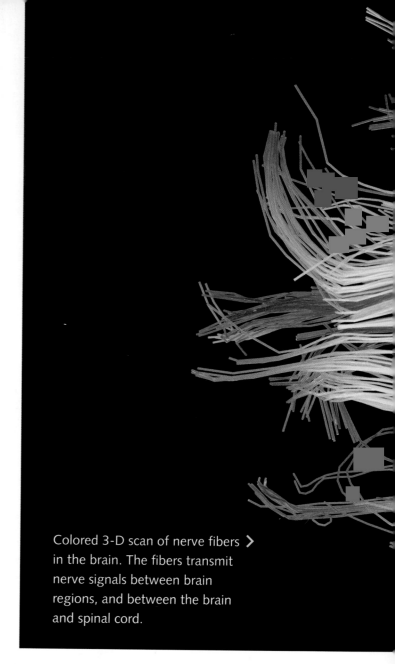

Colored 3-D scan of nerve fibers > in the brain. The fibers transmit nerve signals between brain regions, and between the brain and spinal cord.

images are put in order using a computer. Slowly a three-dimensional image is built— one that the scientists can explore as if they
60 were in a tiny submarine. "Everything is revealed," says Lichtman.

G The problem is that even a mouse brain is unbelievably complex. Lichtman and his colleagues have managed to recreate a piece
65 about the size of a grain of salt. Its data alone is equal to the amount of data in about 25,000 high-definition movies. "It's a wake-up call to how much more complicated brains are than the way we think about them," says Lichtman.
70 When asked if his method could be used to

scan an entire human brain, which contains a thousand times more neurons than a mouse brain, Lichtman says with a laugh, "I don't dwell on that. It's too painful."

**H** 75 When and if Lichtman completes his 3-D portrait of the brain, it will reveal much—but it will still be only an **exquisitely** detailed sculpture. Living neurons, on the other hand, are full of active genes that are integral to brain function. Researchers at the Allen Institute in Seattle, Washington, have developed a method for mapping these genes—the Allen Brain Atlas. First, the donated brains of recently deceased people are scanned using a powerful MRI[6]

85 scanner. This scan is used for reference as a kind of three-dimensional road map. The brain is then sliced into sections so thin that they are nearly invisible, and the slices are mounted on glass. Finally, chemicals are applied to reveal the active genes in the neurons.

---

4 **Psychedelic** art has bright colors and strange patterns.

5 An **electron microscope** is a tool that allows the viewer to see objects as small as an atom.

6 Magnetic Resonance Imaging (**MRI**) is a technique for creating detailed images of organs in the body.

**I** So far, the researchers have mapped the brains of six people. It's a huge amount of data, and they've only just begun to understand the genetic landscape of the brain. The scientists estimate that 84 percent of all the genes in our DNA become active in the adult brain. Certain combinations of genes are activated by neurons to carry out important tasks in different locations. The secret to certain **disorders** may be hiding in these complex networks, as certain genes shut down or switch on abnormally.

**J** Of all the new ways of visualizing the brain, perhaps the most remarkable is one invented by neuroscientist Karl Deisseroth and colleagues at Stanford University. They have found a way to make a mouse brain as transparent as glass, allowing researchers to see inside the brain while it is still intact. The technique involves replacing the naturally occurring substances in the brain with transparent ones. They can then color the brain with chemicals that show different pathways of connecting neurons. "You don't have to take it apart to show the wiring," says Deisseroth.

**K** It's not easy to **dazzle** neuroscientists, but Deisseroth's method, called CLARITY, has left his colleagues awestruck.[7] Wedeen has called the research "spectacular . . . unlike anything else in the field." Deisseroth's ultimate goal is to make a human brain transparent—a far more difficult task, not least because a human brain is 3,000 times larger than that of a mouse. He anticipates that CLARITY may someday help patients with autism[8] or depression, but for now he's keeping those hopes in check. "We have so far to go before we can affect treatments that I tell people, 'Don't even think about that yet.' It's just a voyage of discovery for now."

# Connecting Brain with Machine

**L** For the most part, brain research has yet to change how doctors treat patients. But there is one line of research—brain–machine interfaces[9]—where the mapping of the brain has started to change people's lives.

**M** At 43 years old, Cathy Hutchinson suffered a massive stroke, leaving her unable to move or speak. Lying in her bed in Massachusetts General Hospital, she gradually figured out that her doctors didn't know if she was brain-dead or still aware. Her sister asked Hutchinson if she could understand her, and she managed to answer by moving her eyes up as a signal. "It gave me such a relief," Hutchinson tells me 17 years later, "because everybody talked about me as if I was dying."

**N** Still almost completely unable to move or speak, she communicates by looking at letters on a computer screen. A camera tracks the movement of a tiny metal disk attached to the center of her eyeglasses, thanks to a system developed by Brown University neuroscientist John Donoghue.

**O** Donoghue wanted to find a way to help people with paralysis by using signals from the brain's motor cortex—the area where signals to move muscles **originate**. He spent years developing such a device, testing it on monkeys. Once he and his colleagues knew it was safe, they were ready to start working with human patients.

**P** Surgeons inserted the device into Hutchinson's motor cortex. After she had healed from her surgery, the researchers plugged in wires to send signals from her brain to nearby computers. The computers recognize the

---

7 If a person is **awestruck**, he or she is very impressed and amazed by something.

8 **Autism** is a mental disorder that affects a person's ability to communicate and interact with others.

9 An **interface** is a device or program that enables a person to interact with a computer.

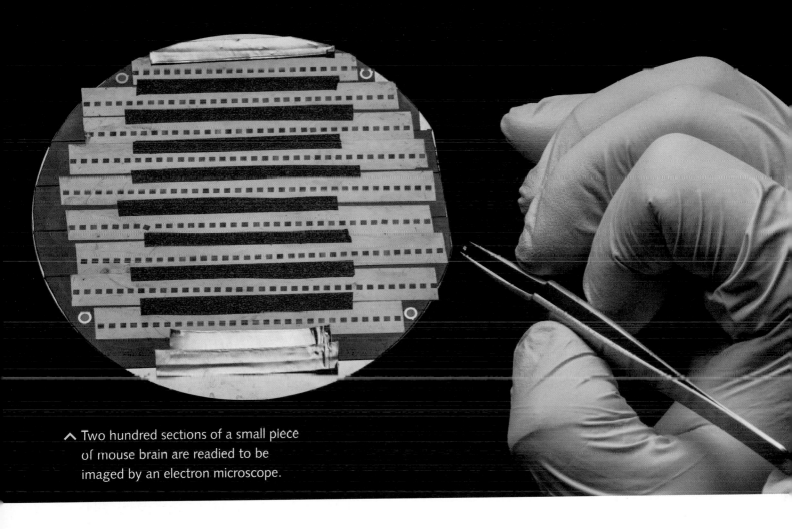

∧ Two hundred sections of a small piece of mouse brain are readied to be imaged by an electron microscope.

# "Eventually brain implants will become as common as heart implants."

— Miguel Nicolelis

170 signals and use them to move a computer cursor around a screen. Two years later, they attached a robot arm with a hand to the computers. Hutchinson quickly learned to use it.

Q 175 "It felt natural," she says. So natural that one day she reached out for a cup of coffee, grabbed it, and brought it to her lips to drink. "Cathy's smile when she put down that drink—that's everything," Donoghue says.

R 180 Today Donoghue and other scientists are building on that success, hoping to create human–machine interfaces that will be powerful, safe, and easy. At Duke University, Miguel Nicolelis has gotten monkeys to 185 control full-body exoskeletons using methods similar to those that helped Hutchinson. "Eventually brain implants[10] will become as common as heart implants," says Nicolelis. Predicting the future is a **tricky** game, 190 however, and advances in the past have inspired expectations that have not been met. But it is clear that current research is moving neuroscience to a remarkable new stage.

---

**10** An **implant** is something inserted into a person's body, especially by surgery.

# First Steps in Understanding the Brain

Scientists are learning so much about the brain now that it's easy to forget that for much of history we had no idea at all how it worked or even what it was. In the ancient world, physicians believed that the brain was made of phlegm.[11] The Greek philosopher Aristotle thought the organ's purpose was to cool off the fiery heart. In the Renaissance, various authorities declared that our perceptions, emotions, reasoning, and actions were all the result of "animal spirits"—mysterious, unknowable vapors that swirled through cavities in our head and traveled through our bodies. It wasn't until the scientific revolution of the 17th century that the British physician Thomas Willis recognized that the brain was where our mental world existed. It would take another century for researchers to understand that electricity travels through the brain and out into the body's nervous system.

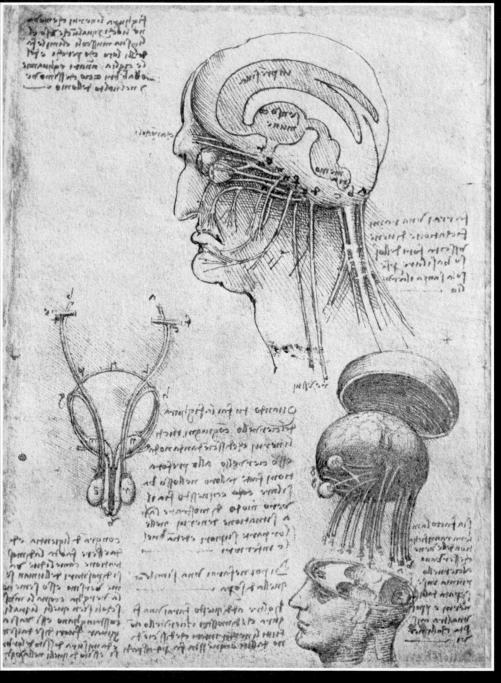

❮ During the Renaissance era, Leonardo da Vinci drew detailed sketches of the human brain based on dissections. His sketches were more anatomically correct than others of his time.

---

11 **Phlegm** is a thick yellow or green substance that you get in your nose and throat when you have a cold.

# Reading Comprehension

**Multiple Choice.** Choose the best answer for each question.

**Detail**

1. Why did the writer get a brain scan?
   a. to help him recollect childhood memories
   b. because the neuroscientist Van Wedeen asked him to
   c. to aid him in reporting on how the brain works
   d. because he wants to learn to suppress feelings of panic

**Paraphrase**

2. When asked if his method could be used to scan an entire human brain, Jeff Lichtman says with a laugh, "I don't dwell on that. It's too painful." What does he mean by his response?
   a. I can't answer that because it's not ethical to do that to a human.
   b. I doubt I would do it since it would cause so much pain.
   c. I find it funny that people would suggest that since the mice died in the process.
   d. I don't think about it much because it would be such a huge challenge.

**Sequence**

3. When mapping genes, what do researchers at the Allen Institute do last?
   a. cut the brain into thin sections
   b. apply chemicals to reveal active genes
   c. scan the brain of a dead person
   d. mount brain slices on glass

**Author Attitude**

4. How does the author feel about the work of Karl Deisseroth?
   a. He is extremely impressed.
   b. He finds it impressive, but he's very skeptical.
   c. He finds it interesting, but feels it's not practical.
   d. He thinks his work will not amount to much in the end.

**Vocabulary**

5. The phrase *in check* (line 128) is closest in meaning to _____.
   a. in focus    b. at a glance    c. under control    d. without fear

**Inference**

6. Which researcher is the farthest along in finding practical ways to use the findings of recent brain research?
   a. Van Wedeen                b. Jeff Lichtman
   c. Karl Deisseroth           d. John Donoghue

**Detail**

7. Which of these is NOT a theory of early physicians?
   a. The brain was where our mental world existed.
   b. The brain was made out of phlegm.
   c. The brain's purpose was to calm the heart.
   d. The brain is the control center of the body.

## Critical Thinking

**Evaluating:** Duke University's Miguel Nicolelis predicts that "eventually brain implants will become as common as heart implants." Do you think that's possible? If they were possible, what ethical ramifications might there be?

_____

**Discussion:** The author described himself as a "guinea pig" for undergoing a brain scan. Would you ever volunteer for a medical test or treatment you didn't need? Under what circumstances?

# Understanding the Use of the Passive Voice

Most sentences in English are in the active voice. However, there are times when the passive is the structure of choice and the writer chooses to omit the agent (the "doer" of the action). These include:

when the person who performed the action is either unimportant or obvious.
*The brain is then sliced into sections.*

when the writer does not know who performed the action.
*A box of chocolates was left on my bedside table.*

when the writer wishes to be vague.
*Advances in the past have inspired expectations that have not been met.*

**A. Noticing.** Read the excerpt from the reading. Underline the verbs in the passive voice.

They begin by slicing preserved mouse brains into thin layers of tissue, each less than a thousandth the thickness of a human hair. An electron microscope is then used to take a picture of each layer, and the images are put in order using a computer. Slowly a three-dimensional image is built—one that the scientists can explore as if they were in a tiny submarine. "Everything is revealed," says Lichtman.

**B. Multiple Choice.** Choose why the writer probably chose to use the passive voice in each sentence.

1. The patient was told that he would need brain surgery.
   a. The person who told the patient is obvious.
   b. The person who told the patient is not known.

2. His mail was delivered to his house while he was in the hospital.
   a. The person who delivered the mail is not important.
   b. The writer wishes to be vague.

3. Irregularities were noticed on several occasions.
   a. The people who noticed the irregularities are not known.
   b. The writer wishes to be vague.

4. The test results appear to have been removed from the file.
   a. The person who removed the test results is not known.
   b. The person who removed the test results is obvious.

# Vocabulary Practice

**A. Completion.** Complete the information using the words from the box. Three words are extra.

| | | | |
|---|---|---|---|
| dazzle | disorder | forefront | neural |
| organ | originate | scrutinize | unprecedented |

What do you see when you look at the moon? In Western cultures, people see "the man in the moon." In East Asia, people point to a rabbit. In India, it's a pair of hands. "The brain is really a predictive **1.** _____," says scientist Nouchine Hadjikhani, a researcher working at the **2.** _____ of brain research. "We try to find sense in the noise all the time, and we fill things with information."

Neuroscientist Joel Voss studies how our brains find meaning in random shapes and lines. In his studies, he has presented people with meaningless shapes and asked them if the shapes resemble something meaningful. He measures **3.** _____ activity by tracking changes in blood flow. He can see regions in the brain becoming active when a person looks at the lines and shapes. The same areas involved in processing meaningful images light up when the lines and shapes are viewed.

Where does seeing images like this **4.** _____? Voss says the brain must quickly **5.** _____ unfamiliar visual information and figure out what's worth paying attention to. Seeing faces and figures in the moon or images formed by groups of stars is a consequence of the brain's tendency to match stored information with new information.

△ Depending on where you're from, you might see a man, a rabbit, or a pair of hands in the full moon.

**B. Words in Context.** Complete each sentence with the best answer.

1. Something that is **unprecedented** has _____ been done or known before.

   a. never            b. frequently

2. If someone has a brain **disorder**, the brain is acting

   a. normally            b. abnormally

3. A **tricky** problem would probably be _____ to solve.

   a. easy            b. difficult

4. Something that is drawn **exquisitely** is drawn _____.

   a. carelessly and too quickly    b. beautifully and in detail

5. If someone or something **dazzles** you, you are _____ by their skill, qualities, or beauty.

   a. impressed            b. disappointed

> **Word Partnership**
> Use **unprecedented**
> with: (*n.*) unprecedented
> **scale**, unprecedented
> **prosperity**, unprecedented
> **growth**; (*adv.*) **absolutely**
> unprecedented, **virtually**
> unprecedented; (*prep. phrase*)
> unprecedented **in history**.

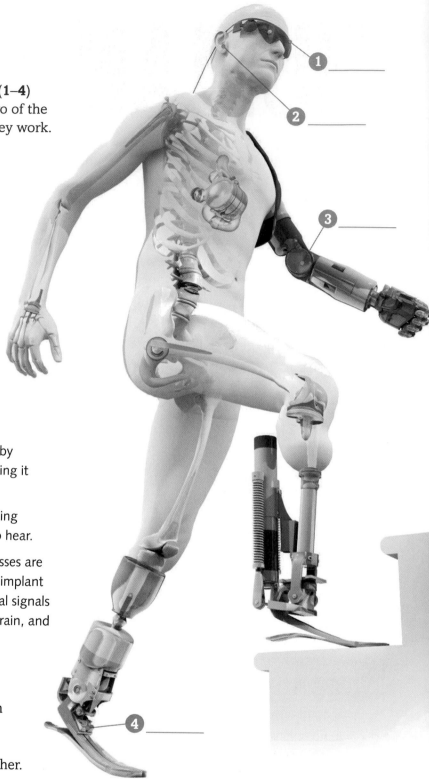

**A. Matching.** Match parts of the bionic body (**1–4**) with the descriptions (**a–d**). Then choose two of the bionic parts and explain to a partner how they work.

## Bionics: from *biology* + electro*nics*

As scientists work to link machine and mind, artificial bones, organs, joints, and limbs (parts shaded green and blue) are gaining many of the capabilities of human ones:

**a.** Signals are transmitted from the brain to the bionic arm via electrodes attached to remaining nerves in the injured arm. The result: a person is able to grasp and manipulate objects.

**b.** A bionic ankle copies the action of a real one by propelling (pushing) the wearer forward, making it possible for the person to walk again.

**c.** Implants stimulate nerves inside the ear, allowing people who are partially or completely deaf to hear.

**d.** Images captured by a video camera in the glasses are converted to signals and sent wirelessly to an implant in the eye. Electrodes in the eye send the visual signals to the optic nerve, which sends them to the brain, and a person is able to "see" the images.

**B. Skim and Predict.** You are going to read an article about a woman with a bionic body part. Skim the passage on pages 151–155 for two minutes to note some information about her. Then read the passage to check your ideas.

| Name | Amanda Kitts |
|---|---|
| Bionic body part | |
| Why she needs it | |
| Things she can now do | |
| Things she can't do yet | |

# HUMAN BIONICS

**A 1** Amanda Kitts is mobbed by four- and five-year-olds as she enters the classroom. "Hey, kids, how're my babies today?" she says, patting shoulders and ruffling[1] hair.
**5** Slender and energetic, she has operated this Knoxville, Tennessee, daycare center and two others for almost 20 years. She crouches down to talk to a small girl, putting her hands on her knees.

**B 10** "The robot arm!" several kids cry. "You remember this, huh?" says Kitts, holding out her left arm. She turns her hand palm up. There is a soft whirring sound. If you weren't paying close
**15** attention, you'd miss it. She bends her elbow, accompanied by more whirring.

**C** "Make it do something silly!" one girl says. "Silly? Remember how I
**20** can shake your hand?" Kitts says, extending her arm and rotating her wrist. A boy reaches out, hesitantly, to touch her fingers. What he brushes against is flesh-colored plastic, fingers
**25** curved slightly inward. Underneath are three motors, a metal framework, and a network of sophisticated electronics. The assembly is topped by a white plastic cup midway up Kitts's biceps, encircling a stump[2] that is
**30** almost all that remains from the arm she lost in a car accident in 2006.

> A new generation of bionic technology provides hope to people with damaged body parts, including amputee Amanda Kitts who lost her arm in a car accident.

---

**1** If you **ruffle** someone's hair, you lightly rub it.

**2** A **stump** is the base portion of a body part that remains after the rest has been amputated.

**D** Almost all, but not quite. Within her brain, below the level of consciousness, lives an intact image of that arm, a phantom. When Kitts
35 thinks about flexing[3] her elbow, the phantom moves. Impulses racing down from her brain are picked up by electrode sensors in the white cup and converted into signals that turn motors, and the artificial elbow bends.

**E** 40 "I don't really think about it. I just move it," says Kitts, who uses both this standard model and a more experimental arm with even more control. "After my accident, I felt lost. These days I'm just excited all the time, because they
45 keep on improving the arm. One day I'll be able to feel things with it and clap my hands together in time to the songs my kids are singing."

**F** Kitts is one of "tomorrow's people," a group
50 whose missing or ruined body parts are being replaced by devices **embedded** in their nervous systems that respond to commands from their brains. The machines they use are called neural prostheses or—using a term made
55 popular by science fiction writers—bionics.

**G** The kind of prosthesis that Amanda Kitts uses is controlled by her brain. A technique called targeted muscle reinnervation uses nerves remaining after an amputation[4] to control an
60 artificial limb. It was first tried in a patient in 2002. Four years later, Tommy Kitts, Amanda's husband, read about the research, which took place at the Rehabilitation Institute of Chicago (RIC). His wife lay in the hospital at the time;
65 the truck that had crushed her car had also crushed her arm, from just above the elbow down.

**H** "I was angry, sad, depressed. I just couldn't accept it," she says. But the news Tommy
70 brought her about the Chicago arm gave her some reassurance, and some hope. "It seemed like the best option out there, a lot better than motors and switches," Tommy says. "Amanda actually got excited about it." Soon they were
75 on a plane to Illinois.

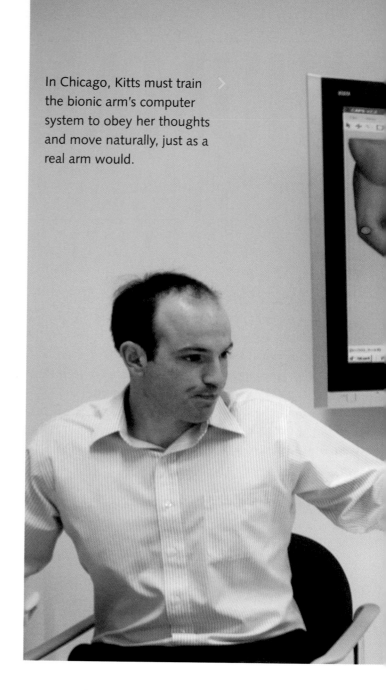

In Chicago, Kitts must train the bionic arm's computer system to obey her thoughts and move naturally, just as a real arm would.

**I** Todd Kuiken, a licensed medical practitioner and biomedical engineer at RIC, was the person responsible for what the institute had begun calling the "bionic arm." He knew that
80 nerves in an amputee's stump could still carry signals from the brain. And he knew that a

---

3 When you **flex** something, usually a muscle, you bend it.

4 An **amputation** occurs when a body part is removed, usually for medical reasons.

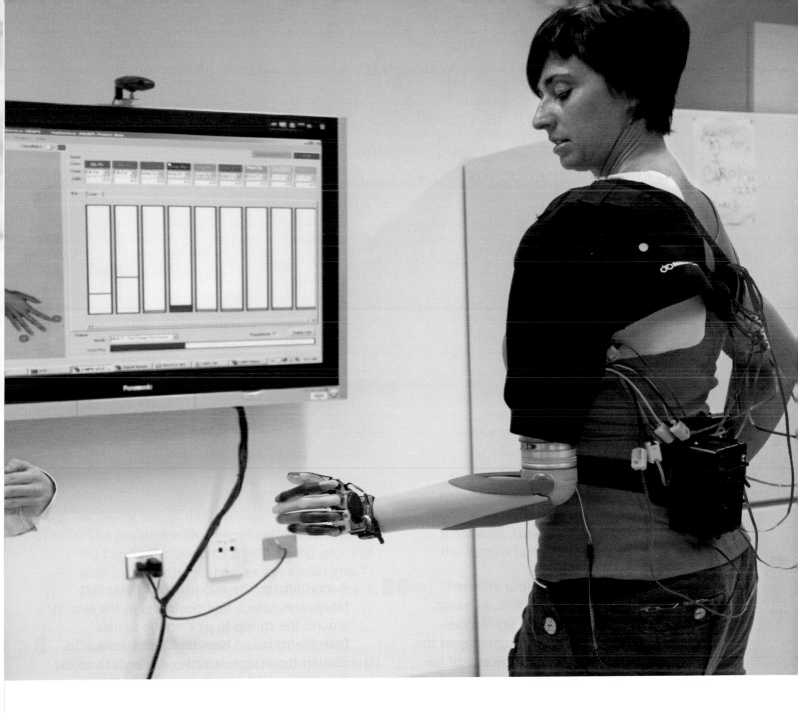

computer in a prosthesis could direct electric motors to move the limb. However, making the connection was far from straightforward.
85 Nerves conduct electricity, but they can't be spliced together with a computer cable. (Nerve fibers and metal wires are not mutually compatible, and an open wound where a wire enters the body would be a dangerous avenue
90 for infections.)

J Kuiken needed an amplifier to boost the signals from the nerves, avoiding the need for a direct contact between nerve and wire. He found one in muscles. When muscles tense, they give
95 off an electrical burst strong enough to be detected by an electrode placed on the skin. He developed a technique to reroute severed nerves from their old, damaged spots to other muscles that could give their signals the
100 proper boost.

K In October 2006, Kitts consented to have Kuiken try out his new technique on her. The first step was to **salvage** major nerves that once went all the way down her arm. "These
105 are the same nerves that work the arm and

# Vocabulary Practice

**A. Completion.** Complete the information by circling the correct word in each pair.

Bionics are being used with increasing frequency and more
**1. (reliability / sensation)** to improve the lives of people who have suffered from the loss of hearing, sight, **2. (vibration / sensation)**, or movement.

For instance, about 250 people have been treated with an experimental technique to restore hand movement lost due to paralysis. A patient can experience some degree of movement, such as the ability to pick up a knife or fork, by means of a sophisticated and **3. (crude / intricate)** piece of equipment **4. (embedded / assigned)** in their chest.

Another bionic success has restored partial hearing to nearly 200,000 people around the world during the past 30 years. In this procedure, 22 electrodes are planted in the part of the inner ear that normally detects sound **5. (vibrations / validities)**. A microphone picks up sounds and sends signals to the electrodes; these then transmit electronic impulses directly to the nerves, allowing some degree of hearing to be restored.

∧ A modern bionic hand allows for a more sophisticated range of movement.

Researchers are even beginning to **6. (assign / salvage)** the power of bionics to the brain itself. Scientists are experimenting with allowing patients to move remote objects with their minds. Researchers believe there is a **7. (crude / reasonable)** chance that one day bionics may even allow us to reactivate the brain area that stores memories in people with memory loss.

**B. Words in Context.** Complete each sentence with the correct answer.

1. Something that is **crude** is _____.
   a. simple and basic       b. complex and refined

2. If something is **embedded** in ice, the ice _____.
   a. is similar to it        b. completely surrounds it

3. A **valid** argument or idea is based on _____ reasoning.
   a. complex                b. sensible

4. If you manage to **salvage** a difficult situation, you are able to get something _____ from it.
   a. useful                 b. unusual

5. People or things that are **reliable** can be _____ to work well.
   a. changed                b. trusted

> **Word Link**
> The root **val** has the meaning of "strength or worth," e.g., *value, valid, valiant, valor, equivalent, evaluate.*

# VIEWING Bionic Mountaineer

## Before You Watch

**A. Matching.** You will hear these words and phrases in the video. What do you think they mean? Match each word or phrase (**1–5**) to its meaning (**a–e**).

1. Exposed to **the elements**, they grew sick and weak.

2. Some [other climbers] accused me of cheating, which was **music to my ears**, . . . that meant that they fully accepted [me] . . .

3. We're at **the brink** of a new age. I can imagine in the coming years . . .

4. [Hugh's ideas] could represent a **revolution** in the field of prosthetics.

5. I can imagine . . . a prosthesis that will enable an **amputee** to run faster than is possible with a biological leg.

   **a.** _____ a big change

   **b.** _____ severe weather conditions

   **c.** _____ the edge, or the moment before something begins

   **d.** _____ a person who has had a limb surgically removed

   **e.** _____ a very good and pleasing thing

‹ Hugh Herr demonstrating his prosthetic legs. These artificial legs give him greater versatility than biological legs in rock climbing.

**B. Discussion.** Discuss these questions with a partner.

1. What are the dangers of rock climbing?

2. What would be especially difficult about mountain climbing with prosthetic legs?

## While You Watch

**A. Multiple Choice.** Choose the correct answer to each question.

1. How long were Hugh and his friend lost on Mount Washington?

   a. three days      b. five days      c. a week

2. When Hugh started to design prosthetic legs for climbing, what body part didn't he need?

   a. the toes      b. the heel      c. the ankle

3. Where does Hugh look to for design ideas?

   a. athletes      b. transportation      c. nature

**B. Fact or Opinion.** The following sentences are based on information from the video. Decide if this information is a fact (**F**) or an opinion (**O**).

1. ____ Hugh and his friend started to lose sensation in their limbs because of frostbite.

2. ____ Hugh and his friend would have died if the woman snowshoeing hadn't found them.

3. ____ The artificial legs that were given to Hugh were designed for the horizontal world.

4. ____ Hugh's artificial legs were in some ways more versatile than his biological legs.

5. ____ Hugh cheated when he used his biological legs to climb.

6. ____ People with biological legs will choose to get their legs amputated so they can have a performance advantage.

∧ With his prosthetic legs, Hugh is able to scale surfaces he could never access before.

## After You Watch

**Discussion.** Discuss these questions with a partner.

1. Hugh mentions that other mountaineers accused him of cheating because his prosthetic legs gave him a climbing advantage. Do you feel that constitutes cheating?

2. The use of bionics can give rise to ethical issues, such as the factors used in determining who receives bionic body parts. What other ethical issues could arise?

3. In the video, Hugh says, "I could imagine that people with biological legs will choose to get their legs amputated so they can achieve the same performance advantage." Do you agree? Why or why not?

# 8

# SOCIAL BEHAVIOR

All adult meerkats—male and female—pitch in to help educate the young in hunting and survival techniques.

## Warm Up

**Discuss these questions with a partner.**

1. What aspects of social behavior are unique to humans?

2. Which animals do you think are closest to us in terms of social behavior?

3. In what ways is the behavior of insects similar to, and different from, our own?

## Before You Read

**A. Quiz and Discussion.** Answer the questions below. Then check your ideas with a partner.

1. Can you match each term with the correct animals?

| bees | elephants | fish | lions |
|------|-----------|------|-------|

   **a.** a swarm of _____  **b.** a herd of _____
   **c.** a pride of _____  **d.** a school of _____

2. What do you think are the advantages and disadvantages for animals of living in large groups?

**B. Skim.** Briefly skim the passage on pages 163–167. Why do you think researchers are interested in how ants and bees behave in groups? Note your answers below. Then read through the passage again to check your ideas.

_____

_____

Insect swarms—like this swarm of ants—live in tight groups, often acting as a single entity.

# THE GENIUS OF SWARMS

A single ant or bee isn't smart, but ant and bee colonies are. The reason, as writer Peter Miller discovers, is something called swarm intelligence.

**A** 1   I used to think ants knew what they were doing. The ones marching across my kitchen counter looked so confident, I just figured they had a **coherent** plan, knew where they were going and what needed to be done. How else could ants create highways, build elaborate nests, organize epic[1] raids, and
5   do all the other things ants do?

**B**   Turns out I was wrong. Ants aren't clever little engineers, architects, or warriors after all—at least not as individuals. When it comes to deciding what to do next, most ants don't have a clue. "If you watch an ant try to accomplish something, you'll be impressed by how inept[2] it is," says
10   Deborah M. Gordon, a biologist at Stanford University.

**C**   How do we explain, then, the success of Earth's 12,000 or so known ant species? They must have learned something in 140 million years. "Ants aren't smart," Gordon says. "Ant colonies are." A colony can solve problems unthinkable for individual ants, such as finding the shortest path to the best
15   food source, allocating workers to different tasks, or defending a **territory** from neighbors. They do it with something called swarm intelligence.

1 If something is **epic**, it is very large or grand.

2 People or animals that are **inept** are awkward, clumsy, or unable to do things.

∧ Nomadic army ant workers working together to build a new bivouac (a temporary shelter)

**D** Where this intelligence comes from raises a fundamental question in nature: How do the simple actions of individuals add up to the complex behavior of a group?

**E** One key to an ant colony is that no one's in charge. No generals command ant warriors. No managers boss ant workers. The queen plays no role except to lay eggs. Even with half a million ants, a colony operates as a single entity without any management at all—at least none that we would recognize. Scientists describe such a system as self-organizing. It relies upon countless interactions between individual ants, each of which is following simple rules.

**F** That's how swarm intelligence works: simple creatures following simple **protocols**, each one acting on local information. No ant sees the big picture, or tells any other ant what to do. Some ant species may go about this with more sophistication than others. (*Temnothorax albipennis,* for example, can rate the quality of a potential nest site using multiple **criteria**.) But in each case, says Iain Couzin, a biologist at Oxford and Princeton Universities, no leadership is required. "Even complex behavior may be coordinated by relatively simple interactions," he says.

**G** Inspired by this idea, computer scientists have been using swarm behavior to create mathematical procedures for resolving complex human problems, such as routing trucks and scheduling airlines.

**H** In Houston, for example, a company named American Air Liquide has been using ant-based guidelines to manage a complex business problem. The company produces industrial and medical gases at about a hundred locations in the United States and delivers them to 6,000 sites, using pipelines, railcars, and 400 trucks. Air Liquide developed a computer model inspired by the foraging behavior of Argentine ants (*Linepithema humile*), a species that, like other ant species, deposits chemical substances called pheromones.

**I** "When these ants bring food back to the nest, they lay a pheromone trail that tells other ants to go get more food," says Charles N. Harper, who oversees the supply system at Air Liquide. "The pheromone trail gets reinforced every time an ant goes out and comes back, kind of like when you wear a trail in the forest to collect wood. So we developed a program that sends out billions of software ants to find out where the pheromone trails are strongest for our truck routes."

**J** Air Liquide used the ant approach to consider every permutation[3] of plant scheduling, weather, and truck routing—millions of possible decisions and outcomes a day. Every night, forecasts of customer demand and manufacturing costs are fed into the model. "It takes four hours to run, even with the biggest computers we have," Harper says. "But at six o'clock every morning, we get a solution that says how we're going to manage our day."

**K** Other companies have also profited by imitating ants. In Italy and Switzerland, fleets of trucks now use ant-foraging rules to find the best routes for bulk deliveries. In England and France, telephone companies improved their network speed by having messages deposit virtual pheromones at switching stations, just as ants leave signals for other ants to show them the best trails.

**L** But ants are not the only insects with something useful to teach us. On a small island off the southern coast of Maine, Thomas D. Seeley, a biologist at Cornell University, has been studying how colonies of honeybees (*Apis mellifera*) choose a new home. In late spring, when a hive gets too crowded, a colony normally splits, and the queen, some drones,[4] and about half the workers migrate a short distance to cluster on

---

3 A **permutation** is one of the ways in which a number of things can be ordered or arranged.

4 A **drone** is a male bee that does not work but can fertilize the queen. The term can also be used to describe one who performs menial or tedious work.

a tree branch. Meanwhile, a small number
105 of scouts go searching for a new site for
the colony.

**M** To find out how, Seeley's team put out five
nest boxes—four that weren't quite big
enough and one that was just about perfect—
110 and released a colony of bees. Scout bees soon
appeared at all five boxes. When they returned
to the main group, each scout performed a
waggle dance urging other scouts to go have
a look. (These dances include a **code** giving
115 directions to a box's location.) The strength of
each dance reflected the scout's enthusiasm
for the site.

**N** The decisive moment didn't take place in the
main cluster of bees, but out at the boxes,
120 where scouts were building up. As soon as the
number of scouts visible near the entrance to a
box reached about 15—a threshold confirmed
by other experiments—the bees at that box
sensed that a quorum[5] had been reached, and
125 they returned to the swarm with the news.
"It was a race," Seeley says. "Which site was
going to build up 15 bees first?"

**O** Scouts from the chosen box then spread
through the swarm, signaling that it was time
130 to move. Once all the bees had warmed up,
they lifted off to **secure** their new home,
which, to no one's surprise, turned out to be
the best of the five boxes. The bees' rules for
decision-making—seek a diversity of options,
135 encourage a free competition among ideas,
and use an effective mechanism to narrow
choices—so impressed Seeley that he now
uses them at Cornell as chairman of his
department.

**P** 140 "I've applied what I've learned from the bees
to run **faculty** meetings," he says. To avoid
going into a meeting with his mind made
up, hearing only what he wants to hear, and
pressuring people to conform, Seeley asks his
145 group to identify all the possibilities, discuss
their ideas for a while, then vote by secret
ballot.[6] "It's exactly what the swarm bees do,
which gives a group time to let the best ideas
emerge and win."

**Q** 150 In fact, almost any group that follows the
bees' rules will make itself smarter, says James
Surowiecki, author of *The Wisdom of Crowds.*
"The analogy is really quite powerful. The
bees are predicting which nest site will be
155 best, and humans can do the same thing,
even in the face of exceptionally complex
decisions." Investors in the stock market,
scientists on a research project, even kids at
a county fair guessing the number of beans
160 in a jar can be smart groups, he says. That is,
if their members are diverse, independent-
minded, and use a mechanism such as voting,
auctioning, or averaging to reach a collective,
**aggregate** decision.

**R** 165 That's the wonderful appeal of swarm
intelligence. Whether we're talking about
ants, bees, or humans, the ingredients
of smart group behavior—decentralized
control, response to local cues, simple rules
170 of thumb—add up to an effective strategy to
cope with complexity.

**S** Consider the way an Internet search engine
like Google uses group smarts to find what
you're looking for. When you type in a search
175 query, the engine surveys billions of Web
pages on its **index** servers to identify the
most relevant ones. It then ranks them by the
number of pages that link to them, counting
links as votes (the most popular sites get
180 weighted votes,[7] since they're more likely to
be reliable). The pages that receive the most
votes are listed first in the search results.

**T** With free collaborative encyclopedias available
to anyone online, "it's now possible for
185 huge numbers of people to think together
in ways we never imagined a few decades
ago," says Thomas Malone of Massachusetts
Institute of Technology (MIT) Center for
Collective Intelligence. "No single person

---

5 A **quorum** is the minimum number of members required
to be present in a meeting or assembly before any business
can be transacted.

6 A **ballot** occurs when people select a representative or
course of action by voting.

7 **Weighted voting** systems are voting systems based on the
idea that not all voters are equal.

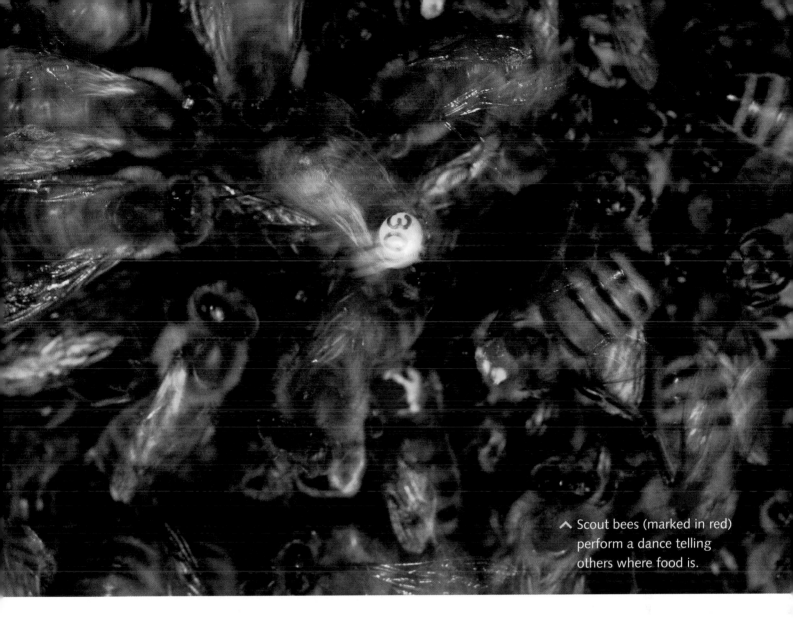

∧ Scout bees (marked in red) perform a dance telling others where food is.

190 knows everything that's needed to deal with problems we face as a society, such as health care or climate change, but collectively we know far more than we've been able to tap[8] so far."

U 195 Such thoughts underline an important truth about collective intelligence: Crowds are wise only if individual members act responsibly and make their own decisions. A group won't be smart if its members **imitate** one another,
200 unthinkingly follow fads, or wait for someone to tell them what to do. When a group is being intelligent, whether it's made up of ants or attorneys,[9] it relies on its members to do their own part. For those of us who
205 sometimes wonder if it's really worth recycling

that extra bottle to lighten our impact on the planet, the fact is that our actions matter, even if we don't see how.

V "A honeybee never sees the big picture any
210 more than you or I do," says Thomas D. Seeley, the bee expert. "None of us knows what society as a whole needs, but we look around and say, oh, they need someone to volunteer at school, or mow the church
215 lawn, or help in a political campaign." If you're looking for a role model in a world of complexity, you could do worse than to imitate an ant or a bee.

---

8 When we **tap** something, like a resource, we access and use it.

9 **Attorneys** is another term used for lawyers.

# Reading Comprehension

**Multiple Choice.** Choose the best answer for each question.

**Gist**

1. What is this reading mainly about?
   a. Although colonies of ants display intelligence, they are not as smart as colonies of bees.
   b. Insects such as ants and bees can teach humans lessons about collective decision-making.
   c. Individual ants and bees are far more intelligent than other types of insects.
   d. A group of humans that uses the bees' methods of decision-making will be smarter than one that doesn't.

**Rhetorical Purpose**

2. Why does the author quote Deborah M. Gordon in paragraph C?
   a. to present an idea that supports his own point of view
   b. to show how much ants have learned in 140 million years
   c. to support the idea that individual ants are not intelligent
   d. to contradict the idea that ant colonies are truly intelligent

**Reference**

3. The word *it* in line 16 refers to _____.
   a. the shortest path          b. an ant colony
   c. solving difficult problems  d. the best food source

**Detail**

4. According to the information in paragraph E, what is the primary role of queen ants?
   a. They manage the worker ants.
   b. They create more members of the colony.
   c. They command warrior ants on raids.
   d. They allow the colony to operate as a single entity.

**Rhetorical Purpose**

5. How does Charles N. Harper explain the concept of a pheromone trail in paragraph I?
   a. by contrasting it with a computer program
   b. by explaining the chemical composition of pheromones
   c. by comparing it with a similar human activity
   d. by giving examples of several types of pheromone trails

**Inference**

6. In paragraph M, the author implies that _____.
   a. scouts communicate information to the swarm by dancing
   b. the researchers had no idea which home the bees would choose
   c. the scouts moved as a group and visited each box in turn
   d. some scouts stayed at the new home while others informed the swarm

**Detail**

7. What is true for both ants and bees?
   a. Leadership is required for decision-making.
   b. Individuals are unable to see the "big picture."
   c. They communicate by elaborate dances.
   d. They need to reach a quorum before a decision is made.

**Critical Thinking**

**Analyzing:** Using information from the reading, explain in your own words the difference between collective intelligence and individual intelligence in both insects and humans.

_____

**Discussion:** What benefits has the Internet brought to the way people think and make decisions? Are there any disadvantages?

# Understanding Inference

Writers often tell readers more than they say directly. They give clues that help you "read between the lines" to get a deeper understanding of a text. Understanding these clues is called inferring, or drawing inferences. When you infer, you draw on background knowledge, common sense, and the details in the text. The following are examples of questions that ask you to infer information from a passage.

*The author implies that …*
*Which statement would the author most likely agree with?*
*According to the passage, we can reasonably infer that …*
*Based on the passage, it could be suggested that …*

**Inference.** Choose the best answer for each question.

1. In the first paragraph, what does the author imply?
   a. He has changed his mind about the behavior of ants.
   b. He has performed research on ants himself.
   c. He was not really interested in ants until he wrote this article.
   d. He now believes that ants can make coherent plans.

2. According to the information in paragraph E, we can reasonably assume that an ant colony would not work as a single entity if _____.
   a. there is more than one queen
   b. the queen started laying fewer eggs
   c. it grew to over half a million ants
   d. someone is in charge

3. Based on what you have read, which of these business-management structures is most likely to be successful?
   a. a structure with a strong management team and workers who follow orders
   b. a structure where workers are not informed about company plans and policies
   c. a structure in which workers question and resist every management decision
   d. a structure in which open communication among employees is encouraged

4. If Thomas Seeley were to advise a company on ways to run meetings, based on what he knows about bees, he would probably first suggest _____.
   a. seeing what other companies have done
   b. brainstorming ideas openly
   c. forming two teams and then comparing ideas
   d. secretly voting on a leader to organize a campaign

5. Which of these could be considered an example of swarm intelligence?
   a. a political party that follows the teaching of a charismatic leader
   b. a blog that identifies companies that are using computers to streamline business
   c. a collaborative travel website where users share tips, resources, and other information
   d. a crowd at a rock concert that refuses to follow any rules or regulations

# Vocabulary Practice

**A. Completion.** Complete the information by circling the correct word in each pair.

For animals in the wild, traveling in large groups offers several advantages: It increases their chances of detecting predators, **1. (imitating / securing)** necessary **2. (territory / criteria)**, and finding food.

Wildlife biologist Karsten Heuer has spent many years observing the annual migration of caribou, one of the longest mass movements in the natural world. Once, he spotted a wolf creeping up to a caribou herd. As soon as the wolf got within a certain distance of the herd, the nearest caribou turned and ran. This sent a(n) **3. (coded / indexed)** message to the rest of the herd. Animals closest to the wolf demonstrated every variation of flight, running in all directions and confusing the wolf, but the rest of the herd ran in a(n) **4. (aggregate / coherent)** and orderly mass. In the end, the entire herd escaped, and the wolf was left exhausted.

Each individual caribou was engaged in its own life or death struggle, and yet the **5. (aggregate / secure)** behavior of the herd was characterized by precision, not fright. Every caribou knew the **6. (criteria / index)** that determined when to run and in which direction to go, even if it didn't know exactly why. No leader was responsible for coordinating the herd. Instead, swarm intelligence ensured that each animal followed simple **7. (faculties / protocols)** evolved over thousands of years of wolf attacks.

Herds of wildebeest climb the banks of the Talek River at the Masai Mara National Reserve, Kenya, during their annual migration.

**B. Definitions.** Use the correct form of words in **red** in **A** to complete the definitions. Two words are extra.

1. _____: to copy behavior

2. _____: logical and well organized

3. _____: factors used to judge or decide something

4. _____: an alphabetical list of items used for reference

5. _____: to obtain something after a lot of effort

6. _____: made up of smaller amounts added together

7. _____: the teaching staff at a university or college

8. _____: an area of land occupied and defended by a group of animals

> **Usage**
> *Code* and *protocol* have similar meanings. A *code* is a set of rules about how people should behave or about how something must be done. A *protocol* is also a set of rules or guidelines about correct conduct, but it is usually used in a formal context, e.g., *He understood the proper protocol for declining a job offer.*

# OF ANTS AND HUMANS

A girl looking at an ant she caught. It is believed that ants have been on Earth for more than 130 million years.

## Before You Read

**A. Matching.** Match each word with its definition.

    **a.** habitation      **b.** scavenger      **c.** organism

    **1.** _____: an animal that feeds on dead or decaying matter

    **2.** _____: an animal or a plant

    **3.** _____: the act of living in a place

**B. Predict.** The passage on pages 172–177 is an interview with the American biologist, researcher, and author Edward O. Wilson. Skim the passage and check (✓) the topics you think the interview will cover. Read the whole passage to check your ideas.

    ☐ how Wilson became a naturalist

    ☐ similarities between ants and humans

    ☐ how unselfish behavior developed among animals

    ☐ Wilson's plans for future expeditions

    ☐ human impact on animals today

    ☐ Wilson's opinions on young people today

E. O. Wilson, one of the world's foremost authorities on biodiversity, discusses his life-long love of the natural world, including its smallest members.

**[A]** **1** **National Geographic:** How did you develop a passion for nature?

**Edward O. Wilson:** When I was nine years old and living in Washington, D.C., I somehow
**5** got excited about the idea of expeditions to far-off jungles to collect the sorts of things you saw in *National Geographic.* So I decided I would do some expeditions to Rock Creek Park,[1] and I got bottles and everything, and
**10** I started collecting there. I would go on my own and wander for hours. Then I went to the National Zoo, which was paradise on Earth for me. How could you avoid becoming a naturalist in that kind of environment?

**[B]** **15** **NG:** Is that kind of exploration a rarer experience for kids today?

**Edward O. Wilson:** I worry about that. I have no data, but it appears to me that many of our young people are staying at
**20** home or being influenced by an increasingly stimulating "artifactual" world. **Fake** nature, sci-fi movies, videos, being drawn into lives that are pursued in front of a computer. That's a trend that would take young people away
**25** from a naturalist's experience. But there are counter-influences. More people go to zoos in the U.S. than attend professional sports; did you know that? There's a strong pull remaining that I think is primal.

**[C]** **30** **NG:** Darwin loved beetles. What was it about ants for you?

**Edward O. Wilson:** Originally I was going to work on flies, because I felt that was a wide-open area to do exploration, but I couldn't get
**35** the special insect pins to collect them. It was 1946, just after the Second World War, and those pins were not available. So I turned to ants, because I could collect them in bottles of alcohol.

**[D]** **40** **NG:** Do some say that this isn't serious science, it's just collecting?

**Edward O. Wilson:** Well, when people say that sort of thing, you can respond quickly that you're not going to get anywhere until you do
**45** this science, and furthermore, you're going to make all sorts of new discoveries while you're doing it. You never know when someone is going to be looking for some kind of lead in this growing body of information from
**50** mapping life on Earth. For instance, someone might say, "What I need for my work is an ant that hunts underwater and walks around submarine fashion and then comes out and goes back to a dry nest. Does any such thing
**55** exist?" It turns out, yes!

**[E]** **NG:** A submarine ant?

**Edward O. Wilson:** Yes, in Malaysia, on the pitcher plant *Nepenthes.* This plant collects water in which insects fall and drown, and
**60** there are substances in the water that help digest the insects. *Nepenthes* gets **organic** material from the insects it captures. There is this ant that lives on *Nepenthes,* and the workers walk in, right down into the mouth of
**65** hell. They just walk right in submarine-like and pick up insects that have fallen to the bottom.

**[F]** **NG:** Are you doing any field trips these days?

**Edward O. Wilson:** I get together with younger ant specialists—they all seem younger
**70** to me, these days—and we go into the field. It's a joyous activity. On a recent trip to the Dominican Republic, we went up to 2.4 kilometers (8,000 feet) above sea level. Most people don't know the Dominican Republic
**75** has mountains. We were all the way up in cold pine forests, discovering new species at every mountain site.

---

**1 Rock Creek Park** is an urban park in Washington, D.C.

Edward O. Wilson is an American biologist who specializes in the study of ants.

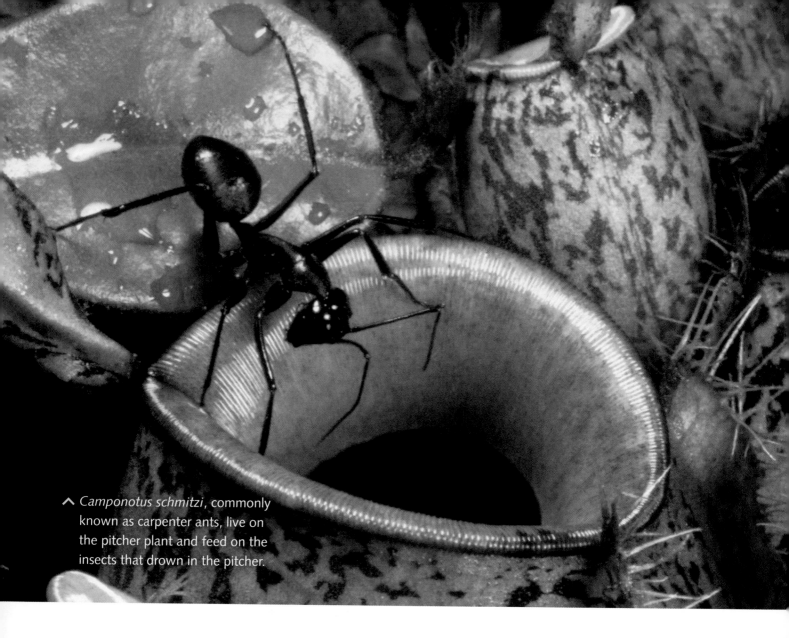

▲ *Camponotus schmitzi*, commonly known as carpenter ants, live on the pitcher plant and feed on the insects that drown in the pitcher.

G **NG:** There's no feeling that the world has been conquered now?

80 **Edward O. Wilson:** Oh, no. That's the point—we're just beginning exploration. For animals, we probably know as few as ten percent of the species. Even in a fairly familiar group like ants, we're discovering them right 85 and left. I estimate that maybe half the ants in the world remain undiscovered.

H **NG:** How well did Darwin know his ants?

**Edward O. Wilson:** Darwin knew his ants very well. He spent a lot of time watching 90 ants. And part of the reason was that ants **exemplified** a peculiarity that he said might have proved **fatal** to his theory of evolution.

And that potential flaw was that worker ants are so completely different from queen 95 ants, yet they are **sterile**. So how would you explain that by natural selection? If worker ants couldn't have offspring,[2] how are their traits developed and passed on?

I **NG:** The problem was how this kind of self-100 sacrifice—tending the queen while giving up reproduction—evolved?

**Edward O. Wilson:** Yes, and Darwin solved the problem: What counts is the group, and that worker ants are just part of the colony, 105 just an extension of the queen. Her heredity

---

2 People's or animals' **offspring** are their children.

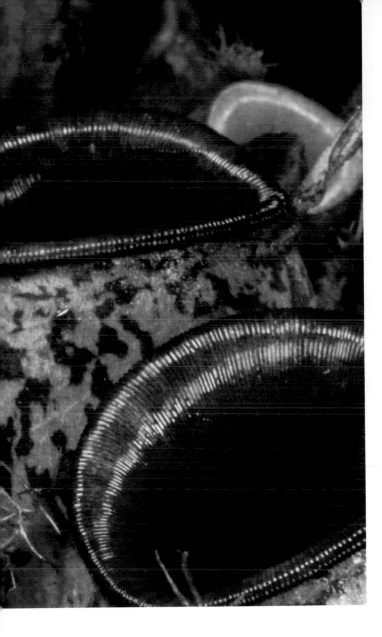

and of evolution. One colony against another is what's being selected. This happens to be close to Darwin's idea but in modern genetic terms.

**K** 125 **NG:** How does this kind of social behavior get started?

**Edward O. Wilson:** It has to do with defense against enemies. Naturalists have discovered more and more groups that have altruistic[5]
130 workers and soldiers—ants, termites, certain beetles, shrimp, and even a mammal, the naked mole rat. What's **consistently** the case is that these animals have a resource, usually a place to live with food, that's very valuable.
135 If you're a solitary individual and you build a chamber like that, somebody could chuck you out.[6] The idea is that these lines are going to find it advantageous to develop sterile castes for maintaining and protecting the colony.

**L** 140 **NG:** So this is a story about community and home.

**Edward O. Wilson:** I've learned my lesson about jumping from ants or sponges to humans! But it does, in my opinion,
145 call for another look at human origins. Anthropologists now pretty much agree that a major factor in human origins was having a habitation, a campsite, which allowed for certain specialization, where some stayed and
150 looked after the site and the young and so on, while others ventured out to bring food back. And the pressures from predators must have been pretty intense.

is what matters. If she is producing separate organisms that serve her purpose, then all together, these colonies can prevail over **solitary** individuals. That was the solution.
110 And actually that isn't too far from the way we see it today. The most recent theories [are] spelled out in a book that Bert Hölldobler and I wrote called *The Superorganism*.[3]

**J** **NG:** Why that title?

115 **Edward O. Wilson:** The colony is the next level of biological organization. The colony, by group selection, has developed traits that could not be possible otherwise— communication, the "caste" system,[4]
120 cooperative behavior. It's a unit of activity

---

3 Bert Hölldobler and Edward O. Wilson, *The Superorganism: The Beauty, Elegance, and Strangeness of Insect Societies*, W.W. Norton & Company, 2008.

4 A **caste system** is a rigid hereditary system of social ranking.

5 Someone who is **altruistic** is unselfish and does things out of concern for the welfare of others.

6 When you **chuck** something **out**, you throw it out.

Leafcutter ants consume almost 20 percent of the annual vegetation growth of the Central American rain forests. They can carry leaf pieces that weigh up to twenty times their own weight.

M **NG:** But we don't have sterile castes.

155 **Edward O. Wilson:** No, we have a division of labor. That is very true. And that's a fundamental difference between us and insects and these other creatures, and that's why we have to be very careful about drawing
160 analogies. Because human beings are so flexible and intelligent, we can divide labor without physical castes.

N **NG:** That system has worked pretty well for ants.

165 **Edward O. Wilson:** They dominate ecosystems. In tropical forests, from one study, ants alone make up four times the weight of all the land vertebrates put together—amphibians, reptiles, birds, mammals. The
170 weight of all the ants in the world is roughly the weight of all the humans, to the nearest order of magnitude.[7] They are the principal predators of small animals, the principal scavengers in much of the world, and the
175 principal turners of the soil.

O **NG:** It's interesting that ants and humans are both social and that both dominate their environment.

**Edward O. Wilson:** Sure enough, we're
180 the one highly social vertebrate with altruism and high levels of division of labor, though not sterility. We're the one species that has reached this level, and we dominate.

P **NG:** We also have a tremendous effect on
185 other species.

**Edward O. Wilson:** More than any kind of ant. But I'm always at risk of having it said, "That nut[8] wants to compare ants and humans." Well, obviously not. Beyond the
190 fact that we both reached high levels of social behavior based on altruism and division of labor, the resemblance between humans and ants pretty much comes to an end. For example, they communicate almost entirely by
195 taste and smell. They live in a sensory world that's totally different from humans. It's like

---

7 An **order of magnitude** is an estimate of size or magnitude expressed as a power of ten.

8 The term "**nut**" is sometimes used to describe someone who is crazy.

ants are from another planet. And ants are constantly at war. Well, so are we! But they are the most warlike of animals.

**Q** 200  **NG:** It makes you wonder whether war and complex societies go together.

**Edward O. Wilson:** It may turn out that highly evolved societies with this level of altruism tend strongly to divide into groups
205  that then fight against each other. We humans are constantly at war and have been since prehistory. I know a lot of people would like to believe that this is just a nasty habit we developed, just a cultural **anomaly**, and all we
210  have to do is get enlightened[9] and drop it. I hope that's true.

**R**  **NG:** Do the ants offer any lessons?

**Edward O. Wilson:** At least not any we would care to put in practice. Ant colonies
215  are all female; males are tolerated only part of the year. Slavery and cannibalism[10] are commonplace. There is one lesson we have already learned, however: Ants keep themselves **fanatically** clean, so epidemics[11]
220  are rare.

**S**  **NG:** But now ants and many other creatures are threatened with extinction. Are you hopeful that we can save enough in time?

**Edward O. Wilson:** Actually, I am. The best
225  funded global conservation organizations are now scoring successes in **persuading** developing countries to set up sustainable reserves—sustainable meaning they provide an actual increase in the quality of life for
230  people living in and around them. That doesn't take as much money as some have thought. It can be achieved in many of these countries where the greatest destruction is occurring because incomes may be just a few hundred
235  dollars a year. There are reasons to believe that where most of the biodiversity occurs—the tropical forest, grasslands, and shallow marine areas—a lot can be saved.

---

9  An **enlightened** person is someone who has great understanding and is therefore tolerant and unprejudiced.
10  **Cannibalism** is the eating of an animal by an animal of its own kind.
11  **Epidemics** are widespread occurrences of a disease.

# Reading Comprehension

**Multiple Choice.** Choose the best answer for each question.

<table>
<tr><td>Detail</td><td>

**1.** Why did E. O. Wilson study ants and not flies?

a. He found ants much more interesting than flies.

b. He couldn't find the equipment he needed to study flies.

c. He was ordered by the military to study ants.

d. He liked the idea that the study of ants was wide open.

</td></tr>
<tr><td>Detail</td><td>

**2.** What are *Nepenthes*?

a. plants that grow underwater

b. insects that are digested by certain plants

c. submarine ants from Malaysia

d. plants that capture insects

</td></tr>
<tr><td>Detail</td><td>

**3.** According to Wilson, what would many people find surprising about the Dominican Republic?

a. that it has mountainous areas

b. that it has cold pine forests

c. that it has many species of ants

d. that it is located in the Caribbean

</td></tr>
<tr><td>Detail</td><td>

**4.** What is the book *The Superorganism* about?

a. newly discovered species of insects and their importance

b. the idea that worker insects were once fertile

c. theories about the role of colonies in the evolution of species

d. species of animals that were researched by Darwin

</td></tr>
<tr><td>Reference</td><td>

**5.** In paragraph L, the word *some* (line 149) refers to some _____.

a. anthropologists    b. ancient humans

c. predators    d. ants or sponges

</td></tr>
<tr><td>Rhetorical Purpose</td><td>

**6.** Wilson mentions the statistics in paragraph N to _____.

a. present the results of some research that he recently completed

b. show that there are more types of ants than of any other animals

c. indicate that ants are one of the world's most dominant species

d. compare the number of ants in the tropics with the number of ants elsewhere

</td></tr>
<tr><td>Main Idea</td><td>

**7.** According to Wilson's responses on pages 175–177, how are humans unique?

a. We are the most warlike of all the creatures on the Earth.

b. We have division of labor but no biological castes.

c. We have a strong effect on other species with which we share territory.

d. We are the only social creatures that do not form colonies.

</td></tr>
</table>

## Critical Thinking

**Analyzing:** Do you think the author of the previous reading, "The Genius of Swarms," would generally agree or disagree with E. O. Wilson? Why do you think so?

**Evaluating:** What does Wilson say about war in paragraph Q (from line 197)? Do you think there may be evolutionary reasons that humans go to war? What other reasons might explain it?

# Scanning for Details (II)

We scan to find specific information that we need from an article. For example, we might scan to locate key information like dates, names, amounts, or places, as well as to identify specific points or ideas that the author is making. In some cases, the specific information we are scanning for may not be mentioned in the passage.

**Scanning.** Scan the article "Of Ants and Humans," and then mark the following items **T** (True), **F** (False), or **NG** (Not Given). Try to locate the information you need as quickly as possible.

1. _____ Wilson first became interested in natural science during a visit to the National Zoo in Washington, D.C.

2. _____ According to Wilson, more people visit zoos in the United States than attend professional sporting events.

3. _____ The insects that fall to the bottom of the water inside the Malaysian pitcher plant are mostly ants.

4. _____ Wilson feels older than most of the other ant specialists he works with now.

5. _____ Darwin spent more time studying ants than he did studying beetles.

6. _____ The naked mole rat is given in the passage as a type of mammal that has altruistic workers and warriors.

7. _____ Solitary animals find it more difficult to maintain and defend a nest than colonial animals.

8. _____ The number of ants in the world is about the same as the number of humans.

9. _____ Ants communicate by taste and smell because they have very poor vision and hearing.

10. _____ Female ants are usually not found in ant colonies.

11. _____ Ants keep themselves so clean that epidemics seldom occur in ant colonies.

12. _____ According to Wilson, setting up sustainable reserves in developing countries is not as expensive as some people predicted.

# Vocabulary Practice

**A. Completion.** Complete the information using the correct form of words in the box. Four words are extra.

| | | | | |
|---|---|---|---|---|
| anomaly | consistent | exemplify | fake | fanatically |
| fatal | organic | persuade | solitary | sterile |

## Warriors on the Move

When it comes to the art of war, army ant colonies **1.** _____ an extreme fighting spirit. With their tough bodies and powerful jaws, army ants are able to kill prey vastly larger than themselves. Although a(n) **2.** _____ ant can do no real damage, a swarm of several hundred thousand can inflict **3.** _____ attacks on tens of thousands of insects and small animals within a matter of hours.

Over many generations, certain insects have developed strategies to avoid becoming ant prey. One of an army ant's traits, for example, is poor vision. So a stick insect will attempt to **4.** _____ its appearance by imitating a piece of vegetation; it will also keep completely motionless, hoping not to send any vibration that will reveal its location. In general, however, army ants tolerate nothing in their path, not even lizards, snakes, and frogs, which they kill but do not eat.

Although violent, attacks by army ants also benefit the forest by helping maintain biodiversity. The ants turn the soil, move nutrients and **5.** _____ matter, and help to disperse seeds. The devastation left by an ant raid also creates opportunities for new species to enter the habitat. Environmentalists therefore feel it is important to **6.** _____ governments to protect their army ant communities because of their long-term benefit to the environment.

∧ Colonies of the army ant *Eciton burchelli* (light brown) can be found in many parts of Central and South America.

**B. Definitions.** Match words from the box in **A** with the correct definition.

**1.** _____: not true; pretending to be something else

**2.** _____: something different from what is usual or expected

**3.** _____: unreasonably or excessively enthusiastic about something

**4.** _____: spending a lot of time alone

**5.** _____: relating to or derived from living things

**6.** _____: to demonstrate a typical example

**7.** _____: to be unable to reproduce

**8.** _____: always behaving in the same way

**9.** _____: resulting in death

**10.** _____: to make someone do something by giving good reasons for it

> **Word Partnership**
> Use *fatal* with:
> (*n.*) fatal **accident**, fatal **illness**, fatal **shooting**, fatal **blow**.

# VIEWING Monarch Migration

## Before You Watch

**A. Discuss.** Look at the map and read the caption. Then discuss these questions.

1. Where do monarch butterflies travel to and from?

2. Why do you think they migrate? When do you think they migrate?

3. Do you know any other animals that travel long distances when they migrate?

Every year, monarch butterflies travel south to their winter roosts in Mexico.

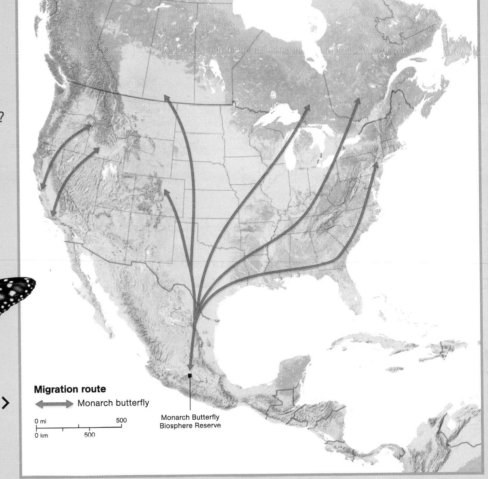

**Migration route**

→← Monarch butterfly

0 mi          500
0 km      500

Monarch Butterfly
Biosphere Reserve

**B. Predict.** Predict the number that you think completes each sentence.

| 50 | 80 | 320 | 250 | 300 | 3,000 |
|----|----|-----|-----|-----|-------|

1. More than _____ million monarch butterflies migrate from North America to Mexico each year.

2. Their trip is about _____ kilometers.

3. Their final resting spot is a forest about _____ kilometers away from Mexico City.

4. A terrible storm in 2002 killed about _____ million monarchs.

5. This accounted for _____ percent of the monarch population.

6. Nearly _____ percent of the forest the butterflies depend on has been destroyed in the last few decades.

# While You Watch

**A. Completion.** While you watch the video, check your predictions in **B** of the *Before You Watch* section.

**B. Completion.** Complete the summary with words from the box. Two words are extra.

| | | | | | |
|---|---|---|---|---|---|
| aggregate | consistent | criteria | fatal | habitat | illegal |
| implement | persuade | population | remote | secure | tolerate |

Every year, millions of monarch butterflies fly south, covering over 3,000 kilometers on their way to their **1.** _____ wintering grounds in Mexico.

But these beautiful creatures are also very fragile animals, and are often unable to **2.** _____ sudden changes to their environment. In fact, such environmental changes can prove **3.** _____ for these delicate creatures. For example, in 2002, a rainstorm and freezing temperatures killed as many as 250,000,000 butterflies, almost 80 percent of the monarch **4.** _____ in the "El Rosario" butterfly sanctuary.

Mike Quinn, a Texas biologist with the organization Monarch Watch, believes **5.** _____ logging may have destroyed sections of the forest that serve as the butterflies' **6.** _____. Usually, the thick forests protect the monarchs, keeping the temperature and environment around them fairly **7.** _____ during the winter months. But logging opens up the forest and lets in the cold air, freezing the places where the monarchs rest.

The Mexican government, along with the World Wildlife Fund, has tried to **8.** _____ laws that will help **9.** _____ the butterflies' future, for instance, by offering payments to landowners to **10.** _____ them not to cut down trees. The hope is that these measures will enable millions of monarchs to continue to take flight each year.

# After You Watch

**Discussion.** Discuss these questions with a partner.

1. The video mentions paying money to persuade loggers not to cut down trees. But would fines work better, or some other incentive? What do you think?

2. The monarch migration is described as "one of the great spectacles of nature." What other great natural spectacles have you seen or heard about?

# 9

# CREATIVITY

A page from Leonardo da Vinci's notebook showing his ideas for a flying machine. Leonardo often wrote backwards—from right to left. The image shown here hasn't been reversed.

## Warm Up

**Discuss these questions with a partner.**

1. Who are the most creative artists, writers, or designers today?

2. Who do you think were the most creative people in the past?

3. To what extent is creativity something that people are born with?

183

# Before You Read

**A. Discussion.** What do you know about Leonardo da Vinci? Discuss your ideas with a partner.

_____

_____

**B. Scan.** Quickly scan the reading on pages 185–190. Which of Leonardo da Vinci's works of art does the author discuss? Note them below.

_____

_____

_____

Despite over 500 years of chipping wall and flaking paint, the brilliance of Leonardo da Vinci's masterpiece *The Last Supper* still shines through.

# DECODING LEONARDO

**A** 1   According to legend, in the year 1505 near the Tuscan town of Fiesole, a great bird rose from Monte Ceceri (Swan Mountain) and took to the air. No witness testimony remains of the event. But if anyone was present on that hillside, the most likely candidate is Leonardo da Vinci, a man whose ambition for many years had been
5   to fly like a bird. Some 50 years later, an acquaintance, Gerolamo Cardano, wrote, "Leonardo da Vinci . . . attempted to fly, but failed. He was an excellent painter."

**B**   To call Leonardo an excellent painter is like labeling Shakespeare a clever wordsmith.[1] He was a true genius, recognized in his own time and idolized in ours. His paintings are as secret and seductive as himself, done with the hand of
10   an angel, the intellect of a scientist, and the soul of a romantic. His drawings are among the most beautiful ever made; his most treasured painting, the *Mona Lisa*, is undoubtedly the most famous in the world.

---

1   A **wordsmith** is someone who is good with words and language.

*Virgin of the Rocks* by Leonardo da Vinci

remains only one enigmatic[2] reference, in a notebook characteristically filled with phrases and sketches, in which he proclaims that his great bird "will bring eternal glory to the nest
35 where it was born . . ."

## Birth of a Genius

E Leonardo da Vinci was born in 1452, the illegitimate child of a peasant girl named Caterina and respected notary[3] Piero da Vinci.
40 Leonardo lived at first with his mother in a three-room stone house on a hill just outside the village of Vinci, some 20 kilometers (12 miles) west of Florence. In that idyllic Tuscan countryside began the youngster's lifelong love
45 of nature—a love that would remain **implicit** in all his later works.

F Around 1469 Leonardo's father took him to Florence, where the statesman Lorenzo de Medici had established an **academy** where
50 all arts were honored. For years, art had been an instrument of religious expression, and the **parameters** of what was **ideologically** acceptable had been decided by the Church. But in the more tolerant atmosphere of
55 Florence, painters represented things as they saw them, rather than as the Church said they must be. It was a society well suited to the ever-questioning country boy.

G Leonardo commenced an apprenticeship at
60 the studio of Andrea del Verrocchio, with whom he studied for at least six years. The boy mastered every medium and continued his studies of nature, discovering so much so fast that it seemed to him that everything
65 must eventually be revealed to his searching. In painting, he not only outshone his more mature colleagues but also his teacher. Assigned to paint the figure of an angel, he gave it a whole new dimension that drew the
70 viewer directly into the painting, in a way that Verrocchio's inhibited style could never do. Some say that Verrocchio never painted again.

C His love of painting notwithstanding, it was knowledge itself that was Leonardo's
15 great love—knowledge, and the experience from which it may be drawn. To acquire it, Leonardo turned to a diverse array of fields: mathematics, geometry, optics, astronomy, geology, botany, zoology, hydraulics,
20 mechanics, and anatomy, as well as painting and drawing. As an engineer, he could think in four dimensions, visualizing not only the shapes of mechanical parts but also their interrelated motions.

D 25 Among his designs for flight, Leonardo imagined parachutes, landing equipment, even an aerial screw that acted like the blades of a helicopter. But, like so much else in his life, Leonardo's attempts to actually create a
30 workable flying machine are a mystery. There

---

**2** A person, thing, or situation that is **enigmatic** is mysterious or puzzling.

**3** A **notary** is a clerk licensed to prepare legal documents.

## Early Masterworks

[H] Leonardo left Florence in 1482 at the age
75 of 30. He stayed away for 18 years. The
young Florentine hoped to find the glory he
sought in the court of Ludovico Sforza, ruler
of Milan. A practical city, Milan cared more
for knowledge than for the arts. It housed no
80 great artists but counted many learned men.
Leonardo came as a musician but presented
himself as an engineer, describing in a long
boastful letter his inventiveness in the field
of weapons. Almost as an afterthought, he
85 assured Sforza that, ". . . also I can do in
painting whatever may be done, as well as any
other, whoever he may be."

[I] It was as an artist that Leonardo was accepted.
He established an art factory much like
90 Verrocchio's shop in Florence and at once
accepted assignments. These included a portrait
of Sforza's beautiful and learned mistress,
Cecilia Gallerani (see page 189, *Lady with an
Ermine*), a portrait of a musician that some
95 scholars believe is really a self-portrait, and a
brilliant early version of *Virgin of the Rocks*,
begun in 1483 and now in the Louvre.

[J] Around 1485 he began his notebooks. These
are detailed, cryptic[4] compilations of material
100 on a seemingly **arbitrary** range of topics,
from geology and geometry to anatomy and
astronomy, all interwoven and superimposed
as one burning interest gave way to the next.
His notes are written left-handed from right
105 to left, and there are sketches everywhere
that complement his text. His discussions
were addressed to himself, leaving us an
extraordinary record of the movements of his
mind.

---

4 Something that is **cryptic** is mysterious in meaning,
puzzling, or ambiguous.

## 110 Bronze Horse and Last Supper

[K] Along with his varied duties at court, which
ranged from painting to plumbing, two great
works mark Leonardo's years with Sforza. One
was to be a bronze statue of the duke's late
115 father as a conquering hero riding a horse. The
other, ordered by Sforza for his favorite church,
was a "Last Supper." The themes were not
unlike other **commissions** of the time, but if
the subjects lacked originality, their treatment
120 did not.

[L] The horse was to be colossal, in a pose full of
motion and life. The concept was so bold, so
ambitious, that it finally brought the artist the
praise he sought. His contemporaries thought
125 it could not be created, but Leonardo devised
workable plans. Sadly, he was **denied** the
chance to complete his project. War broke out,
and the bronze was used for cannon instead.

[M] *The Last Supper*, too, was presented as never
130 before. Leonardo arranged the 13 figures in
a brilliant composition reflecting the terrible
moment following Christ's words, "One of
you shall betray me." He gave the figures
deep emotions, varying according to their
135 natures, perfectly illustrating the intention of
each subject's soul.

[N] Unfortunately, Leonardo's brilliance was not
matched by his planning. He hated deadlines
and fixed schedules; painting fresco (that is,
140 on freshly prepared plaster) imposed both. So
he worked with oil mixtures, which could be
applied whenever the mood struck him. The
technique suited the artist, but not the wall.
The paint soon blistered and began to peel
145 away from the damp surface.

[O] With his doomed masterworks behind him, and
with the French army of Louis XII approaching
the city, Leonardo left Milan, and in the spring
of 1500, he was back in Florence.

# Battle of the Giants

**[P]** **150** Leonardo came home a famous man. No one knew or cared much about his science and his inventions, but everyone had heard of his horse and his *Last Supper*.

**[Q]** **155** Many of his competitors had either died or gone to Rome. His most serious rival was Michelangelo Buonarroti, 23 years his junior, surly,[5] ambitious, and a great painter. The two Florentines hated each other wholeheartedly.

**[R]** **160** Once again, two great works drew Leonardo's artistic effort. One was a huge mural for the Council Chamber depicting the Battle of Anghiari, an important political victory for Florence. The other was a life-size portrait **165** of a middle-class woman. He worked on the paintings **concurrently**, the portrait offering him pleasant relief from the subject of the battle.

**[S]** Some say the subject of the portrait is Lisa, **170** wife of Florentine merchant Francesco del Giocondo, while others suggest different identities. Known today as *Mona Lisa*, it hangs in the Louvre, glass shrouded and guarded. Its colors have suffered a strange change, as **175** if bathed in undersea light, but the lady still glows with an inner radiance, both troubling and serene.

**[T]** The battle scene thrust Leonardo into an artistic rivalry with Michelangelo, who was **180** to paint another wall of the same chamber. The rivals did their **preliminary** sketches in separate quarters. Both sketches were magnificent in their own way: The younger man's picture of male bathers interrupted by **185** a call to arms was as dynamic as Leonardo's cavalry[6] confrontation. Benvenuto Cellini, who saw them both while they were still intact, wrote that "they were the school of the world."

**[U]** **190** Michelangelo never transferred his **draft** to the Council Chamber wall. Leonardo did, or at least, he began to. Forgetting the fate of his *Last Supper* (or perhaps not yet aware of it), he again used an oil paint for greater freedom **195** and brighter colors. The paint soon began to flake and run. The work was doomed, another masterpiece lost—at least until its traces were rediscovered in the 1970s.

# A Life Unfinished

**[V]** **200** Leonardo now turned from art to his old love: flight. By this time, his knowledge went far beyond the limits of his age and was approaching the understanding that much later gave men wings. But his efforts, including **205** his legendary attempt on Monte Ceceri, brought him no satisfaction, only the certainty that he himself would never fly or witness manned flight.

**[W]** In 1513, Leonardo journeyed south to Rome **210** to work for the new pope, Leo X; three years later, he set out once again, this time for France, on the last journey of his homeless life. France's young new king, Francis I, regarded Leonardo as the wisest of men and wanted him **215** nearby, whether he painted or not. Thus, he lived the three remaining years of his life in a small chateau among the peaceful landscape of the river Loire.

**[X]** In his heart, Leonardo felt defeat. His greatest **220** works crumbling, his great knowledge undisclosed, Leonardo grieved for what might have been, for all the wondrous, unfinished projects that forever filled his extraordinary mind. He had no way to know that the few **225** magnificent works he did complete would alone make his name immortal. And so the universal man—symbol of his time and anticipator[7] of ours— passed into eternal fame.

---

5 Someone who is **surly** is usually bad-tempered and rude.

6 The **cavalry** is the part of an army that is mounted on horseback.

7 An **anticipator** is someone who foresees future events.

# Secrets of the *Mona Lisa*

Recent analysis by researchers and scientists has revealed some of the secrets of the Mona Lisa, Leonardo da Vinci's most famous masterpiece.

The Mona Lisa's famous smile, which seems to disappear if you look directly at it, "is an illusion that [results from] the way the human eye processes images," says Harvard professor Margaret Livingstone. Leonardo used "shadows that we see best with our peripheral [indirect] vision. This is why we have to look her in the eyes or somewhere else in the painting to see her smile."

According to Italian researcher Dr. Vito Franco, the Mona Lisa shows clear signs of a buildup of fatty acids under her skin, caused by too much cholesterol. There also seems to be a lipoma, or benign fatty-tissue tumor, near her right eye.

What happened to the Mona Lisa's eyebrows? According to French engineer Pascal Cotte, they were probably removed during an attempt to clean the painting years ago. Using an ultra-high resolution scan, he was able to find the brushstroke of a single eyebrow hair—perhaps the only one that remains.

Cotte's multi-spectrum analysis also revealed why the Mona Lisa's wrist rests so high on her stomach. "If you look deeply in the infrared, you understand that she holds a cover with her wrist," Cotte says. The hidden cover, or blanket, has almost completely disappeared.

The sky behind the Mona Lisa was once a glowing blue, far different from today's gray-green shades, says Cotte, who says the darkened coloring is the result of 500 years of aging.

In 2010, researcher Philippe Walter revealed that Leonardo applied up to 30 layers of paint over several years to create his transitions from light to dark, a technique known as sfumato. The layers add up to about half the thickness of a human hair—"an amazing achievement even by today's standards," says Walter.

∧ It is believed that Leonardo da Vinci started painting the Mona Lisa between the years 1503 to 1506.

Was the Mona Lisa pregnant? Beneath its surface layer, the painting has traces of a veil around the woman's shoulders, of a type that "was typical of the kind worn in early 16th-century Italy by women who were pregnant or who had just given birth," says researcher Bruno Mottin.

Close examination reveals a small patch of damaged paint next to the woman's left elbow, caused when an enraged man threw a rock at the painting in 1956. The painting is now kept in the Louvre behind bulletproof glass.

# Reading Comprehension

**Multiple Choice.** Choose the best answer for each question.

**Detail**

1. What does the author say about Leonardo in paragraph B?
   a. Today he is considered much more talented than Shakespeare.
   b. He was known in his own era and is greatly respected today.
   c. His drawings are thought to be more beautiful than his paintings.
   d. His painting *Mona Lisa* was not well known when he first painted it.

**Reference**

2. The word *it* in line 16 refers to _____.
   a. love     b. experience     c. knowledge     d. painting

**Inference**

3. In paragraph G, the author implies that Verrocchio _____.
   a. was not able to teach Leonardo much because he was not
      a very good painter
   b. was a great inspiration for his apprentice Leonardo
   c. taught Leonardo more about nature than about the art of painting
   d. stopped painting because he was not as skillful as Leonardo

**Detail**

4. The metal for the bronze horse sculpture was eventually _____.
   a. used to create other works of art
   b. stolen by enemies of Milan
   c. used to make weapons
   d. used for plumbing in a palace

**Inference**

5. The section title "Battle of the Giants" refers to _____.
   a. Cellini's criticism of Michelangelo and Leonardo
   b. Florence's victory at the battle of Anghiari
   c. the dispute about the identity of the subject of *Mona Lisa*
   d. the competition between Leonardo and Michelangelo

**Paraphrase**

6. What does the author mean when he says, *"He had no way to know that the few magnificent works he did complete would alone make his name immortal"* (lines 224–226)?
   a. Leonardo could not predict that the few great works he finished would be enough to make him famous for years to come.
   b. Leonardo could not decide which of the works he produced were best and would make him famous after his death.
   c. At the end of his career, Leonardo had no way to be certain how many of his great works were still in existence.
   d. Although he produced many great works, Leonardo would be surprised to know that only a few are still famous.

**Detail**

7. What have researchers NOT discovered about the *Mona Lisa*?
   a. She is holding a cover with her wrist.
   b. The sky behind Mona Lisa was once glowing blue.
   c. She was probably Leonardo's wife.
   d. Her smile is an illusion that results from the way the human eye processes images.

## Critical Thinking

**Analyzing:** The term "Renaissance man" is used to describe a person who can do many things well. Using information from the article, write a list of the fields in which Leonardo worked and one or more of his accomplishments in those fields.

**Discussion:** Do you think it would be possible today to work successfully in as many fields as Leonardo did? Why or why not?

# Relating Textual Information to a Map

In an article that mentions a number of dates and place names, you will have a clearer understanding of the sequence of events if you follow the flow of the article on a map. This provides a useful visual of some key information from the text.

**Labeling.** Use information from the article to trace Leonardo's movements during his life. Write either the missing place name or the year in which Leonardo arrived in each place (**1–6**). Then draw arrows on the map to show Leonardo's key movements over the course of his life.

**1.** Place: _____
   From: 1452

**2.** Place: Florence
   From: _____

**3.** Place: _____
   From: 1482

**4.** Place: _____
   From: 1500

**5.** Place: Rome
   From: _____

**6.** Place: _____
   From: _____

# Vocabulary Practice

**A. Completion.** Complete the information using the correct form of words in the box. Three words are extra.

| academy | arbitrary | commission | concurrent | deny |
|---------|-----------|------------|------------|------|
| draft | ideology | implicit | parameter | preliminary |

Leonardo da Vinci was perhaps the greatest multitasker of all time, a genius who could work **1.** _____ as an painter, sculptor, inventor, engineer, and architect.

During his career as an artist, Leonardo received numerous **2.** _____ from some of the wealthiest and most powerful people in Italy. Yet his artwork represents just a fraction of what he wanted to achieve. The pages of his notebooks are filled with scientific sketches and notes on a seemingly **3.** _____ range of topics. However, only a few of Leonardo's original artworks survive, and very few practical examples of his designs. Most of these are kept in museums and, until recently, **4.** _____ to a wider international audience.

Recently, a traveling exhibition, *Da Vinci—The Genius,* has opened Leonardo's life to the world. The show features reproductions of Leonardo's most famous paintings—from detailed early **5.** _____ to finished works—and a range of full-scale models, including **6.** _____ designs for a glider, a parachute, and a submarine. These have all been carefully constructed using the detailed sketches in Leonardo's notebooks. The exhibition also includes a section devoted to French engineer Pascal Cotte's analysis of the *Mona Lisa,* which reveals the sophisticated ideas **7.** _____ in Leonardo's most famous work of art.

**B. Definitions.** Match the definitions to words from the box in **A.**

1. _____ : beginning, introductory

2. _____ : institution for teaching and learning

3. _____ : limit, guideline

4. _____ : to refuse access

5. _____ : early version

6. _____ : expressed in an indirect way

7. _____ : happening at the same time

8. _____ : not based on any system or plan

9. _____ : piece of work that is requested and paid for

10. _____ : set of beliefs on which actions are based

∧ A man flies a flying machine inspired by Leonardo's drawings.

> **Word Partnership**
> Use *deny* with:
> (*n.*) deny **a charge**, deny **access**, deny **entry**, deny **a request**, deny **the chance**.

## Before You Read

**A. Matching.** The following words appear in the passage on pages 207–211. Use the words to complete the definitions (**1–3**).

| compound | exposure | pollutants |
|----------|----------|------------|

A helicopter sprays pesticide over crops. These pesticides can make their way up the food chain and end up in the human body—causing harmful effects on human health.

1. In chemistry, a(n) _____ is a substance that consists of two or more elements.

2. Examples of _____ are gases from vehicles and poisonous chemicals produced as waste by industrial processes.

3. _____ to something dangerous, such as a poison, means being in a situation where it might affect you.

**B. Read and Predict.** Read the first two paragraphs of the article on pages 207–211. What "experiment" is the author taking part in? What does he want to find out? Then read the rest of the passage to check your ideas.

_____

_____

_____

# HIDDEN HAZARDS

Modern chemistry makes life more convenient and helps save lives. But at what price? Writer David Ewing Duncan begins a journey of chemical self-discovery.

**A** 1   My experiment is taking a **disturbing** turn. A Swedish chemist is on the phone, talking about flame retardants, chemicals added for safety to just about any product that can burn. Found in carpets, electronic circuit boards, and automobiles, flame retardants save hundreds of lives a year
5   in the United States alone. These, however, are where they should not be: inside my body.

**B**   Åke Bergman of Stockholm University tells me he has received the results of a chemical analysis of my blood, which measured levels of flame-retarding compounds called polybrominated diphenyl ethers (PBDEs).
10   In mice and rats, high doses of PBDEs **interfere** with thyroid[1] function, cause reproductive problems, and slow neurological[2] development. Little is known about their impact on human health.

**C**   "I hope you are not nervous, but this concentration is very high," Bergman says with a light Swedish accent. My blood level of one
15   particularly toxic PBDE, found primarily in U.S.-made products, is ten times the average found in a study of U.S. residents, and more than 200 times the average in Sweden. The news about another PBDE variant is nearly as bad. My levels would be even higher if I were a worker in a factory making the stuff, Bergman says.

1   The **thyroid** is a large gland in the neck that produces hormones to regulate growth and metabolism.

2   If a medical condition or disorder is **neurological**, it involves the nerves or the nervous system.

**D** 20 In fact, I'm a writer participating in a journey of chemical self-discovery. Last fall I had myself tested for 320 chemicals I might have picked up from food, drink, the air I breathe, and the products that touch my skin—the

25 secret compounds I have acquired by merely living. It includes older chemicals that I might have been exposed to decades ago, such as DDT and PCBs. It also includes pollutants like lead, mercury, and dioxins; newer pesticides

30 and plastic ingredients; plus other compounds that hide beneath the surface of modern life— making shampoos fragrant,[3] pans nonstick, and fabrics water-resistant and fire-safe.

**E** The fee for the tests is expensive, and only

35 a few labs have the **technical** expertise to detect the amounts involved. I submitted myself for them to learn what substances build up in a typical person over a lifetime, and where they might come from. Prior to

40 the tests, I had little knowledge of what was lurking inside my body. Now I'm learning more than I really want to know.

**F** First, Bergman wants to solve my flame-retardant mystery. Have I recently bought

45 new furniture or rugs? No. Do I spend a lot of time around computer monitors? No, I use a titanium laptop. Do I live near a factory making flame retardants? Nope, the closest one is over 1,600 kilometers (1,000 miles)

50 away. Then I come up with an idea. "What about airplanes?" I ask. "Yah," he says, "do you fly a lot?" "I flew almost 300,000 kilometers (200,000 miles) last year," I say. In fact, as I spoke to Bergman, I was sitting in an

55 airport waiting for a flight from my hometown of San Francisco to London.

**G** "Interesting," Bergman says. He tells me that he has long been curious about PBDE exposure inside airplanes, whose plastic and

60 fabric interiors include flame retardants to meet safety regulations. "I have been wanting to apply for a **grant** to test pilots and flight attendants for PBDEs," Bergman says. But for now the airplane connection is only a

65 hypothesis. Where I picked up this chemical remains a mystery. And there's a bigger question: How worried should I be?

**H** The same can be asked of other chemicals I've absorbed from air, water, the nonstick

70 pan I used to scramble my eggs this morning, my faintly scented shampoo, my cell phone. I'm healthy, and as far as I know have no symptoms associated with chemical exposure. In large doses, some of these substances can

75 have horrific effects. But many toxicologists[4] insist that the minimal amounts of chemicals inside us are, on the whole, nothing to worry about.

**I** "In toxicology, dose is everything," says Karl

80 Rozman, a toxicologist at the University of Kansas Medical Center, "and these doses are too low to be dangerous." A standard unit for measuring most chemicals inside us is a **ratio** of one part per billion (ppb)—an amount

85 so small, it's like putting half a teaspoon (two milliliters) of dye into an Olympic-size swimming pool. Moreover, some of the most feared substances, such as mercury, normally dissipate[5] within days or weeks unless the

90 individual is constantly re-exposed.

**J** Even though many health **statistics** have improved over the past few decades, a few illnesses are rising mysteriously. From the early 1980s through the late 1990s, autism

95 increased tenfold; from the early 1970s through the mid-1990s, one type of leukemia[6] was up 62 percent, male birth defects doubled, and childhood brain cancer was up 40 percent. Some experts, **albeit** with little firm evidence,

100 suspect there is a link to the man-made chemicals in our food, water, and air. Over the years, several chemicals that were thought to be harmless turned out to be otherwise once the facts were in.

---

3 Something that is **fragrant** has a pleasant or sweet smell.

4 **Toxicologists** study the effects of poisons and the treatment of poisoning.

5 When things **dissipate**, they disperse, scatter, and break up.

6 **Leukemia** is a cancer of the blood or bone marrow.

**K** 105 The classic example is lead. In 1971, the U.S. Surgeon General declared that lead levels of 40 micrograms per deciliter[7] of blood were safe. It's now known that any detectable lead can cause neurological damage in children. From 110 DDT to PCBs, the chemical industry has released compounds first and discovered damaging health effects later. Regulators have often allowed a standard of innocent until proven guilty. Leo Trasande, a pediatrician[8] and environmental 115 health specialist at Mount Sinai Hospital in New York City, calls it "an uncontrolled experiment on America's children."

**L** Each year the U.S. Environmental Protection Agency (EPA) reviews an average of 1,700 120 new compounds that industry is seeking to introduce. Yet the 1976 Toxic Substances Control Act legally requires that they be tested before approval only if there is evidence of potential harm—which is seldom the case for 125 new chemicals. The agency approves about 90 percent of the new compounds without any restrictions. Only a quarter of the 82,000 chemicals in use in the U.S. have ever been tested for toxicity.

---

7 A **deciliter** is a metric unit of volume equal to one-tenth of a liter.

8 A **pediatrician** is a doctor who specializes in treating children.

⌄ Author David Ewing Duncan cooks breakfast at home, exposed to the potentially dangerous chemicals found in plastic containers, pans, and other everyday household items.

M 130 Studies by an environmental organization known as the Environmental Working Group found hundreds of chemical traces in the bodies of volunteers. Until recently, no one had measured average levels of exposure

135 among large numbers of Americans. No regulations required it, the tests are expensive, and the technology sensitive enough to measure the tiniest levels didn't exist.

N So why take a chance on these chemicals?
140 Why not immediately ban them? In 2004, Europe did just that for penta- and octa-BDEs, which animal tests suggest are the most toxic of the compounds. California banned these forms in 2008. In 2004 Chemtura, an
145 Indiana company that is the only U.S. maker of pentas and octas, agreed to **phase** them **out**. Currently, there are no plans to prohibit the much more prevalent deca-BDEs. They reportedly break down more quickly in the
150 environment and in people, although their breakdown products may include toxic pentas and octas.

⌄ An X-ray shows chips of lead paint present in the body of a child. Chemicals such as lead, if allowed to build up inside the body, can severely affect human health.

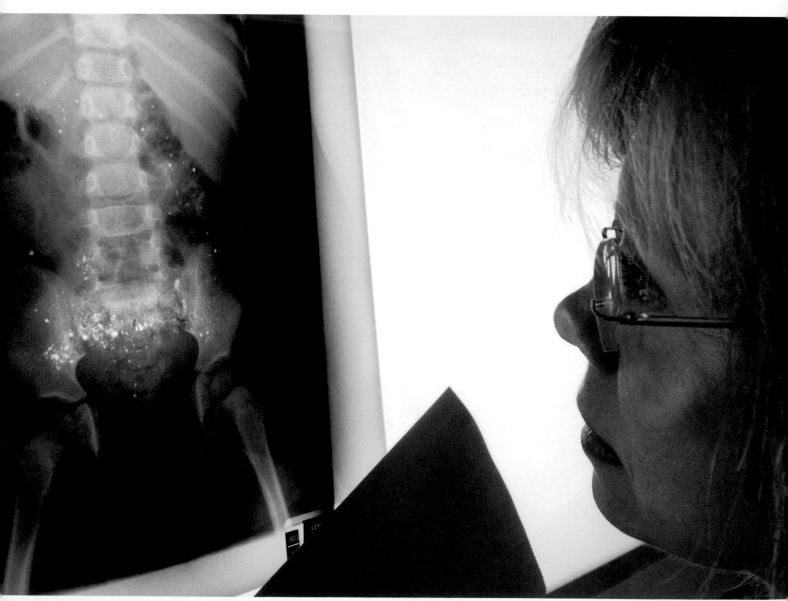

**O** Nor is it clear that banning a suspect chemical is always the best option. The University of Surrey in England recently assessed the risks and benefits of flame retardants in consumer products. In its summary, the report concluded that the "benefits of many flame retardants in reducing the risk from fire outweigh the risks to human health."

**P** Except for some pollutants, every industrial chemical was created for a purpose. Even DDT, the chemical whose toxic effects helped launch the modern environmental movement, was once seen as a **miracle** substance. It saved countless lives because it was able to kill the mosquitoes that carry malaria, yellow fever, and other diseases. Eventually it was banned in much of the world because of its danger to wildlife. "Chemicals are not all bad," says Scott Phillips, a medical toxicologist in Denver. "While we have seen some cancer rates rise," he says, "we also have seen a doubling of the human life span in the past century."

**Q** The key is to know more about these substances, so we are not blindsided[9] by unexpected hazards, says California State Senator Deborah Ortiz, chair of the Senate Health Committee and the author of a bill[10] to monitor chemical exposure. "We benefit from these chemicals, but there are consequences, and we need to understand these consequences much better than we do now."

**R** In 2006 the European Union gave initial approval to a measure called REACH—Registration, **Evaluation**, and Authorization of Chemicals—which requires companies to prove the substances they market or use are safe, or that the perceived benefits outweigh any risks. The bill, which the chemical industry and the U.S. government opposed, encourages companies to find safer alternatives to suspect flame retardants, pesticides, solvents,[11] and other chemicals. That would give a boost to the so-called green chemistry movement, a search for alternatives that is already under way in laboratories on both sides of the Atlantic.

**S** As disturbing as my journey of chemical self-discovery was, it left out thousands of compounds, among them pesticides, plastics, and solvents. Nor was I tested for chemical cocktails—mixtures of chemicals that may do little harm on their own but act together to damage human cells. Mixed together, pesticides, PCBs, phthalates,[12] and others "might have additive effects, or they might be antagonistic," says James Pirkle of the CDC, "or they may do nothing. We don't know."

**T** Soon after I receive my results, I show them to my internist,[13] who admits that he too knows little about these chemicals, other than lead and mercury. But he confirms that I am a healthy adult, as far as he can tell. He tells me not to worry. So I'll keep flying, and scrambling my eggs on Teflon, and using my scented shampoo. But I'll never feel quite the same about the chemicals that make life better in so many ways.

---

9 When a person is **blindsided**, he or she is surprised by something, usually with harmful consequences.

10 A **bill** is a draft of a proposed law presented for approval to a legislative body, as well as the law that results from the draft.

11 **Solvents** are substances, usually liquids, that are capable of dissolving another substance.

12 **Phthalates** are substances added to plastic to increase its flexibility, transparency and durability.

13 An **internist** is a doctor of internal medicine, a branch of medicine that deals with the prevention, diagnosis, and treatment of adult diseases.

# Reading Comprehension

**Multiple Choice.** Choose the best answer for each question.

**Purpose**

1. What is the author's main purpose in writing this article?
   a. to discuss the research done by a Swedish scientist on the health dangers of flame retardants
   b. to report on an experiment he conducted on himself regarding common toxic chemicals
   c. to contrast U.S. government policies regarding chemical pollutants with European government policies
   d. to argue that dangerous chemicals such as flame retardants should be immediately banned

**Inference**

2. Bergman suspects that the author's PBDE levels are probably due to _____.
   a. flame retardants used on new furniture and rugs
   b. exposure to radiation from computer monitors
   c. pollution from a factory that manufactures PBDEs
   d. flame retardants used inside airplanes

**Detail**

3. According to the article, which of the following illnesses has seen the greatest rise in recent decades?
   a. autism
   b. leukemia
   c. male birth defects
   d. childhood brain cancer

**Rhetorical Purpose**

4. The author provides the statistics in paragraph L to show that _____.
   a. a large number of new chemicals are introduced each year
   b. products of the U.S. chemical industry are largely untested
   c. more and more chemicals are tested for toxicity every year
   d. chemicals in the environment are becoming more toxic

**Reference**

5. The word *its* in line 157 refers to _____.
   a. the flame retardant       b. the best option
   c. a suspect chemical         d. the university's report

**Cohesion**

6. Where would be the best place to insert this sentence in paragraph O? *After all, flaming beds and airplane seats are not an inviting prospect either.*
   a. before the first sentence       b. after the first sentence
   c. after the second sentence       d. after the third sentence

**Detail**

7. Which of the following is NOT true about DDT?
   a. It has saved many lives.
   b. It is dangerous to animals.
   c. It can help stop the spread of some diseases.
   d. Its use is supported by environmentalists.

## Critical Thinking

**Evaluating:** Consider this statement:

*Chemicals such as PBDEs and pesticides are dangerous to human health and should be banned.*

Find information in the article for and against this point of view.

_____

**Discussion:** What chemicals do you think you are exposed to in your daily life?

# Identifying Theory and Fact

Scientific articles often present a combination of theories and facts. Facts are statements that are definitely true. The author, or one of the experts that he or she quotes, may also speculate about concepts that *might* be true. These are theories.

An author may use signal words or phrases to mark theories. These words often indicate uncertainty or doubt:

*perhaps . . . it is believed/suspected that . . . maybe . . . In theory, . . . possibly . . . it is possible/conceivable that . . . might . . . No one knows for certain, but . . .*

**Scanning/Classification.** Read each statement and locate the section in the passage that it relates to. According to the information in the passage, circle if each statement is a **F** (Fact) or a **T** (Theory). Underline any signal words or phrases in the passage that help you decide.

1.  In laboratory animals, large doses of PBDEs can cause health problems. (paragraph B)     **F**    **T**

2.  The level of PBDEs in the author's blood was much higher than the level typically found in Swedish people. (paragraph C)     **F**    **T**

3.  The flame retardants used in airplanes caused the high levels of PBDEs in the author's blood. (paragraph G)     **F**    **T**

4.  Some of the most dangerous chemicals, such as mercury, normally disappear from a person's body unless that person encounters the chemical again and again. (paragraph I)     **F**    **T**

5.  There is a link between dangerous chemicals and the rising incidence of autism, childhood brain cancer, and birth defects in male babies. (paragraph J)     **F**    **T**

6.  Any measurable amount of lead in a child's blood can cause damage to the child's nervous system. (paragraph K)     **F**    **T**

7.  Only 25 percent of the chemicals now in use in the United States have been tested to see if they are dangerous. (paragraph L)     **F**    **T**

8.  When certain chemicals such as pesticides and PCBs mix inside the human body, they become stronger or they interact in a negative way. (paragraph S)     **F**    **T**

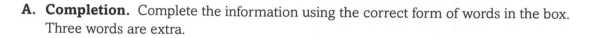

# Vocabulary Practice

**A. Completion.** Complete the information using the correct form of words in the box. Three words are extra.

| | | | | |
|---|---|---|---|---|
| **albeit** | **disturbing** | **evaluate** | **grant** | **interfere** |
| **miracle** | **phase out** | **ratio** | **statistics** | **technical** |

When people think of the Arctic, they probably imagine a pure and beautiful—**1.** _____ harsh—environment. So it is a(n) **2.** _____ thought that the region's native animals and people are among the most chemically contaminated on Earth.

Recently, various studies were conducted to **3.** _____ the levels of toxic chemicals in the bodies of Arctic animals, as well as in the native Inuit people. The **4.** _____ are worrisome. Both the animals and the Inuit who participated in the studies showed unusually high levels of man-made toxins. These included older pollutants like dioxins and PCBs which many governments have been trying to **5.** _____ since the 1970s. Such chemicals are known to **6.** _____ with our hormones and damage the immune system.

∧ Arctic animals such as polar bears have layers of fatty tissue to keep them warm. Toxins that break down slowly can collect in these tissues over several years.

The studies also found newer compounds building up in the bodies of the Inuit people at a(n) **7.** _____ of five to one compared to levels found in other Canadians. Experts say the reason is diet. Whale skin and other contaminated animal fats are important foods in Inuit communities. There is now great concern that over time such chemicals will have a serious impact on the health of the Inuit people.

**B. Definitions.** Match the definitions to the words from the box in **A**.

**1.** _____: amazing event not easily explained

**2.** _____: causing anxiety

**3.** _____: involving machines, processes, and materials

**4.** _____: even though

**5.** _____: to gradually stop using something

**6.** _____: to have a damaging effect on a process or activity

**7.** _____: a comparison between two things, expressed in numbers

**8.** _____: an amount of money given for a specific purpose, such as research

**9.** _____: numbers used to show the results of a study or investigation

**10.** _____: to consider something in order to make a judgment about it

> **Usage**
> **Albeit** is used to introduce a fact or comment that reduces the force or significance of what has just been said, e.g., *My friend appeared on the talkshow, albeit briefly.*

# ELEMENT HUNTERS

## Before You Read

**A. Discussion.** Look at the photos and captions on pages 215–217. Discuss these questions with a partner.

  **1.** Which of the elements in the periodic table (pages 216–217) are you familiar with? What uses do they have?

  **2.** Why do you think scientists are interested in creating new elements?

**B. Scan.** Scan the article on pages 216–221 for information about the three scientists below. Then match the names to their accomplishments.

  **1.** _____ Georgy Flerov     **a.** led a team that created the first atom of element 114

  **2.** _____ Glenn Seaborg     **b.** helped launch Soviet nuclear weapons research

  **3.** _____ Yuri Oganessian   **c.** helped create an atomic bomb for the U.S. military

Georgy Flerov (right) was a prominent Soviet Union nuclear physicists who launched the country's nuclear weapons research.

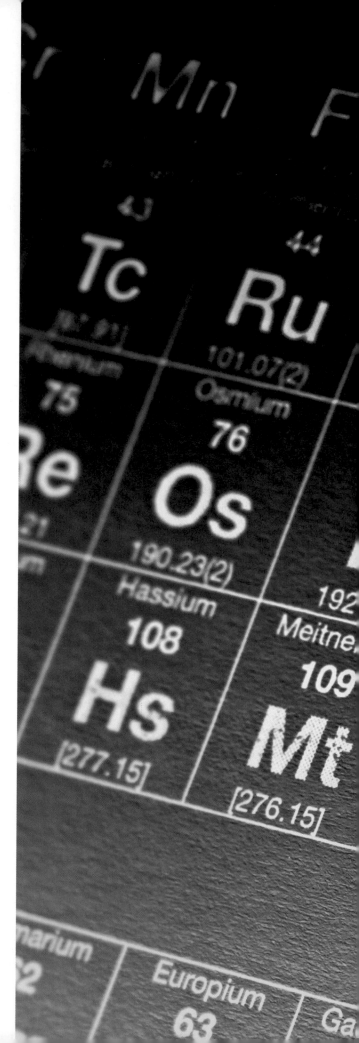

**A** 1  All the elements found in nature—the different kinds of atoms—were found long ago. To find a new one these days, you need to create it.

**B** 5  Everything you know and love on Earth, and everything you don't, is built of elements—the different types of atoms. Most of them are billions of years old, scattered into space by the big bang[1] or exploding stars. They were then incorporated
10  into the newly born Earth, endlessly recycled as they moved from rock to bacteria, president, or mouse. In the late 1800s, the Russian chemist and inventor Dmitry Mendeleyev tried to make sense of them all, grouping them by mass—the scientific term
15  for weight—and other **attributes** in his periodic table of the elements. Later, scientists connected the order of elements in the periodic table to the structure of atoms. Each element got a number: its atomic number, the number of protons in its atomic
20  nucleus.

**C**  By 1940, researchers had discovered every element on Earth, right up to uranium (element 92). They had filled in every gap Mendeleyev had left in his table, but they weren't finished. Beyond uranium
25  lay a world of possibilities—elements too radioactive and unstable to have survived billions of years. To explore that world, you have to create it first.

**D**  The first steps of creation not only extended the periodic table, they played a fateful[2] role in world
30  history. It was 1940, the year after World War II began, and U.S. scientists led the race to create new elements. Element 93, Neptunium, was created in a laboratory at the University of California, Berkeley. The next year, Glenn Seaborg and his colleagues
35  at the same university produced element 94, plutonium. Seaborg was promptly recruited to the Manhattan Project[3] to create an atomic bomb for the United States military.

---

1  The **big bang** theory suggests that the universe was created as the result of a massive explosion.

2  If an action is **fateful**, it is considered to have an important and often disastrous effect on future events.

3  The **Manhattan Project** was the name of the U.S. government project that developed the first atomic bombs during World War II.

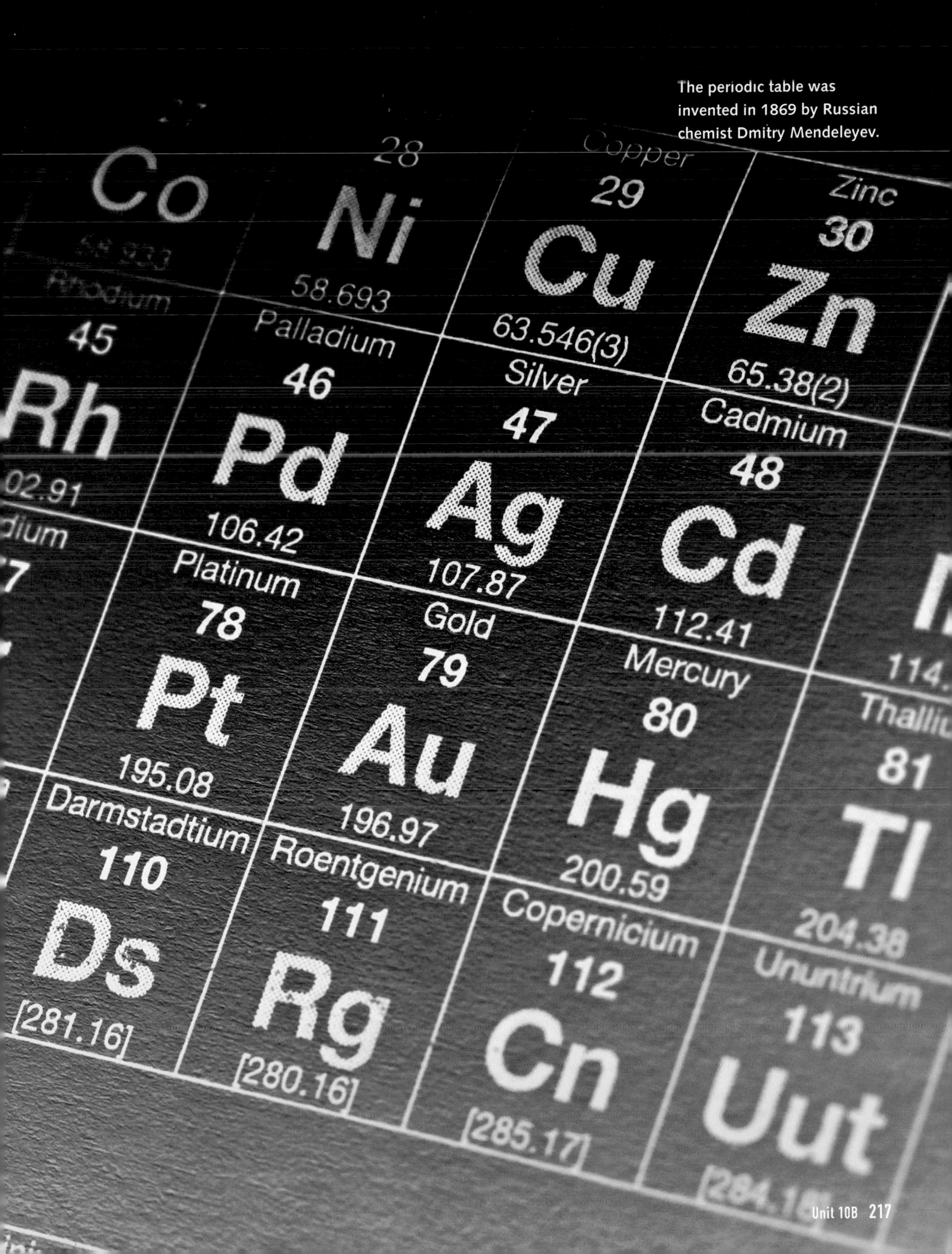

Co

58.933

Rhodium
45
Rh
102.91

dium
7

28
Ni
58.693
Palladium
46
Pd
106.42
Platinum
78
Pt
195.08
Darmstadtium
110
Ds
[281.16]

Copper
29
Cu
63.546(3)
Silver
47
Ag
107.87
Gold
79
Au
196.97
Roentgenium
111
Rg
[280.16]

Zinc
30
Zn
65.38(2)
Cadmium
48
Cd
112.41
Mercury
80
Hg
200.59
Copernicium
112
Cn
[285.17]

114.
Thalliu
81
Tl
204.38
Ununtrium
113
Uut
[284.1

**E**
40 The intensified level of nuclear research in the United States did not go unnoticed by the world's other superpower at the time—the Soviet Union. Georgy Flerov was a prominent physicist who had helped launch that country's nuclear weapons research. Early in World War
45 II, Flerov had noticed that the flow of articles about radioactive elements from U.S. and German scientists had suddenly stopped. This heightened secrecy led him to suspect that they were building atomic bombs. He wrote
50 to Soviet leader Joseph Stalin in April 1942. Flerov's suspicions were confirmed, and Stalin asked Russian physicists to build a bomb, too.

**F**
For his part in the war effort, Flerov was rewarded with a car, a house, and, most
55 significantly, a laboratory in the town of Dubna, north of Moscow. There, Flerov focused his attention on the hunt for new elements. His American **counterpart**, Glenn Seaborg, returned to Berkeley after helping
60 to engineer the bomb that the United States military dropped on Nagasaki at the end of the war. He continued to make new elements, with less fateful **applications**—smoke detectors, for instance—or no applications
65 at all. By 1955, his team had gotten as far as element 101. He named it mendelevium.

**G**
For a time it seemed Mendeleyev's table might end there, with his namesake.[4] The protons in an atomic nucleus are always trying to tear
70 it apart; their positive electric **charges** repel[5] one another. Neutrons—electrically neutral particles that outnumber the protons—help **bind** the nucleus together. But that binding force works only at extremely close range.
75 It weakens sharply as the size of the nucleus increases. So there has to be a final box on the periodic table, a maximum size beyond which an atom won't be stable even for an instant. With mendelevium, which has a half-life[6] of
80 51.5 days, researchers seemed to be getting close to the final box.

# Beyond Mendelevium

**H**
The Berkeley team continued its research regardless, rivaled by the Flerov's team in
85 Dubna. From 1965 to 1974, Berkeley claimed to have produced elements 102, 103, 104, 105, and 106—but so did the Dubna lab. Although those short-lived elements died within hours, the tense **disputes** over
90 who made them first were fueled by the competitive atmosphere of the Cold War.[7] In the end, a spirit of compromise **prevailed**: Element 105 was named dubnium and element 106 seaborgium.

**I**
95 Meanwhile, theorists had given a new purpose to the **quest** for elements. They calculated that a very large nucleus might be surprisingly stable if it had "magic numbers" of protons and neutrons. That insight, if correct, would
100 change everything. It would mean that there could be an "island of stability" where extremely heavy elements might last minutes, weeks, or even thousands of years. Although the exact magic numbers of protons and
105 neutrons weren't known, the theory suggested these elements should contain 184 neutrons and 114, 120, or 126 protons.

**J**
Around the time that this new theory appeared, a brilliant physicist named Yuri
110 Oganessian joined Flerov's lab in Dubna. The island of stability had captured his imagination. However, reaching it seemed to him an impossible task at that point. The Berkeley and Dubna labs had gotten only as far as element
115 106 by shooting light atoms against heavy ones with such force that they joined to create a single superheavy nucleus. But beyond 106, the **collisions** were so energetic that they

---

4 Someone's or something's **namesake** has the same name as that person or thing.

5 When two charged particles **repel** each other, they push each other away.

6 **Half-life** is the time needed for half the atoms in a radioactive substance to disintegrate.

7 The **Cold War** is the name given to the period of hostility between the United States and the Soviet Union from the end of World War II in 1945 until the collapse of the Soviet Union in 1991.

were ripping the new nucleus apart before it even formed. To overcome this problem, Oganessian proposed that shooting slightly heavier atoms at lighter targets might create gentler collisions that were more likely to create new elements. Unfortunately, before he could put his proposal into action, a lab in Darmstadt, Germany, used the idea to make elements 107 through 112. Oganessian's historic moment would have to wait another quarter century.

K 130 In the coming years, the Dubna lab went through hard times. Flerov died in 1990; the Soviet Union collapsed in 1991. The lab went months without being able to pay its researchers. Scientists gathered mushrooms in the forests and fished in the Volga River. Oganessian, now in charge of the lab, could have directed it toward more practical goals and made some money for himself and his staff. He decided instead to continue toward element 114 and the promised island of stability.

## Achieving the Dream

L To make element 114 (with 114 protons), Oganessian would shoot calcium (with 20 protons) at plutonium (with 94). He persuaded U.S. physicists at the Lawrence Livermore National Laboratory in California—who just a few years earlier had been his rivals—to give him a small amount of plutonium. The plan was to use a cyclotron[8] to shoot a beam of calcium atoms at high speed into a thin sheet of metal covered with the precious plutonium atoms. Among the trillions of atoms spraying out the other side—the metal sheet was thinner than hair—Oganessian expected at most one atom of element 114. His team— along with Livermore's—invented a new device to detect it.

M They turned the cyclotron on in November 1998. It wasn't a very **trustworthy** piece of machinery, and it required constant attention. Nevertheless, in late November, the cyclotron managed to produce a single

atom of element 114. It lasted only a few seconds—but that was thousands of times longer than would be expected if there were no island of stability. It also proved that the calcium method worked. Dubna and other labs have since made elements 115, 116, 117, and 118, and isotopes with different numbers of neutrons. They are still nowhere near the island's peak, where an element might last years. But the creation of element 114 was the great breakthrough that Oganessian had been dreaming about for decades.

N It wasn't until 2011, however, that element 114 was officially admitted to the periodic table. This is because no newly discovered element is officially recognized until another laboratory can duplicate[9] the experiment, which sometimes takes years. Element 114 was given the name flerovium. This belated[10] but welcome recognition came when Oganessian was 78 years old. After such a triumph, other scientists might have decided it was time to retire to a quiet and grateful life— but not Yuri Oganessian.

O The island of stability still captures his imagination, inspiring him on to further discoveries. As he put it, "We have discovered the island. Now it is time to explore it, to walk along its western beach." Techniques must be developed to shoot the magic number of neutrons, 184, into flerovium, to reach its peak of stability. Scientists need to discover if there are other peaks at elements 120 or 126. Although at the moment those goals seem almost impossible, Oganessian has no intention of giving up the hunt for new elements.

---

8 A **cyclotron** is a device that can accelerate charged atoms, protons, or other particles, direct them into a beam, and "shoot" them at a target.

9 If you **duplicate** something that has already been done, you repeat or copy it.

10 A **belated** action happens later than it should have.

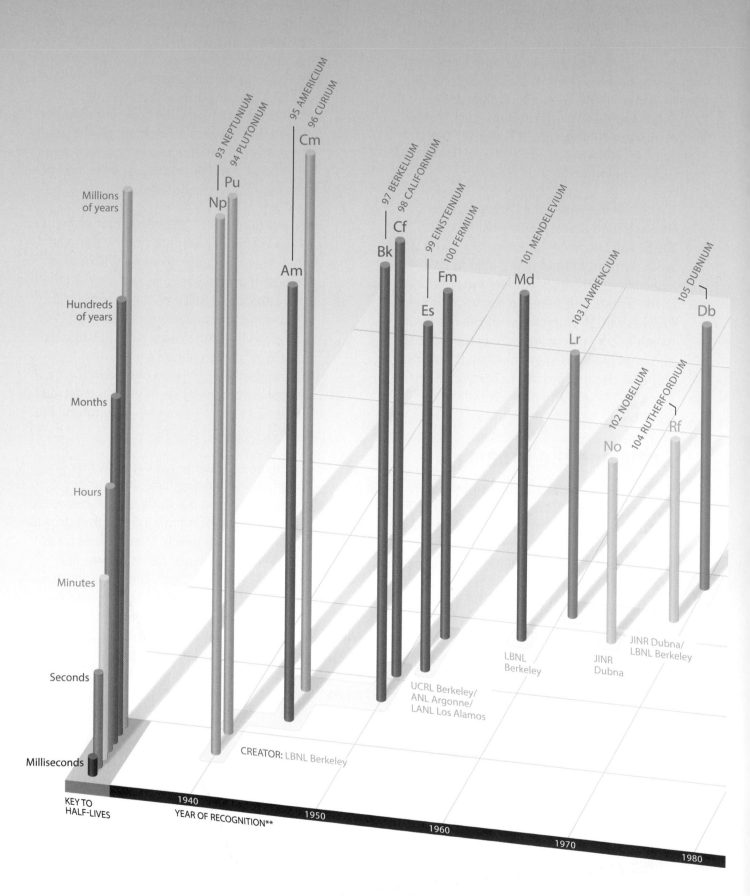

Millions
of years

Hundreds
of years

Months

Hours

Minutes

Seconds

Milliseconds

KEY TO
HALF-LIVES

YEAR OF RECOGNITION**

93 NEPTUNIUM
94 PLUTONIUM
Np
Pu

95 AMERICIUM
96 CURIUM
Cm
Am

97 BERKELIUM
98 CALIFORNIUM
Bk
Cf

99 EINSTEINIUM
100 FERMIUM
Es
Fm

101 MENDELEVIUM
Md

103 LAWRENCIUM
Lr

102 NOBELIUM
No

104 RUTHERFORDIUM
Rf

105 DUBNIUM
Db

CREATOR: LBNL Berkeley

UCRL Berkeley/
ANL Argonne/
LANL Los Alamos

LBNL
Berkeley

JINR
Dubna

JINR Dubna/
LBNL Berkeley

1940

1950

1960

1970

1980

# Twenty-Six New Elements

Over the past 73 years, scientists have probed the frontiers of the atomic nucleus, synthesizing heavier elements one by one. The first step beyond uranium (the heaviest natural element) was neptunium, number 93 in the periodic table. The synthetic atoms are all radioactive: They decay into lighter elements, sometimes within milliseconds. In general, the heavier the element, the shorter its half-life. For decades researchers have been crossing a sea of short-lived elements in search of the "island of stability," where "magic numbers" of protons and neutrons might combine to make superheavy atoms that last long enough to be studied.

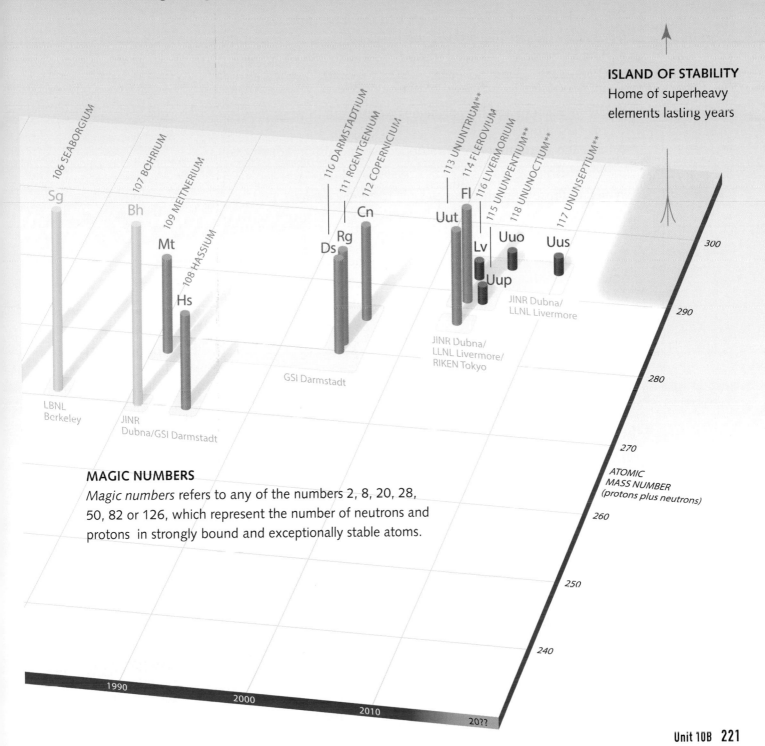

ISLAND OF STABILITY
Home of superheavy elements lasting years

106 SEABORGIUM
107 BOHRIUM
109 MEITNERIUM
108 HASSIUM
116 DARMSTADTIUM
111 ROENTGENIUM
112 COPERNICIUM
113 UNUNTRIUM**
114 FLEROVIUM
116 LIVERMORIUM
115 UNUNPENTIUM**
118 UNUNOCTIUM**
117 UNUNSEPTIUM**

Sg
Bh
Mt
Hs
Ds
Rg
Cn
Uut
Fl
Lv
Uup
Uuo
Uus

LBNL Berkeley
JINR Dubna/GSI Darmstadt
GSI Darmstadt
JINR Dubna/ LLNL Livermore/ RIKEN Tokyo
JINR Dubna/ LLNL Livermore

ATOMIC MASS NUMBER
(protons plus neutrons)

300
290
280
270
260
250
240

1990
2000
2010
20??

## MAGIC NUMBERS

*Magic numbers* refers to any of the numbers 2, 8, 20, 28, 50, 82 or 126, which represent the number of neutrons and protons in strongly bound and exceptionally stable atoms.

# Reading Comprehension

**Multiple Choice.** Choose the best answer for each question.

Detail

**1.** What contribution to science is Dmitry Mendeleyev noted for?
a. the discovery of the element uranium
b. the understanding that elements have different weights
c. the creation of the periodic table of elements
d. the connection of elements in the periodic table to atoms

Cause and Effect

**2.** What led Georgy Flerov to suspect that the Americans and Germans were building atomic bombs?
a. The Russians had already started to build atomic weapons.
b. Glenn Seaborg and his colleagues had recently discovered plutonium.
c. Glenn Seaborg and his colleagues were about to work on a military project.
d. U.S. and German scientists stopped writing about radioactive elements.

Sequence

**3.** Which of these elements was the last to be discovered?
a. flerovium          b. dubnium
c. mendelevium        d. neptunium

Detail

**4.** What evidence is there that the Berkeley and Dubna teams were able to compromise?
a. Element 105 was named dubnium and element 106 seaborgium.
b. The teams worked together to produce 102, 103, 104, 105, and 106.
c. They reached agreement on who discovered each element first.
d. Flerov worked with Seaborg to jointly discover mendelevium.

Detail

**5.** Why were physicists excited about the theory of the "island of stability"?
a. They could increase the number of protons in a nucleus.
b. They could create an unlimited number of new elements.
c. Heavy elements could exist for a significant amount of time.
d. It allowed them to study the nucleus in great detail.

Cohesion

**6.** Where would be the best place in paragraph O to insert this sentence? *In other words, there is more work to do before we understand how the new elements behave alone and in reaction with others.*
a. after the first sentence
b. after the second sentence
c. after the third sentence
d. after the fourth sentence

Understanding Infographics

**7.** Since 2005, how many newly created elements have lasted longer than a few milliseconds (page 220–221)?
a. none       b. two       c. four       d. five

## Critical Thinking

**Analyzing:** How has world history been shaped by the hunt for elements?

**Discussion:** There continue to be scientific rivalries in the quest for discoveries. For example, scientists all over the world continue to search for a cure for AIDS. Do you think these scientists would find a cure faster if they worked together in a single place, or do these rivalries help the search for discoveries?

# Understanding Long Sentences

Long sentences are easier to understand if you break them down into shorter, more manageable parts.

Identify the subject and object of the key clause(s). Ask yourself questions like:
*Who/What does what? Who/What is it being done to?*
*How did they/it do it? Why did they/it do it? Where did they/it do it? When did they/it do it?*

**Example**

*He [Oganessian] persuaded U.S. physicists at the Lawrence Livermore National Laboratory in California, who just a few years earlier had been his rivals, to give him a small amount of plutonium.*

1. Who did he persuade?
   *The U.S. physicists at the Lawrence Livermore National Laboratory in California*

2. What did he persuade them to do?
   *Give him a small amount of plutonium*

**Analyzing.** Answer the questions to check your understanding of the sentences below.

1. His [Flerov's] American counterpart, Glenn Seaborg, returned to Berkeley after helping to engineer the plutonium bomb that the United States military dropped on Nagasaki, Japan, at the end of the war.

   a. Who returned to Berkeley? _____

   b. What did he help engineer? _____

   c. When was it used? _____

2. The Berkeley and Dubna labs had gotten only as far as element 106 by shooting light atoms against heavy ones with such force that they joined to create a single superheavy nucleus.

   a. What were the names of the two labs? _____

   b. How far did they get with their experiments? _____

   c. How did they get this far? _____

   d. What happened when the atoms joined? _____

## Vocabulary Practice

**A. Completion.** Complete the information by circling the correct word in each pair.

The **1. (bind / quest)** for new elements begins with expensive ingredients: rare, heavy isotopes of calcium and an existing heavy element like plutonium. When the two kinds of atoms **2. (collide / prevail)** at high speed, they sometimes fuse into a new superheavy one. Here are the key steps.

A. Bake a solid calcium compound in a(n) **3. (applied / trustworthy)** oven at 700 degrees Celsius (1,300 degrees Fahrenheit). The calcium vaporizes, forming a gas that can be shaped into a high-energy beam.

B. Ionize the calcium atoms by stripping off some of their electrons. The positively **4. (charged / disputed)** ions can now be accelerated by electric and magnetic fields.

C. Accelerate the ions in a cyclotron.

D. Smash the calcium ions into a spinning target. The foil is coated with plutonium or another heavy element.

E. Detect the new element and its **5. (disputes / attributes)**. The first step is to catch everything in a disk.

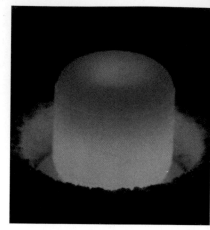

∧ Pellet of plutonium-238 glowing from its own heat. Plutonium-238 is used to fuel space probes.

**B. Words in Context.** Complete each sentence with the correct answer.

1. If a husband and wife are having a **dispute**, they are having _____.
   a. a good laugh          b. a disagreement

2. Someone interested in the **application** of a new technology is interested in

   _____.
   a. how it was created          b. how it can be used

3. If you **prevail** in a lawsuit, you eventually _____.
   a. win          b. give up

4. If you have a **counterpart** in another office, that person has

   _____.
   a. a job similar to yours          b. a job you will likely take over

5. _____ are two things that help **bind** things.
   a. String and rope          b. Scissors and knives

6. Someone on a **quest** is _____ something.
   a. searching for          b. running away from

> **Word Link**
> The prefix **counter-** has the meaning of "opposite," "complementary," and "duplicate," e.g., **counter**act, **counter**balance, **counter**feit.

# VIEWING  Secrets of Toothpaste

## Before You Watch

**A. Definitions.** Here are some words you will hear in the video. Match the words with their definitions.

1. _____: staggering
2. _____: remedy
3. _____: nasty
4. _____: catch on
5. _____: cavity
6. _____: abrasive
7. _____: foam
8. _____: stain

a. very unpleasant
b. to become popular
c. very rough
d. a hole in a tooth
e. to form small bubbles
f. to discolor
g. a treatment
h. very large or surprising

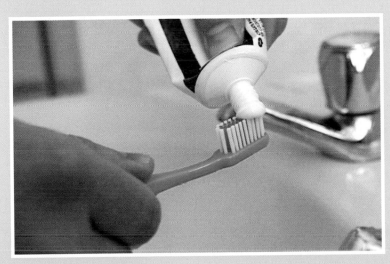

❮ It is believed that the Egyptians were the earliest people to start using paste to clean their teeth.

**B. Predict.** What do you know about toothpaste and tooth care?
Mark your predictions **T** (True) or **F** (False). Then compare with a partner.

| | | |
|---|---|---|
| 1. Toothbrushes were invented by ancient Egyptians. | **T** | **F** |
| 2. An important additive in toothpaste today is fluoride. | **T** | **F** |
| 3. The number one ingredient in modern toothpaste is a whitener. | **T** | **F** |
| 4. You can make homemade toothpaste with baking soda. | **T** | **F** |

## While You Watch

**A. Noticing.** As you watch the video, check your answers to part **B** of the *Before You Watch* section.

**B. Multiple Choice.** Choose the correct answer for each question.

1. How many times will the average U.K. citizen brush his or her teeth in a lifetime?

   a. 40,000        b. 80,000        c. 140,000

2. Where is the oldest surviving tooth care formula from?

   a. Babylon        b. Egypt        c. Greece

3. The first tooth care formula included salt, pepper, and _____.

   a. blood        b. thorium        c. mint

4. Fluoride was added to toothpaste in the _____ century.

   a. 18th        b. 19th        c. 20th

5. What does chalk act as in some toothpastes?

   a. an abrasive        b. a whitener        c. a binding agent

6. What is NOT mentioned as an ingredient in the recipe for homemade toothpaste?

   a. licorice        b. peppermint        c. salt

## After You Watch

**A. Discussion.** Discuss these questions with a partner.

1. Why do you think teeth are also referred to as "pearly whites"?

2. You can fix a CD scratch by gently rubbing toothpaste on it. You can get rid of a pimple by placing a small amount of toothpaste on it. Can you think of any other uses for toothpaste?

**B. Matching.** Look at these other everyday household items. Try to match them to their "other" uses. Then check your answers below. Do you know any other uses like these?

| | |
|---|---|
| 1. _____ : lemon | **a.** to cut cheese |
| 2. _____ : olive oil | **b.** to relieve an insect bite |
| 3. _____ : paper coffee filter | **c.** to put out a small fire |
| 4. _____ : dental floss | **d.** to use as shaving cream |
| 5. _____ : nail polish | **e.** to remove fingerprints from a painted wall |
| 6. _____ : baking powder | **f.** to lessen the effect of a camera flash |
| 7. _____ : bread | **g.** to remove stains from plastic |

# 11

# ISLAM AND THE WEST

Al-Masjid al-Haram (*The Sacred Mosque*) in Mecca, Saudi Arabia, is the largest mosque in the world and surrounds one of Islam's holiest places—the Ka'aba.

## Warm Up

**Discuss these questions with a partner.**

1. Who is the most respected leader in your country's history? Why is that person admired?

2. What have been the most significant turning points in your country's history? What impact did those events have?

3. Which are the most important religious or cultural places in your country today? Why are they important?

## EMPIRE OF THE OTTOMANS

The Ottoman Empire lasted from the end of the 13th century to the beginning of the 20th—a period of more than 600 years. Occupying a strategic position at the junction of three continents, the empire rose to become a major world power under Süleyman the Magnificent (1494–1566). From his capital Constantinople (modern Istanbul), Süleyman personally accompanied his army on 13 campaigns, expanding his territory from central Europe to the southern coast of what is now Iraq. He created a powerful navy that secured coastlines along the Red Sea and eastern Mediterranean and brought most of the North African coast under Ottoman control.

Map labels: Szigetvar, Belgrade, Istanbul (Constantinople), Malta, Rhodes, Mediterranean Sea, Red Sea, Mecca, EUROPE, ASIA, AFRICA, Arabia

◇ Extent of Ottoman Empire, 1566
✗ Battle site

# Before You Read

**A. Discussion.** Look at the map and information above, and answer the questions.

1. Which modern-day countries did the Ottoman Empire include at the height of its power?

2. Who was Süleyman the Magnificent? When did he live and why was he important?

3. Where was the Ottoman capital? How is it known today? What advantages did its location offer?

**B. Scan.** The article on pages 229–234 mentions various people associated with Süleyman. Scan the passage and match the people (**1–6**) to their descriptions (**a–f**).

| | | | |
|---|---|---|---|
| 1. _____ Selim | | **a.** victor of the siege of Malta |
| 2. _____ Selim II | | **b.** the first Ottoman sultan |
| 3. _____ Osman | | **c.** Süleyman's wife |
| 4. _____ Jean Parisot de la Valette | | **d.** Süleyman's father |
| 5. _____ Mehmed the Conqueror | | **e.** Süleyman's great-grandfather |
| 6. _____ Roxelana | | **f.** Süleyman's son |

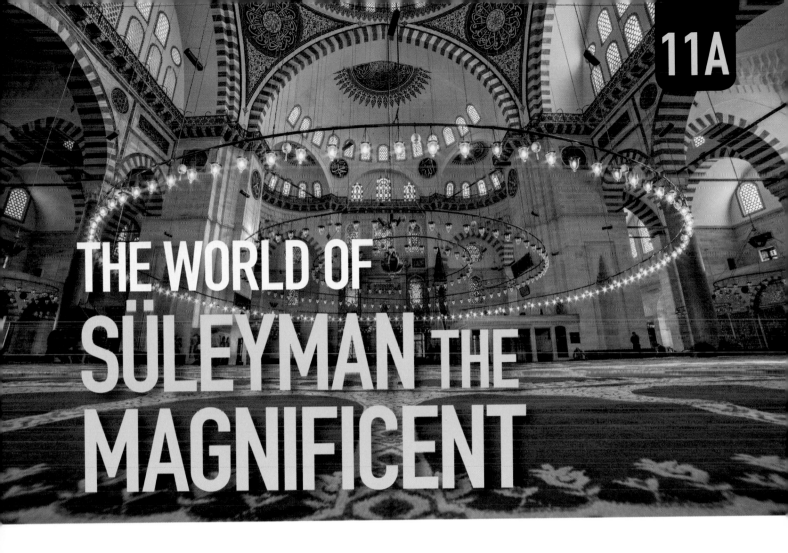

# THE WORLD OF SÜLEYMAN THE MAGNIFICENT

**A** 1  Writer Merle Severy examines the legacy of one of the giant historical figures of the 16th century—a ruler who stood at the crossroads of East and West.

The interior of the Süleymanlye Mosque in Istanbul displays the glory of the Ottoman Empire.

**B** 5  Near the Hungarian town of Szigetvár, a road sign caught my eye: "Szulimán." It was a dying village, the young having moved away, the old hanging on.

**C**  "It was named for a sultan who came long ago," a man in his garden told me.

**D**  "What did he do here?"

**E** 10  "I heard that he died here," a woman said, the lines of many years etching[1] her face. "The old folks would know. But they are all dead now." My curiosity led me finally to a churchyard amid cornfields in the nearby countryside. A church without a village must mark some special spot. I went through the gate, past a large crucifix,[2] and on 15  the church facade saw an Ottoman Turkish inscription. A crescent stood by the wall, bathed in the light of the setting sun.

**F**  It was at this site, I read, that was buried the heart of Sultan Süleyman.

1 If lines are **etched** on a surface, they are cut or carved into that surface.

2 A **crucifix** is a symbol of Christianity, a model cross with a figure of Christ on it, most commonly associated with the Catholic Church.

The Süleymaniye Mosque is the largest work of the renowned Ottoman architect Sinan.

**G** THE 16TH CENTURY was an age notable
for the overlapping **reigns** of giant historical
20 figures: Spanish Emperor Charles V, protector
of the Christian Church; his rival Francis I, King
of France; Henry VIII of England; Ivan the
Terrible, all-powerful ruler of Russia.

**H** Yet, even among this **hierarchy** of great
25 leaders, one ruler arguably stood taller than
the rest: Süleyman, Commander of the
Faithful, Shadow of God on Earth, Protector
of the Holy Cities of Mecca, Medina, and
Jerusalem, Lord of the Lords of the World, East
30 and West. Revered by his people as "Kanuni,"
the Lawgiver, and feared and admired by the
West as "the Magnificent," Süleyman brought
the Ottoman Empire to the peak of its power.

**I** Süleyman was born at a time of world war,
35 of East against West, with two superpowers
locked in mortal conflict on the lands and seas
of three continents. Time and again, Christian
and Muslim forces clashed in the seas around
the Indian Ocean, the Red Sea, and the
40 Mediterranean, and on land in Europe from
Turkey to Austria.

**J** Away from what the Ottomans called the
Realm of War, the frontier against their unholy
enemies, was the Realm of Peace, where races
45 and religions coexisted with the sultan acting
as a great mediator of peoples. At its heart
was Constantinople (present-day Istanbul),
a cosmopolitan crossroads of continents that
grew so large that no other European capital
50 overtook it until the start of the 19th century.

**K** It was Süleyman's great-grandfather, Mehmed
the Conqueror, who turned Constantinople
into the greatest of all European cities.
Mehmed was a descendant of nomadic
55 tribesmen from central Asia who became
followers of Osman, the first Ottoman sultan,
in the 13th century. From these humble
origins, Mehmed rose in power, carrying

the banner[3] of Islam in a series of conquests
60 through Serbia, Greece, and Eastern Europe;
only his death in 1481 prevented him from
pressing the conquest of Italy and taking
Rhodes, the last Christian stronghold in
the east.

**L** 65 Mehmed's dream of achieving Alexander the
Great's ambition—of building a world empire
that brought together East and West—would
eventually be taken up by his great-grandson,
Süleyman. As a young man, the future sultan
70 was educated in a river valley near the Aegean
Sea where he had been assigned as governor.
Well read in history, the Koran, politics,
science, astrology, and poetry, and skilled in
horsemanship and archery, Süleyman had been
75 carefully prepared for his role as a future world
leader.

**M** On hearing of his father Selim's death in
1520, Süleyman rode for three days until he
arrived in Constantinople. As he approached,
80 Süleyman looked with fresh eyes at the city
that would become his capital: the fortress
with its great cannons; the dome of the
magnificent Hagia Sophia, a church that
had been converted to Muslim worship; the
85 wooden houses sheltering immigrant families.
In this crowded city, Spanish Moors and Jews
expelled by Ferdinand and Isabella[4] joined with
Turks, Greeks, and Armenians in the shops and
stalls that filled the city's covered bazaar.[5]

**N** 90 On September 30, eight days after Selim's
death, Süleyman took up the sword of Osman
in an elaborate ceremony and was declared
sultan. From that time on, he held absolute
power over the welfare of his people, with
95 the right of instant death over any subject.
But as he first rode from his palace, his people
gathered to raise their voice in a ritual warning
to a new monarch: "Be not proud, my sultan.
God is greater than you!"

---

**3** Someone **carrying the banner** of a specific cause or idea stands for that idea.

**4** **Ferdinand** of Aragon (1452–1516) **and Isabella** of Castile (1451–1504) were rulers of Spain.
See Unit 11B, "When the Moors Ruled Spain."

**5** A **bazaar** is a market area, usually a street of small stalls.

**O** 100 **SÜLEYMAN'S FIRST OFFICIAL ACTS** were to order a tomb, mosque, and school built in honor of his father; to free 1,500 Egyptian and Iranian captives; and to pay back merchants for goods that Selim had taken from them.
105 These won him popular approval for piety, magnanimity,[6] and justice. "It seemed to all men," one observer commented, "that a gentle lamb had succeeded a fierce lion."

**P** But the lamb proved to be a lion in disguise.
110 A revolt in Syria was put down savagely. Then Süleyman set out to achieve what Mehmed the Conqueror had failed to do. In his first European campaign,[7] the city of Belgrade—the key to Christian defenses in the Balkans—fell
115 after weeks of massed attacks.

**Q** The next summer, in 1522, he besieged[8] the Christian stronghold of Rhodes, which stood between his capital and the ports of Egypt and Arabia, including the Islamic holy city of
120 Mecca. The siege began on July 29 and lasted 145 bloody days, until the knights'[9] desperate defense ended.

**R** Having brought into submission the strongest fortified city in Christendom, Süleyman offered
125 generous terms. Knights and mercenaries could leave freely within 12 days; citizens could depart at any time within three years. Again he won admiration for his magnanimity. Little did he realize the price he would pay
130 later for letting the knights go.

**S** As success followed success in his campaigns, contemporaries wrote with awe of the glories of the sultan's empire. "I know of no State which is happier than this one," reported the
135 Venetian ambassador in 1525. "It is furnished with all God's gifts. It controls war and peace with all; it is rich in gold, in people, in ships, and in obedience; no State can be compared with it. May God long preserve the most just
140 of all Emperors."

**T** **THE VENETIAN AMBASSADOR'S** glowing, and no doubt somewhat **biased**, description is perhaps understandable considering the spectacular show that was put on to welcome
145 visitors to the Ottoman capital. A foreign ambassador's reception was carefully designed to show Ottoman grandeur and power at its most impressive.

**U** On approaching the sultan's Topkapi Palace,
150 the envoy first saw the heads of executed traitors hanging from the Imperial Gate. Passing the executioner's chambers, the envoy entered a shining portico.[10] There he was met on the sultan's behalf by the monarch's vizier,
155 or grand advisor, who, on special occasions, led the envoy past 2,000 bowing officials and heaps of silver coins. The visitor was then offered a "hundred dishes or thereabout, most boiled and roasted."

**V** 160 Then on to the sacred inner precincts.[11] Visitors spoke of the silence—the "silence of death itself." The ambassador was robed in gold cloth while his royal presents were inspected, since the sultan was "not to be
165 approached without gifts." At the door of the throne room, two officials held the visitor firmly by the arms; at no time would they let go. The visitor was led across the room, then forced to **subordinate** himself by kneeling
170 down and kissing the sultan's foot. He was then raised to deliver his message.

**W** The sultan, heavy with silk, gold and silver threads, sat on a jewel-studded throne. Süleyman might make a comment or indicate
175 with a nod that the audience was over. The

---

6 **Piety** is dutiful devotion, usually with reference to a particular theology (religion); **magnanimity** is generosity in forgiving an insult or injury.

7 A **campaign** is a series of coordinated activities designed to achieve a goal, such as a military objective.

8 If soldiers **besiege** a place, they surround it in order to stop the people inside from resisting.

9 In medieval times, a **knight** was a man of noble birth who fought for his king or lord.

10 A **portico** is a porch or covered walkway with columns supporting the roof.

11 **Precincts** are districts, as of a city, or the parts or regions immediately surrounding or within a place.

ambassador was then led backwards out of the room, never turning his back on the sultan. The sultan's response might come much later, usually via the grand vizier.

**X** 180 The envoys who met Süleyman in this way would scan his features for signs of his health and character. From their descriptions, we know something of how the great sultan looked, how he acted. But we know very little 185 of his thoughts, of what really was in the mind of the Lord of Lords.

**Y** **WHAT SORT OF MAN** was Süleyman? Of his private life—his attitudes and his thoughts— we can **infer** very little. His campaign diaries 190 are written in the third person, without emotion. For example, from his third campaign: "The Emperor, seated on a golden throne, receives [his] viziers . . . ; massacre of 2,000 prisoners; the rain falls in torrents."

**Z** 195 Glimpses[12] of humanity are rare, but revealing. After the siege of Rhodes, Süleyman **consoles** the knights' leader for his loss, praises his brave defense, then **confides** to a follower: "It is not without regret that I force this brave 200 man from his home in his old age."

**AA** We know that Süleyman showed wisdom as a lawgiver, creating a new code of laws and giving legal protection to minorities. He was also pious, **consulting** theologians on crucial 205 decisions; just, allowing no corruption or injustice to go unpunished; and, usually, fair.

**BB** Ironically, it was an act of generosity that led, years later, to his greatest defeat. As a young man, Jean Parisot de la Valette fought against 210 Süleyman in the siege of Rhodes, but was later released. Just over four decades later, la Valette led the defense of the great Christian stronghold of Malta. The surprise defeat at the hands of the Christian knights marked the 215 beginning of the end of Ottoman domination in the Mediterranean.

**CC** As the siege of Malta ended, Süleyman was entering his 73rd year, making him the longest-reigning of all Ottoman monarchs.

220 During his reign, he had extended his Islamic empire through southeastern Europe, across much of the Middle East, and in north Africa as far west as Algeria. His code of laws, known as the *kanun-i Osmanî* 225 ("Ottoman Laws"), was to last more than 300 years. And he presided over some of the greatest architectural achievements in the Islamic world.

**DD** Despite these achievements, Süleyman's mood 230 became increasingly dark. To wipe out the disappointment of Malta, he set out on May 1, 1566, to capture Vienna. The journey was painfully slow. The sultan could no longer sit on a horse but had to ride in a carriage. 235 Suddenly, word came that a Hungarian count[13] had executed one of Süleyman's governors and was now hiding in Szigetvár. In a fury, Süleyman diverted his entire army to avenge the injustice.

---

12 **Glimpses** are brief views or vague indications.

13 A **count** is a nobleman in European countries.

A fresco portrays the 1565 Ottoman siege of Malta where Jean Parisot de la Valette defeated Süleyman's army.

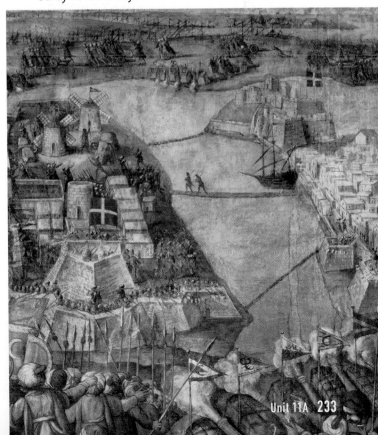

EE 240 Even with only 2,500 defenders, Szigetvár held off the Ottomans for a month, until the fortress was finally shattered by explosives. Holding up his jeweled sword in surrender, the count came out with his survivors. But there 245 was no sultan to greet him. Süleyman had died in the night in his tent.

FF **FOLLOWING SÜLEYMAN'S DEATH**, the Ottoman empire was squeezed by Russian expansion in the east and European 250 domination of southern Asia. Ottoman possessions in the Mediterranean lost their strategic role. Western technology overtook Ottoman military might, and—with no new lands, taxes, or manpower—imperial decline 255 set in. During the 19th century, the empire became known as the "Sick Man of Europe." Nevertheless, when more than a dozen nations emerged from its umbrella in the early 20th century, their languages, religions, and cultures 260 had been largely preserved—a legacy, in part, of Süleyman's tolerance of minorities.

GG Three weeks after the emperor's death, the sultan's **successor** was announced, and Selim, the son of Süleyman and his queen Roxelana 265 (see below), became the new Sultan Selim II. According to Ottoman custom, Süleyman's heart was buried where he died, and the rest of his embalmed[14] remains began the long journey home. When the sultan's body 270 reached the capital, the army fell silent, as did the people who followed behind in a long procession. Their leader all their lives, he raised their sacred empire to its golden age. Their descendants would look back on it with pride 275 and **nostalgia**. But they would never see his like again.

---

14 A dead body that is **embalmed** is preserved by the use of chemicals and oils.

# The Slave Who Became Queen

Süleyman was strongly influenced by two slaves he raised to power: Ibrahim, whom he promoted to grand vizier, and Hürrem—"laughing one"—a captive Russian known to the West as Roxelana, who became his wife.

To gain influence over Süleyman, Roxelana first set out to remove Ibrahim, who had served as grand vizier for 13 years. With prompting from Roxelana, Süleyman began to suspect Ibrahim was acting as if he were the sultan. One evening, Ibrahim was invited to dine with Süleyman. The next morning, he was found strangled.

Next, in order to strengthen the position of her own sons, Roxelana needed to remove Mustafa, Süleyman's firstborn son. He, too, was found strangled in his father's tent. Eventually, one of Roxelana's sons, Selim, succeeded Süleyman to the throne. Rising from slavery to royalty, this strong-willed woman played a man's game with great skill for the highest stakes.

∧ Queen Roxelana was one of the most powerful and influential women in Ottoman history.

# Reading Comprehension

**Multiple Choice.** Choose the best answer for each question.

Vocabulary **1.** The phrase *overlapping reigns* in line 19 indicates that the leaders mentioned in this paragraph _____.
  a. were more powerful than kings in previous centuries
  b. ruled their lands during some of the same years
  c. lived longer lives than previous monarchs
  d. ruled during a time of war and trouble

Detail **2.** Which of the following leaders made Constantinople the most important city in Europe?
  a. Süleyman    b. Osman    c. Mehmed    d. Selim

Detail **3.** Which of the following is NOT true about Constantinople at the time of Selim's death in 1520?
  a. It contained diverse groups of people.
  b. It was where Süleyman was living.
  c. It was located in the Realm of Peace.
  d. It was the heart of the Ottoman Empire.

Paraphrase **4.** Choose the sentence that is closest in meaning to this sentence from line 109: *But the lamb proved to be a lion in disguise.*
  a. Süleyman was not interested in warfare, only in peace.
  b. Süleyman proved that it was better to be powerful than kind.
  c. Süleyman proved to be much fiercer than people first thought.
  d. Süleyman seemed fierce, but was actually very gentle.

Inference **5.** What does the author imply in paragraph R?
  a. The "generous" terms offered were not really very generous.
  b. Although Rhodes was thought to be strong, it fell very easily.
  c. The knights were allowed to become citizens of Rhodes.
  d. Süleyman would later regret treating the knights so liberally.

Rhetorical Purpose **6.** Why does the author quote from Süleyman's campaign diaries in paragraph Y?
  a. to show his writing revealed little about his true personality
  b. to support the idea that the third campaign was his most important
  c. to demonstrate that he was not only a military genius but also a skillful writer
  d. to point out the impact of bad weather on military operations

Detail **7.** What does the author say about the siege of Malta?
  a. It was considered Süleyman's most brilliant campaign.
  b. It was the final battle in which Süleyman fought.
  c. The siege did not last as long as Süleyman had predicted.
  d. Jean Parisot de la Valette's victory there was unexpected.

## Critical Thinking

**Evaluating:** The author frequently emphasizes the power and wealth of Süleyman. List five ways in which he supports the idea that Süleyman was a rich and powerful leader, and note in which lines you found this information.

**Discussion:** In what ways do you think Süleyman's leadership is similar to, and different from, that of world leaders today?

# Creating a Mental Map of a Text

The text of an article is often divided into sections, each corresponding to an important supporting idea of the whole article. Sometimes each section has its own title; in other cases (as in "The World of Süleyman the Magnificent"), the start of new sections may be indicated by spacing or typography (e.g., the use of a different font). Section titles usually refer to the overall main idea or point of the section, rather than to a specific detail. Titles and opening lines of sections are often useful for creating a mental map of the organization and scope of an article.

Süleyman the Magnificent (1494–1566) raised the Ottoman Empire to the height of its glory.

**Matching.** Find the six most appropriate section titles from the list (**a–h**) and put them in the correct order below.

a. Birth of a Leader

b. The End of the Dream

c. The Secret Sultan

d. The Capture of Vienna

e. An Audience with Süleyman

f. The Lamb and the Lion

g. A Dying Village

h. The Lord of Lords

# The World of Süleyman the Magnificent

Section 1 (from paragraph A): _____

Section 2 (from paragraph G): _____

Section 3 (from paragraph O): _____

Section 4 (from paragraph T): _____

Section 5 (from paragraph Y): _____

Section 6 (from paragraph FF): _____

# Vocabulary Practice

**A. Definitions.** Complete the information using the correct form of words in the box. Four words are extra.

| | | | | |
|---|---|---|---|---|
| biased | confide | console | consult | hierarchy |
| infer | nostalgia | subordinate | successor | reign |

During his **1.** _____ in the 12th century, Salah al-Din Yüsuf ibn Ayyüb—better known to the western world as Saladin—was a great war leader. At the height of his power, he ruled over the lands of Egypt, Syria, Mesopotamia, and Yemen, defending his homeland against European invaders.

Saladin began his life as a soldier under his uncle, an army commander, and quickly rose up the military **2.** _____. After taking control of Egypt in 1171, he seized power in Syria following the death of its king. Some saw this as an act of treason against the king's son, who was also the king's intended **3.** _____, but Saladin felt his actions were justified by his mission—to unite the Muslim lands and defend them from the Christian Crusaders arriving from Europe.

While historical accounts of the Crusades are usually **4.** _____ and somewhat unreliable, contemporary accounts of Saladin's actions—from both sides—allow us to **5.** _____ that he was in fact a fair and generous ruler, despite the ruthlessness he showed in battle. For example, he mediated truces between other Muslim leaders, he frequently **6.** _____ with his councils, and he also showed mercy to many of his prisoners.

⌃ Saladin, leader of the Muslim forces against the Crusaders, was also the first sultan of Egypt and Syria.

**B. Definitions.** Match the definitions to words from the box in **A**.

1. _____: a system of organizing people into different levels of importance

2. _____: a person who replaces someone else

3. _____: to make a deduction from evidence given

4. _____: to ask for advice

5. _____: a sentimental longing for a period in the past

6. _____: the time period for which a monarch rules

7. _____: to discuss inner thoughts or secrets

8. _____: to comfort, e.g., after a loss

9. _____: in favor of one group or idea over another

10. _____: someone who is in a lower position

> **Word Link**
> The prefix **bi-** has the meaning of "two," e.g., **bi**ennial, **bi**monthly, **bi**ased, **bi**cycle, **bi**noculars, **bi**lingual, **bi**national.

# Before You Read

**A. Matching.** The following words appear in the reading passage. Match each word with its definition. Two words are extra.

The narrow Strait of Gibraltar, which passes between Morocco's Jabal Musa and the Rock of Gibraltar, separates Africa from Europe by just 15 kilometers (9 miles).

| cathedral   clergy   creed   mosque   prayer   prophet   shrine |
| --- |

1. _____: a set of beliefs, or principles, that strongly influence the way a person lives and works

2. _____: a person who is believed to speak for a divine authority

3. _____: a place of worship associated with a holy person or object

4. _____: the leaders of the religious activities of a group of believers

5. _____: an important church that has a bishop in charge

**B. Skim and Predict.** Look quickly through the article on pages 239–243. Check (✓) the topics you think the author discusses. Then read through the passage to check your ideas.

☐ origins of the Moors

☐ how the Moors came to Spain

☐ Moorish architecture

☐ Moorish poetry

☐ Moorish paintings

☐ how the Moorish era ended

# WHEN THE MOORS RULED SPAIN

**A** 1 From the Rock of Gibraltar, writer Thomas J. Abercrombie set out to explore a forgotten corner of Europe's past.

**B** 5 "Perfect weather for a morning's sail—or an intercontinental passage," said my Spanish shipmate, Rafa, as I scanned the rising mists ahead. Suddenly a silhouette of our destination appeared above the haze ahead: 10 Gibraltar.

**C** "Wow, what a beauty!" Rafa exclaimed.

**D** A beacon for mariners since the dawn of seafaring, the famous Rock of Gibraltar was one of the Pillars of Hercules (Jabal Musa, 15 behind us on the northern coast of Africa, formed the other). For ancient Romans and Greeks, the pillars marked the boundary of the known world. For me, the stronghold marked the first stop on a journey into a neglected 20 corner of Europe's history, a distant time when Muslims ruled Spain and Islam had a powerful influence on the West.

**E** "Only recently have the Spanish begun to approach their Islamic past," Rafa told me. 25 In recent years, Rafa had presided over a Madrid-based institute that promotes cultural exchange between Spain and its Muslim neighbors. "We are finding that much of what we think of as 'pure Spanish,' our architecture, 30 our temperament,[1] our poetry and music— even our language—is a blend from a long Arabic heritage."

**F** Rafa and I were sailing in the wake of Tariq ibn Ziyad, a Muslim general. With soldiers and 35 horses in four boats, he crossed from Ceuta on the African side—as did we—and set up his beachhead on the narrow ledge below, where the town of Gibraltar sits today. In the spring of 711, he marched northward with 12,000 40 Muslims. At the Rio Barbate, south of Cadiz, the invaders met the hastily assembled forces of Spain's Visigoth[2] king, Roderic. "Before us is the enemy; behind us, the sea," shouted Tariq, drawing his scimitar[3] and **invoking** Allah for 45 his blessing and support. "We have only one choice: to win!"

**G** The battle of Barbate proved a mortal wound for the weak Visigoth ruler. King Roderic was slain; his body was never recovered. Whole 50 battalions of soldiers fled, and the Christian army collapsed. The Islamic conquest of Spain had begun.

**H** The creed of Islam had been revealed to the seventh-century prophet-statesman 55 Muhammad in distant Arabia. It spread swiftly, embracing the entire desert peninsula[4] by the time of his death in 632. Six years later, Syria and Palestine fell to the Muslims. From their new capital in Damascus, Muslim armies

---

1 Your **temperament** is your basic nature, such as how you react to situations.

2 The **Visigoths** were a tribe who settled in France and Spain in the 4th century A.D.

3 A **scimitar** is a sword with a curved blade.

4 A **peninsula** is a narrow strip of land projecting from the mainland into a sea or lake.

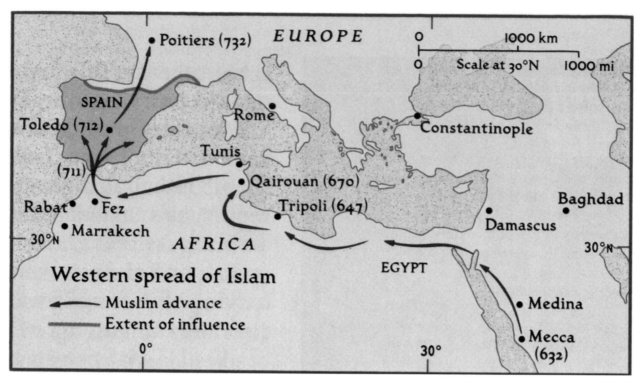

In a mere hundred years, the Prophet Muhammad's followers spread the word of Islam westward from Mecca through northern Africa to Spain and France, where their advance was halted in 732.

among the Moors. Instead, they channeled
190 creative energy into language. With its wealth of vocabulary, its distinctive sounds, its flowing calligraphy, Arabic is well suited to the task.

**U** "Little has been translated," he said, but he quoted some lines that survived the journey
195 into Spanish and English. From Ibn al-Sabuni:
*I present you a precious mirror*
*Behold there the beauty that consumes me*
*O furtive love, your reflection is more yielding*
*And better keeps its promises*

**V** 200 The Nasrid rulers' mansions of the Alhambra make up the most visited site in Spain. It is a miracle that they survived the centuries. They have been abused by squatters,[10] eroded by neglect, and suffered various **appendages**,
205 including a massive addition built during the Renaissance by Charles V. The **integrity** of the Alhambra endures nonetheless, a sublime Moorish mix of artifact and nature.

**W** Here the walls themselves speak—if you know
210 Arabic. We found quotations and poems in the calligraphy of the walls, archways, and

fountains. One marble fountain declared:
*No greater mansions I see than mine*
*No equal in East or West.*

**X** 215 I had to agree. Even in the oil-rich Arab countries of today, architects with unlimited budgets have yet to match the Alhambra.

**Y** The marriage of Ferdinand and Isabella sealed the fate of the weakening Granada sultans.
220 In 1492, the same year that they launched Christopher Columbus on his historic voyage across the Atlantic, the king and queen rode into Granada to preside over the abdication[11] of the last Moorish ruler, Muhammad Abu-
225 Abdullah—Boabdil, as the Spanish call him.

**Z** On the way out of Córdoba, I paused at a pass above the city called *Suspiro del Moro*, the Sigh of the Moor. It was here Boabdil stopped to look back and shed a tear over

---

10 **Squatters** are people who live in unused buildings without having a legal right to do so.

11 An **abdication** occurs when a person gives up being king or queen.

230 his lost kingdom. According to legend, his domineering mother, Aisha, berated[12] him for passively allowing his kingdom to fall: "Fitting you cry like a woman over what you could not defend like a man."

**AA** 235 The remote villages of the Alpujarras, halfway up the southern slopes of Mulhacén, Spain's highest peak, were the last domains of the Moors in Spain until they were finally driven into exile in 1609. Many towns still wear their
240 Arabic names, as does Mount Mulhacén—and the Alpujarras itself. I descended from the mountains via a series of sharp turns, to a very different world: Spain's Costa del Sol—tropical, cosmopolitan, and booming. "Last year 50
245 million visitors came to Spain," Costa del Sol Tourist Board promotion manager Diego Franco told me, "one for every Spaniard and then some. It's an invasion—but a peaceful one."

**BB** 250 All over the coastal region are signs that modern-day Moors have joined the "peaceful invasion"; signs in Arabic script point you to the Lebanese Delicatessen, the Banco Saudi-Espanol, to Arab doctors, a
255 Muslim cemetery . . .

**CC** Near the Andalucía Plaza Casino, I drank coffee with Mokhles "George" El-Khoury, a Christian Arab who moved here from Beirut to run a building-management firm. "[Andalucía]
260 reminds me of Lebanon—without the wars and politics," George said. "You have the mountains, the sea, the fine climate of olives and palm trees. The Spanish are a warm people, not stiff and formal like many
265 Europeans. The food is much like ours, so is the shape of the houses and the towns. To an Arab—well, Andalucía feels like home."

**DD** Nowhere is this more true than in the old Muslim capital of Córdoba, where I spent
270 my last Spanish days. I was awakened there early one morning by the noise of workmen at the Mezquita across the street. No other artifact more richly evokes the golden age of the Moors, a stormy millennium that
275 brought together two faiths, two cultures,

two continents. Throughout, while king and sultan fought bitterly for the hand of Spain, ordinary life prospered as people of different backgrounds worked together to create the
280 brilliant civilization that helped lead Europe out of the Dark Ages.[13]

**EE** Ultimately the Moors themselves faded into history, leaving behind their scattered dreams. But Spain and the West stand forever in
285 their debt.

---

12 When someone is **berated**, they are scolded angrily.

13 The **Dark Ages** refers to a period of cultural and economic decline in Western Europe following the end of the Roman Empire.

# Flamenco

Arabic poetry was crafted, above all, for recital and song. In Morocco and Spain, the soul-stirring music of *cante jondo*, the deep song of Gypsy flamenco, is still played and sung by descendants of ethnic minorities who survived the Inquisition centuries ago.

Throughout Spain the art of flamenco is threatened by its commercialization in shows called *tablaos*, characterized by dramatic lighting and loud amplifiers. Sacrificed in the process is flamenco's most distinctive aspect, its *duende*: soul. But after midnight, it is still possible to sample flamenco *puro* ("pure Flamenco") in the bars of Granada's Albaicin area, when Gypsies gather to recall the moods and rhythms of a lost age.

# Reading Comprehension

**Multiple Choice.** Choose the best answer for each question.

Inference/
Tone

**1.** The author's general attitude toward the Moors is best described
as _____.

   a. questioning        b. neutral

   c. bitter             d. respectful

Detail

**2.** What does the author say about the word *Moors*?

   a. It was applied only to the North African Berber soldiers.

   b. It was used because the invaders came to Spain from
Morocco.

   c. It was what the Muslim conquerors called themselves.

   d. It was originally applied to the Visigoth conquerors of Spain.

Detail

**3.** The name *Gibraltar* comes from the name of a _____.

   a. Visigoth ruler

   b. Christian king

   c. Moorish war leader

   d. Galician slave

Inference

**4.** From the information in paragraph K, we can infer that _____.

   a. at least some of Toledo's scholars could understand Latin

   b. Alfonso X was the Spanish leader who recaptured Toledo
from the Moors

   c. Ibn Sina helped translate his medical textbook from Arabic to
Spanish

   d. speaking or writing in Arabic in Toledo after 1085 was
forbidden

Reference

**5.** The word *their* in line 115 refers to _____.

   a. Muslims and Jews

   b. Moorish rulers to the south

   c. Ferdinand and Isabella

   d. Spanish Christians

Vocabulary

**6.** The word *banal* in line 165 is closest in meaning to _____.

   a. ordinary and unexciting

   b. small and inconspicuous

   c. strange and unlikely

   d. unholy and insulting

Detail

**7.** Which of these is NOT true about the Alhambra?

   a. Nasrid rulers lived there.

   b. There are quotations and poems in Arabic on the walls.

   c. It is the least visited site in Spain.

   d. It has been vandalized and neglected over the years.

## Critical Thinking

**Analyzing:** How
does the author use
metaphoric language
(paragraph O) to
make an analogy
(comparison) between
the Moors' cultivation
of land and Moorish
culture? What other
words or expressions
could the author have
used?

**Discussion:** Think of
a nation or culture that
has been influenced
by being conquered,
ruled, or occupied
by another culture.
In what ways was
the original culture
changed? How does its
experience compare
with the conquest of
Spain by the Moors
as described in this
article?

# Inferring an Author's Attitude

Authors may write about topics in a completely neutral and objective way. However, in many articles, authors express their own positive or negative feelings about the main topic and subtopics in an article. Authors commonly reveal their attitude through the use of words with positive or negative connotations. The use of this language suggests how the author feels about something. Often, these words are adjectives, but other methods—such as the use of metaphoric language—can express positive or negative opinions as well.

Examples:
We found the service in that restaurant *terrible*, but the food was *exceptionally good*.
Natalie is a *graceful* dancer, but her partner dances like an *awkward elephant*.

**Scanning and Inferring.** Find the discussion of the topics listed below in the article. Decide if the author's attitude toward the topic is positive or negative, and note words or phrases that signal the author's attitude.

| Topic | Author's attitude (+ or -) | Words/phrases that indicate the author's attitude |
|---|---|---|
| Toledo in the two centuries after its reconquest (paragraphs K–L) | | |
| the rule of Ferdinand and Isabella (paragraphs M–N) | | |
| Andalucía (paragraphs O–P) | | |
| Córdoba (paragraphs P–Q) | | |
| the cathedral inside the Mezquita (paragraph R) | | |
| Arabic language and poetry (paragraphs T–U) | | |
| changes to the Alhambra since its construction (paragraph V) | | |
| *tablaos* shows (feature article: Flamenco) | | |

# Vocabulary Practice

**A. Completion.** Complete the information using the correct forms of the words in the box. Three words are extra.

| | | | | |
|---|---|---|---|---|
| amend | appendage | empirical | initiate | integrity |
| invoke | liberal | persecute | splendid | violate |

Ruled in turn by the Romans, Moors, and Christians, the city of Toledo in Spain stands as a **1.** _____ showcase of Spanish history, an enduring meeting place of cultures and peoples.

From A.D. 712, under the rule of the Moorish Caliphate of Córdoba, Toledo enjoyed the benefits of a(n) **2.** _____ society in which Muslims, Jews, and Christians co-existed. But Moorish rule was only temporary. On May 25, 1085, Alfonso VI of Castile officially reclaimed Toledo for Christian Spain.

During his reign, Christian, Muslim, and Jewish scholars continued to collaborate, translating Arabic and Hebrew documents into Spanish and Latin, and **3.** _____ advancements in education that lasted over several centuries. These included **4.** _____ studies in science and mathematics. However, in the 1400s, intolerance flared in Toledo. Muslims and Jews were **5.** _____ and their religious freedoms were **6.** _____ . Many were expelled from Spain. It was a dark time that continued well into the 1800s.

⌃ El Greco's *View of Toledo* is considered among the best-known depictions of the sky in Western art and a masterpiece of the Spanish Renaissance.

In 1941, the city of Toledo was declared a national monument and laws were set up to protect the **7.** _____ of Toledo's surviving buildings and monuments.

**B. Words in Context.** Complete the sentences with words from the box in **A**.

1. When something is attached to a larger object, it can be called a(n) _____ .

2. Someone who is _____ believes people should have a lot of freedom in deciding how to think or act.

3. Something that is _____ is very impressive and beautiful.

4. If you _____ something that has been written, you change it.

5. If you _____ something or someone, you refer to it or them to help you.

> **Word Partnership**
> Use ***violate*** with: (*n.*)
> violate **an agreement**, violate **the law**, violate **rights**, violate **rules**, violate **someone's privacy**, violate **(religious) freedom**.

# VIEWING  Heritage of Spain

## Before You Watch

**Quiz.** What do you know about Spain? Work with a partner and complete the quiz.

**(left)** Casa Battlo was designed by famous architect, Antonio Gaudi. **(middle)** Tapas are a wide variety of appetizers in Spanish cuisine. **(right)** Flamenco is a form of Spanish folk music and dance from the region of Andalucía.

1. Spain lies at the crossroads of _____.
   a. Europe and Asia    b. Asia and Africa    c. Africa and Europe    d. Europe and South America

2. What is the capital of Spain?
   a. Madrid    b. Barcelona    c. Granada    d. Seville

3. Antonio Gaudí was a famous Spanish Modernist _____.
   a. painter    b. fashion designer    c. sculptor    d. architect

4. Spain is famous for its small appetizers known as _____.
   a. sagradas    b. paella    c. tapas    d. alhambras

5. Flamenco is composed of three disciplines. Which of these is NOT one of them?
   a. guitar    b. violin    c. voice    d. dance

6. It is believed that flamenco began when _____ arrived in Spain.
   a. Gypsies    b. Jews    c. Moors    d. Christians

7. Where is the Alhambra?
   a. Madrid    b. Barcelona    c. Granada    d. Córdoba

## While You Watch

**A. Completion.** Watch the video and check your answers to the quiz. Make any corrections.

**B. Completion.** Watch the video again and complete the concept map.

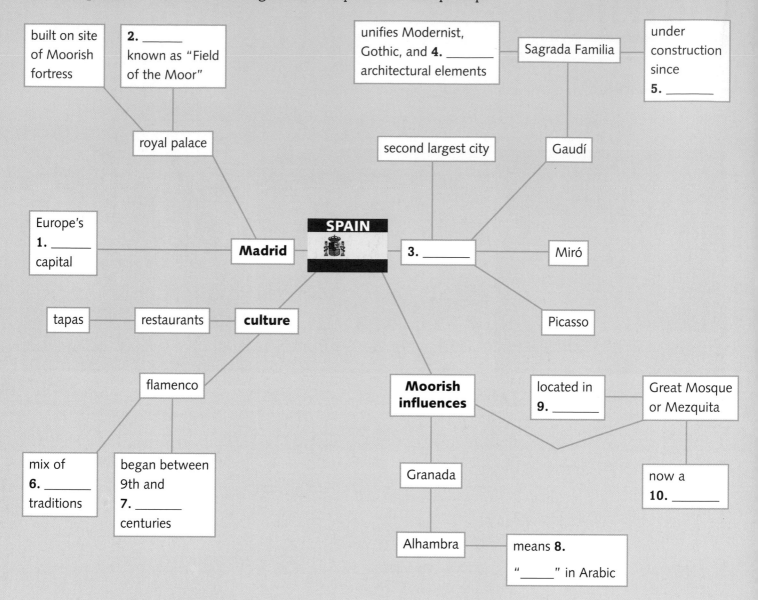

## After You Watch

**Discussion.** Discuss these questions with a partner.

1. Flamenco is the product of Moorish, Jewish, Christian, and Gypsy influences. Do you know any other art forms, customs, or traditions that are the product of more than one culture? How did they develop?

2. Which art forms, customs, or traditions do you think are the most representative of your country's culture?

3. Do you think cultures will, in general, become more mixed in the future? Why or why not?

# 12

# WEALTH AND FINANCE

A woman receiving a gold facial. Consisting of a metallic sheet of liquid gold, the luxurious treatment is said to lift and firm the skin, reducing the appearance of sun damage and lines.

## Warm Up

**Discuss these questions with a partner.**

1. How would you define "price"? How does it compare with the "value" of something?

2. How many different methods of payment do you use for buying items? What are the pros and cons of each one?

3. What social and economic role does gold play in your country?

## Before You Read

**A. Matching.** The following money-related words appear in the passage on pages 251–256. Use the words to complete the definitions. Two words are extra.

| balance | bill | exchange rate | inflation |
|---------|------|---------------|-----------|
| interest | mint | reserve | treasury |

1. _____ is an increase in the prices of goods and services in a country.

2. The _____ is the place where the official coins of a country are made.

3. A(n) _____ is a supply of something that is available for use when needed.

4. The revenues or funds of a government are referred to as the _____.

5. The _____ of a country's unit of currency is the amount of another country's currency that you can get for it.

6. _____ is extra money you receive if you have invested a sum of money; it is also the extra money you pay if you have borrowed money or are buying something on credit.

**B. Skim and Predict.** Skim the following passage. Check (✓) which of the following have been used as money. Then read the passage to check your predictions.

☐ clamshells      ☐ a bronze drum      ☐ a block of salt      ☐ beads

# FROM CLAMS TO CREDIT CARDS

**A** 1 Writer Peter T. White traces the history of one of humanity's oldest creations: from the beginnings of coinage in antiquity to the emergence of a cashless society.

Two monks in Bangkok, Thailand, withdraw money from automatic teller machines (ATMs).

**B** 5 What is money? In its usual definition, money is anything that is accepted as a medium of exchange and a store of value because it exists in limited quantities and, above all, because people have confidence in it. But at a market in Yemen, I found quite a few people who retained a more traditional view on what sort of money can be considered sound.

**C** 10 At Suq al Talh, a Saturday market close to the ancient city of Sadah, I found bearded money changers sitting on concrete steps, curved daggers strapped around their waists, automatic rifles resting on their laps. In front of them were bundles of bank notes—Yemeni rials—and stacks of silver coins. The coins were all dated 1780, and the lady portrayed on them was the Austrian
15 empress Maria Theresa. A man had just bought a thousand of them for 75,000 rials; I asked him why.

**D** "It is the main currency," he said. But isn't that what the rial is? He explained that in this area these coins are *omla saaba*, meaning hard currency. He then

20 walked off with 27 kilograms (60 pounds) of silver in a woven bag. "He bought them to make a profit," another man told me—they'd been going up in price; or, one might say, the rial had been going down.

**E**
25 "The people you saw in Sadah may be illiterate, but they know economic **affairs**," said Dr. Mohamed Said Al-Attar, when I visited him at the Ministry of Trade in Yemen's capital, Sana'a. He told me that in the 18th century, when French traders came to the port of
30 Mocha to buy coffee, the Yemenis didn't want French money, but they liked the Austrian coin, called a *taler*, because of its high silver content. (From *taler*, incidentally, comes the word *dollar*.)

**F** 35 The reputation of the Austrian taler spread through much of the Arabian Peninsula and to Ethiopia, where the coin circulated until the 1950s. "We introduced the rial bank note,"

40 Dr. Al-Attar added, "after the 1962 revolution had ousted[1] the monarchy. But for years we had difficulty getting people to trust paper money."

**G**
The official Austrian mint in Vienna continues to turn out Maria Theresa talers, still dated
45 1780. So do foreign imitators, said a merchant in the Sana'a *suq*, or market. "They have agents in Yemen buy talers, which are 83 percent silver," Dr. Al-Attar told me. "They melt them down, strike new ones, and send
50 them back to Yemen—less than 80 percent silver." Alas,[2] debasing[3] coinage for a bit of profit is almost as old as coinage itself.

---

**1** When a ruler, leader, or government is **ousted** from power, they are ejected or removed, usually against their will.

**2** The word **Alas** is used in literary or religious English to express sorrow, grief, pity, or concern.

**3** **Debasing** something means lowering its character, quality, or value.

∧ Cowrie shell money and terracotta coins that were during the Srivijaya reign in Thailand

*Despite these initial setbacks, paper money would eventually become the norm.*

## Coins, Notes, and Clams

**H**

55 Many of today's currencies—the Turkish lira, the British pound, and the Mexican peso—are named for units of weight once used to measure amounts of metal. Silver, gold, and copper have functioned as money throughout most of recorded history. The earliest
60 documented use of silver for payment appears around 2500 B.C. in Mesopotamian cuneiform tablets.

**I**

Some of the oldest known coins were made in the ancient kingdom of Lydia[4] in the seventh
65 century B.C.—tiny, thumbnail-size lumps of electrum, a pale yellow alloy of gold and silver, washed down by streams from limestone mountains. The coins were likely conceived as a convenience to the state, to be used as
70 a standard medium for payments to officials and for public expenditures. They were also useful for the collection of taxes **levied** by ancient rulers. But merchants, long used to settling accounts in precious metals, must have
75 found them useful, too; by using coins, they didn't have to do as much weighing for each **transaction**.

**J**

The idea of coinage spread from Asia Minor across the Mediterranean world. By the fourth
80 century B.C., a weight unit called the shekel lent its name to silver coins in the Middle East; gold was coined into the aureus of the Roman Empire, the dinar of Muslim lands, the florin of Florence, and the ducat of Venice.

**K** 85 The earliest paper currency issued by a government appeared in China in the 11th century. A couple of centuries later in Persia, the Mongol ruler Geikhatu tried to enforce the use of paper money, but merchants refused to
90 accept it. They closed their shops and hid their goods. Trade stopped. Facing revolt, Geikhatu **revised** his decision (the official who had originally suggested it was torn to pieces in a bazaar).

**L** 95 Despite these initial setbacks, paper money would eventually become the norm. The first European bank notes were printed in Sweden in 1661, when coins were in short supply. Soon after, paper notes were widespread
100 across continents.

**M**

But money hasn't always been metal or paper. One of the oldest forms may have been a shiny white or straw-colored mollusk[5] shell, just a couple of centimeters long, from the
105 Indian Ocean. It's called the cowrie, and from it derives the Chinese character *cai* (财), representing wealth, or money. I once saw a display of other forms of money collected by John Lenker of the International
110 Primitive Money Society—a bronze drum from Malaysia, a block of salt from Ethiopia, a bowl with 11 legs from Fiji. And wampum, once prized by North American Indians—tiny clamshell pieces drilled and strung together
115 like beads. "All these tell stories just as coins do," said Mr. Lenker.

---

4 **Lydia** was an ancient kingdom in western Turkey.

5 **Mollusks** are soft-bodied invertebrate animals, such as clams.

# A Means of Exchange

**N** The historian Fernand Braudel has pointed
out how, in the Middle Ages,[6] the role of
120 money—and hence trade and the entire
economy of Europe—got a boost from Italian
ingenuity. A new scheme was found to get
around the ban imposed by the Church on the
lending of money at interest. Merchants of
125 Tuscany, especially from Siena and Florence,
employed this new system at the fairs of
northeastern France in the 13th century. It
was called the bill of exchange, and it opened
the door to modern banking.

**O** 130 I asked Michele Cassandro, professor of
modern economic history at the University
of Siena, to **clarify** for me how it worked:
"It would say, for example, 'Signor A, having
received so many Sienese scudi, will pay
135 to Signor B so many Florentine florins at
such and such a place on such and such a
date.' That looks like a currency exchange
transaction, but in fact it is a loan agreement,
with the interest hidden in the amount of
140 florins Signor A will be paying." But there's
nothing that **specifies** it's a loan, and there's
no **clause** in the agreement that mentions
interest—so there's nothing illegal.

**P** Outside the Renaissance palace of the Monte
145 dei Paschi di Siena bank, I found another
example of Italian ingenuity: a foreign-
exchange machine, operating around the
clock for the convenience of tourists. Put
in bank notes in any of a dozen currencies,
150 such as the Japanese yen, the British pound,
or the Australian dollar. In no more than 15
seconds, a compartment opens, and there's
the equivalent in euros, down to the last
small coin. An electronic display shows the
155 exchange rates, fluctuating daily.

**Q** For many years after World War II, foreign-
exchange rates were pretty much fixed. I
remember seeing a Washington, D.C., exhibit
of bank notes from nearly every country in
160 the world, each with a notation of its value
in terms of the U.S. dollar; under the dollar
bill, it said "equal to one thirty-fifth of a troy
ounce[7] of gold." During this time, foreign
governments were allowed to redeem[8] dollars
165 for gold at the U.S. Treasury. But eventually
the demand increased so much that the
"gold-exchange standard" was suspended in
1971 and formally abandoned in 1978.

**R** Not that the world's governments have
170 discarded their gold bars—they keep lots of
them as part of their reserves. In the world's
largest gold depository, the subterranean
vaults of the Federal Reserve Bank of New
York, some 60 countries store over nine
175 million kilograms (10,000 tons) of gold
bullion.[9] The U.S. Treasury holds thousands of
tons more, mainly in the famous vaults at Fort
Knox, Kentucky; at West Point, New York;
and in Denver, Colorado.

**S** 180 The abandoning of the gold standard led to
a **paradigm** shift in the way currencies are
rated. Ever since the world's nations ceased
relying on a direct link between currency and
gold, currencies have been "floating" against
185 each other, at prices reflecting demand and
supply. Governments try to keep such prices
within certain limits, but—as has often been
the case in recent years—market forces
can bring about drastic fluctuations. In any
190 case, today's worldwide foreign-exchange
market is the biggest trading system ever,
with an estimated daily turnover[10] of one
trillion dollars.

---

**6** The **Middle Ages** (also called the medieval period) is a period of European history from the fifth century to the 15th
century, following the fall of the Western Roman Empire in 476 A.D.

**7** The **troy ounce** is the unit of weight traditionally used for precious metals such as gold and platinum (1 troy ounce =
0.0311 kilograms).

**8** If you **redeem** a debt or money that has been promised to you, it means you receive that money.

**9** **Bullion** refers to quantities of precious metals, such as bars of gold, being kept in storage as part of a country's reserves.

**10** The **daily turnover** of a company is the amount of revenue it receives per day.

# The Value of Money

**T** 195 Back home I came across a **formula** that bankers and financial analysts know, that in fact everybody should know—the rule of 72. No one is certain who first discovered the rule, but the principle is quite simple: Divide any 200 annual rate of return into 72 and the answer is the number of years it will take for a sum to double in financial terms.

**U** For instance, imagine you are charged 18 percent interest on the unpaid balance 205 of your credit-card account. Eighteen goes into 72 four times—so the debt will double in four years. The same will be true of any investment. Say your annual salary raise is 6 percent; that number goes into 72 twelve 210 times, so in twelve years your salary will double. And what if, at the same time, inflation runs at 6 percent a year? Then after a dozen years, your money will be worth half as much   so in a sense you'll be back where you 215 started!

**V** But look what can happen when inflation doesn't run at 6 percent, but rises at a much faster rate. That can occur when governments issue more and more currency to cover 220 increasing **obligations** as prices rise. When that happens, inflation can run wild.

A shopper pays a vendor at the Pettah market in Colombo, Sri Lanka—continuing the never-ending circulation of money.

**W** In 1986, Peru's currency—the sol, which is Spanish for sun—fell to 14,000 to the U.S. dollar. So the government cut off three zeros
225 and called it the inti, which means sun in Quechua, a language spoken by indigenous Peruvians. By mid-1991, a cup of coffee cost 500,000 intis. The government cut off six more zeros and called it the sol again. Over
230 five years, the inflation rate was 2,200,000 percent!

**X** The most drastic inflation ever? Hungary, 1946, after World War II, when Germany had taken away the national bank's
235 gold reserves. By June the Hungarian pengo appeared in notes of a million million billion, which would look like this: 1,000,000,000,000,000,000,000. Then the gold came back, confidence returned, and in
240 August, Hungary had a stable new currency, the forint.

∨ Credit cards have created a cashless society, by eliminating the hassle of carrying large sums of money around.

## Toward a Cashless Society?

**Y** Less than ten years after World War II, a new means for payment in place of currency
245 began to spread from the U.S. to much of the world—the use of so-called plastic money, meaning charge cards and credit cards. ATM cards for use in automated teller machines have since proliferated[11] across much of the
250 globe, while charge card payments are now commonplace everywhere from gas stations to supermarkets. In cities from London to Singapore, electronic scanners now allow road toll payments to be automatically deducted
255 without drivers having to slow their car.

**Z** From metal to notes to plastic, money has come a long way since its early days in ancient Mesopotamia more than four millennia ago. Soon, perhaps, we will all be living in a world
260 where money is virtual, where notes, coins, and plastic cards are things of the past. In whatever form it takes, money will likely continue to play a central role in our lives, providing the fuel that keeps society moving.

---

11 If something has **proliferated**, it has increased and spread at a rapid rate.

# Reading Comprehension

**Multiple Choice.** Choose the best answer for each question.

**Gist**

1. The best alternative title for this reading would be _____.
   a. Coins Now and in the Past
   b. From China to the World
   c. A Brief History of Money
   d. The Gold Standard

**Vocabulary**

2. The word *sound* in line 9 is closest in meaning to _____.
   a. distinctive          b. expensive
   c. old-fashioned        d. reliable

**Detail**

3. To the Yemenis in this article, *omla saaba* (hard currency) is represented by _____.
   a. Austrian talers       b. 18th-century French coins
   c. U.S. dollars          d. Yemeni rials

**Detail**

4. Which of the following is NOT true about the first bills of exchange?
   a. They provided a way for merchants to lend money despite a religious ban.
   b. They involved an exchange of different forms of currency.
   c. They represent an early stage in the development of modern banking.
   d. They were based on a fixed interest rate set by the government.

**Inference**

5. It can be inferred from paragraph Q that, in the 1970s, U.S. officials _____.
   a. wanted to increase the rate at which dollar bills could be exchanged for gold
   b. were worried that too much gold was flowing out of the U.S. Treasury
   c. decided to lower the rate at which the dollar was traded for other currencies
   d. thought that the exchange rate should be fixed as it had been after World War II

**Paraphrase**

6. Which of the following is closest in meaning to this sentence from lines 220–221? *When that happens, inflation can run wild.*
   a. When that happens, inflation can go down quickly.
   b. When that happens, inflation starts to go up little by little.
   c. When that happens, inflation can be out of control.
   d. When that happens, inflation can never be stopped.

**Detail**

7. Which of these forms of currency suffered the worst inflation?
   a. the sol      b. the inti      c. the pengo      d. the forint

**Critical Thinking**

**Evaluating:** Look through the article again, and list five things you did not previously know about money and five things you already knew. Compare your list with other students'.

**Discussion:** Do you agree with the author that the future of money is likely to be virtual? What do you think would be the pros and cons of a world without any physical money?

# Applying Information from a Text

To truly comprehend a text, it's important for readers to demonstrate that they can apply what they have learned. Applying information learned in a text can be done in various ways. For example, a reader may show comprehension by predicting what could happen in a certain situation, solving a problem using ideas put forth in a text, determining if statements are supported or contradicted by the text's claims, or drawing a logical conclusion based on ideas in the text.

**Application.** Based on information in the article, choose the best answer for each question.

1. Which of these scenarios would the Church have accepted in the Middle Ages?

    a. A man borrows money from a lender. He agrees to pay it back in six months with interest.

    b. A farmer receives a horse from a merchant. They agree that in one year the farmer will give the merchant two cows.

    c. A trader lends a man 100 Sienese scudi, on the condition that in ten days he will pay it all back, plus an extra three silver scudi.

    d. A bank lends a vendor 100 Florentine florins. After one month, the vendor pays the bank back the original 100 Florentine florins, plus 10 additional florins.

2. What could the world's governments do if they wanted to eliminate currency speculation by investors?

    a. print more money

    b. get inflation down to 0 percent

    c. release more gold into the market

    d. reintroduce the gold-exchange standard

3. According to the rule of 72, if you borrow $1,000 at an interest rate of 9% and do not pay any of it back, when will you owe $2,000?

    a. in 4 years      b. in 12 years      c. in 8 years      d. in 18 years

4. Which statement would the writer probably agree with the most?

    a. There will not be money in the future.

    b. The form may change, but there will always be money.

    c. Credit cards will continue to be a popular form of payment.

    d. Societies will go full circle and start using gold as money again.

# Vocabulary Practice

**A. Completion.** Complete the information using the correct form of words in the box. Two words are extra.

| | | | | |
|---|---|---|---|---|
| **affair** | **clarify** | **clause** | **formula** | **levy** |
| **obligated** | **paradigm** | **revise** | **specify** | **transaction** |

For centuries, porters carried heavy loads of tea from southwest China to Lhasa in Tibet. For these porters, who were **1.** _____ to travel hundreds of kilometers on foot, every pound of tea was worth a pound of rice. But as records of taxes **2.** _____ in ancient China show, the true reward for exporting tea to Tibet was horses.

Tea was first brought to Tibet in about A.D. 641, and quickly became popular as a hot drink in a cold climate. Moreover, a simple **3.** _____ of tea, yak butter, and salt could be stored for days, providing meals for herders working in harsh weather. By the 11th century, tea had become the main currency of China. In a typical **4.** _____, 130 pounds of tea were exchanged for a single Tibetan horse, based on a rate of exchange **5.** _____ by the Sichuan Tea and Horse Agency, established in 1074.

Soon, China was trading millions of pounds of tea for some 25,000 horses a year, a state of **6.** _____ that continued until the mid-19th century. When China's need for horses faded, traders **7.** _____ their strategies, returning instead with hides, precious metals, and medicinal plants that thrive only in Tibet. Today, the **8.** _____ for trade here has shifted to a very different arrangement. The Tibetans who once traded horses now trade dried caterpillars, highly in demand as a cure-all for aging bodies, in exchange for motorbikes and modern luxuries.

∧ Horses adapted to life on the Tibetan Plateau were renowned for being tireless and sure-footed.

**B. Definitions.** Use the correct form of words in the box in **A** to complete the definitions. Four words are extra.

1. An act of buying or selling is a(n) _____.

2. When you _____ something, you explain it to make the situation clearer.

3. If an organization or a government _____ a sum of money, you have to pay it.

4. When something is _____, it is changed to make it more appropriate for a particular purpose.

5. A legal document usually contains a number of _____.

6. When you are _____ to do something, it is your duty to do it.

> **Word Partnership**
> Use **obligation** with:
> (*adj.*) **legal** obligation, **moral** obligation; (*n.*) **sense of** obligation; (*v.*) **feel an** obligation, **fulfill an** obligation, **meet an** obligation.

< A mother and daughter looking at gold jewelry for sale at a shop in Dubai, United Arab Emirates

# Before You Read

**A. Understanding Charts.** Read the information on page 263 and circle whether each statement below is true (**T**) or false (**F**).

1. Without adjustment for inflation, the first time gold reached US$1,000 per ounce was in 2008.      **T**     **F**

2. With adjustment for inflation, gold's highest value ever was during the American Civil War.      **T**     **F**

3. More gold is used for exchange-traded funds than for electronics.      **T**     **F**

4. More gold is used for jewelry than all other uses combined.      **T**     **F**

**B. Skimming for Main Ideas.** The author breaks the main part of the article (pages 261–265) into five sections, indicated by section breaks. Look quickly through the article and match each section with its topic. Then read the passage to check your ideas.

Section 1 _____      a. how big mining companies are excavating the world's gold

Section 2 _____      b. the working life of a female truck driver at a gold mine

Section 3 _____      c. the attraction of gold from ancient to modern times

Section 4 _____      d. how a female truck driver feels about the pros and cons of her job

Section 5 _____      e. the influence of gold on India's economy and society

# GOLD FEVER

**A** 1 From an open mine in an Indonesian rain forest to an elaborate wedding ceremony in southern India, writer Brook Larmer follows the path of humanity's most desired commodity.

**B** 5 **AS A GIRL GROWING UP** on the remote Indonesian island of Sumbawa, Nur Piah heard tales about vast quantities of gold buried beneath the mountain rain forests. They were legends—until geologists from a U.S. company, Newmont Mining Corporation, discovered a curious green rock near a dormant[1] volcano about 13 kilometers (eight miles) from her home. 10 The rock's mossy color meant it contained copper, an occasional companion to gold, and it wasn't long before Newmont began setting up a mine named Batu Hijau, meaning "green rock."

**C** Nur Piah, then 24, replied to a Newmont ad seeking "operators," thinking that she might be able to get a job answering phones. When she arrived for 15 training, her boss showed her a different kind of operating booth—the cab of a Caterpillar 793, one of the world's largest trucks. Standing six meters (21 feet) tall and 13 meters (43 feet) long, the truck was bigger than her family home. Its wheels alone were double her height. "The truck terrified me," Nur Piah recalls. Another shock soon followed when she saw the 20 mine itself. "They had peeled the skin off the Earth!" she says. "I thought, whatever force can do that must be very powerful."

**D** Ten years later, Nur Piah, the daughter of a Muslim cleric, is part of that force herself. Pulling a pink head scarf close around her face, she smiles demurely[2] as she starts up the Caterpillar's engine and heads into the pit at 25 Batu Hijau. Her vehicle is part of a fleet of more than a hundred trucks that removes close to a hundred million tons of rock from the ground every year.

**E** For millions of years, a 550-meter (1,800-foot) volcano stood here; however today, no hint of it remains. Layers of rock have been removed, and the space the volcano once occupied has been turned into a 1.6-kilometer- 30 (one-mile-) wide pit that reaches more than a hundred meters (345 feet) below sea level. By the time the gold supplies at Batu Hijau have been **depleted**, the pit will be about 450 meters (1,500 feet) below sea level. The environmental impact doesn't concern Nur Piah anymore. "I only think about getting my salary," she says.

1 When a volcano is **dormant**, it is inactive but may become active in the future.

2 If an action is done **demurely**, it is done in a modest and reserved manner. The term is most often used with reference to young women.

**F** 35 **THERE IS ONE THING,** however, that Nur Piah finds curious: In a decade at Batu Hijau, she has never seen a speck of the gold she has helped mine. The engineers monitoring the process track its presence in the copper 40 compounds that are extracted. And since the gold is shipped out to smelters[3] overseas, nobody on Sumbawa ever sees the hidden treasure that has transformed their island.

**G** 45 Newmont is one of several giant mining corporations that are pursuing gold to the ends of the Earth, from the lowlands of Ghana to the mountaintops of Peru. Part of the challenge of mining for gold is that there is so little of it. In all of history, only about 160,000 50 tons (145 million kilograms) of gold have been mined, barely enough to fill two Olympic-size swimming pools. More than half of that has been extracted in the past 50 years. Now the world's richest deposits—particularly those in 55 the U.S., South Africa, and Australia—are fast being depleted, and new discoveries are rare.

**H** In recent years, attracted by the benefits of operating in the developing world—lower costs, higher yields, fewer regulations— 60 Newmont has generated tens of thousands of jobs in poorer regions of the world. But it has also come under attack from conservationists, who have **filed** complaints about **unrestrained** ecological destruction 65 and the forced relocation of villagers. At Batu Hijau, where Newmont is responsible for the mine's operation, the company has responded by spending more on its community development and environmental programs— 70 and by dismissing its critics.

**I** "Why is it that activists thousands of miles away are yelling, but nobody around the mine complains?" asks Malik Salim, Batu Hijau's former senior external relations manager. 75 "Gold is what drives everybody crazy."

**J** **GOLD HAS BEEN DRIVING** people crazy for millennia. The desire to possess gold has driven people to extremes, fueling wars and conquests, boosting empires and 80 currencies, leveling mountains and forests.

Gold is not vital to human existence; it has, in fact, relatively few practical uses. Yet its chief attractions—its unusual density and malleability,[4] along with its imperishable[5] 85 shine—have made it one of the world's most desired commodities, a symbol of beauty, wealth, and immortality. From pharaohs (who chose to be buried in what they called the "flesh of the gods") to financiers (who, 90 following Sir Isaac Newton's advice, made it the foundation of the global economy), nearly every society has invested gold with an almost mythological status.

**K** 95 Humankind's feverish attachment to gold shouldn't have survived the modern world. Few cultures still believe that gold can give eternal life, and every country in the world— the United States was last, in 1971—has done away with the gold standard, which the 100 economist John Maynard Keynes[6] famously called "a barbarous[7] relic." But gold's appeal not only endures; fueled by global uncertainty, it grows stronger.

**L** Aside from extravagance,[8] gold is also 105 **reprising** its role as a safe haven in financially unstable times. Gold's recent surges have been amplified by concerns over a looming global recession. In 2007, demand exceeded mine production by 59 percent. "Gold has 110 always had this kind of magic," says Peter L. Bernstein, author of *The Power of Gold*. "But it's never been clear if we have gold—or gold has us."

---

3 **Smelters** are people or companies that melt ores in order to extract the metals they contain.

4 **Malleability** refers to the ease with which an object or a person can be altered and changed.

5 If a thing is **imperishable**, it never dies out or disappears.

6 **John Maynard Keynes** (1883–1946) was an influential British economist.

7 If something is described as **barbarous**, it is considered primitive and uncivilized.

8 **Extravagance** is the spending of more money than is reasonable or than you can afford.

# What It's Worth

In coins and later backing for paper money, the price of gold has fluctuated with world crises and market forces. After 1971, when the dominant U.S. dollar was no longer tied to gold, the metal became a freely traded commodity. It reached US$1,000 per ounce for the first time in March 2008, but in real terms, its actual value was still well below its peak in the early 1980s.

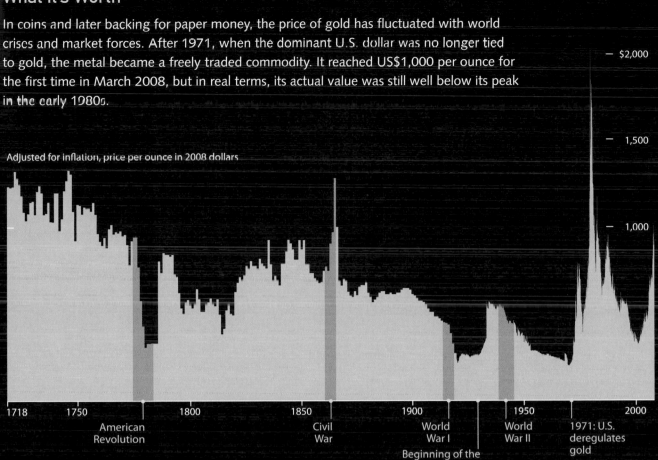

Adjusted for inflation, price per ounce in 2008 dollars

— $2,000
— 1,500
— 1,000

1718    1750    1800    1850    1900    1950    2000

American Revolution

Civil War

World War I

Beginning of the Great Depression

World War II

1971: U.S. deregulates gold

# How It's Used

Jewelry dominates gold consumption. The metal is also widely used in electronics as an efficient and reliable conductor of electricity. Gold-backed investment funds (exchange-traded funds, or ETFs) became popular as a "safe option" during the financial crisis beginning in mid-2008.

JEWELRY

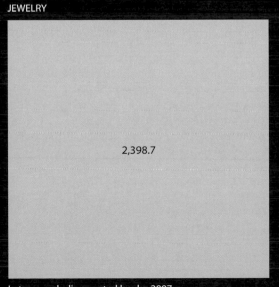

2,398.7

In tons, excluding central banks, 2007

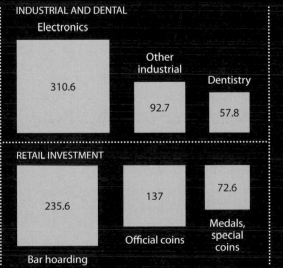

INDUSTRIAL AND DENTAL

Electronics
310.6

Other industrial
92.7

Dentistry
57.8

RETAIL INVESTMENT

Bar hoarding
235.6

Official coins
137

Medals, special coins
72.6

EXCHANGE-TRADED FUNDS
253.3

**M**
While investors flock to gold-backed funds, jewelry still accounts for two-thirds of the demand, generating a record $53.5 billion in worldwide sales in 2007. In the U.S., an activist-driven "No Dirty Gold" campaign has persuaded many top jewelry retailers to stop selling gold from mines that cause severe social or environmental damage. But such concerns have little impact on the biggest consumer nations, namely China—which surpassed the U.S. in 2007 to become the world's second largest buyer of gold jewelry—and, above all, India.

**N**
**NOWHERE IS THE GOLD OBSESSION** more culturally entrenched[9] than in India. Per capita income in this country of 1.2 billion people is $2,700, but it has been the world's runaway leader in gold demand for several decades. In 2007, India consumed 773.6 tons of gold, about 20 percent of the world gold market and more than double that purchased by either of its closest followers, China (363.3 tons) and the U.S. (278.1 tons). India produces very little gold of its own, but its citizens have hoarded[10] up to 18,000 tons of the yellow metal—more than 40 times the amount held in the country's central bank.

**O**
India's obsession stems not simply from a love of extravagance, or the rising prosperity of an emerging middle class. For Muslims, Hindus, Sikhs, and Christians alike, gold plays a central role at nearly every turning point in life—most of all when a couple marries. There are some ten million weddings in India every year, and in all but a few, gold is crucial both to the spectacular event itself and to the transaction between families and generations. "It's written into our DNA," says K.A. Babu, a manager at the Alapatt jewelry store in the southwestern city of Kochi. "Gold equals good fortune."

**P**
The importance of gold is most obvious during the springtime festival of Akshaya Tritiya, considered the most **auspicious** day to buy gold according to the Hindu calendar. The quantity of gold jewelry Indians purchase on this day—49 tons in 2008—so exceeds the amount bought on any other day of the year throughout the world that it often pushes gold prices higher.

**Q**
"We grow up in an atmosphere of gold," says Renjith Leen, a magazine editor based in Kerala, a relatively prosperous state on India's southern tip that claims just 3 percent of the country's population but 7 to 8 percent of its gold market. When a baby is born, a grandmother rubs a gold coin in honey and places a drop of the liquid on the child's tongue for good luck. When the child is three years old, a learned family member takes a gold coin and traces words on the child's tongue to give the gift of eloquence.[11]

**R**
Aside from its cultural significance, gold is also the bedrock of the Indian economy. "Gold is the basis of our financial system," says K.A. Babu. "People see it as the best form of security, and nothing else lets you get cash as quickly." Hoarding gold as an intergenerational family nest egg[12] is an ancient tradition in India. So, too, is pawning[13] gold jewelry for emergency loans—and then buying it back.

**S**
As the price of the metal goes up, however, poor Indian families are having a harder time raising the gold they need for dowries.[14] Rajam Chidambaram, a 59-year-old widow living in a slum on the outskirts of Kochi, recently found a young man to marry her only daughter, age 27. The groom's family, however, demanded a dowry far out of her reach: 25 sovereigns, or 200 grams (seven

---

9 If a custom or an idea is **entrenched**, it is firmly established and difficult to change.

10 When something is **hoarded**, it is accumulated and kept hidden away for future use.

11 Someone who has the gift of **eloquence** can write and speak very well.

12 Someone's **nest egg** refers to their monetary savings, which have been put aside for later use.

13 **Pawning** is the act of giving or depositing personal property as security for payment of money borrowed.

14 **Dowries** are portions of money or property given by a bride's family to her husband at marriage.

ounces), of gold (worth more than $9,000 today). Chidambaram, a cleaning woman, has only the two earrings she wears; the gold necklace she once owned went to pay off her deceased husband's hospital bills. "I had to agree to the groom's demand," Chidambaram says, wiping away tears. "If I refuse, my daughter will stay home forever."

In the end, local financiers advanced a loan for her daughter's dowry. Her daughter may now be married, but Chidambaram is now faced with a debt that she may spend the rest of her life trying to repay.

**FOUR THOUSAND KILOMETERS** (2,500 miles) away, in her new house in the village of Jereweh, Nur Piah is focused more on the present than the future. "So many people depend on me," she says. Her husband makes some money as a timber trader, but Nur Piah's salary—about $650 a month—paid for their two-story concrete home. As if in tribute, she has hung a large painting of the yellow Caterpillar 793 on her wall.

Nur Piah's job is not without its **hardships**. Maneuvering the enormous truck over a 12-hour shift is especially stressful, she says, when the pit's graded roads are slicked by torrential rains. But now, after a long day, she smiles contentedly as her child, age six, falls asleep on her lap. The girl's middle name? Higrid, the Indonesian approximation of "high-**grade**," the best ore in the mine.

# A Golden Wedding

The gold ornaments come out of the velvet boxes one by one, family treasures that Nagavi, a 23-year-old Indian bride, always knew she would wear on her wedding day. The eldest daughter of a coffee plantation owner in the southern Indian state of Karnataka, Nagavi grew up marveling at the weddings that mark the **merger** of two wealthy Indian families. But not until the morning of her own arranged wedding to the only son of another coffee plantation family does she understand just how beautiful the golden tradition can be.

By the time Nagavi is ready for her wedding, the university graduate has been transformed into an Indian princess, covered in gold. An elaborately crafted hairpiece is so heavy—two and a half kilograms (5.5 pounds)—that it pulls her head back. Three gold necklaces and a dozen other pieces of jewelry act as effective counterweights. As the family members **convene**, Nagavi walks slowly out of her home, trying to keep her balance as she tosses rice over her head in a traditional gesture of farewell.

The gold treasures Nagavi wears are not a traditional dowry. In this circle of coffee growers around the town of Chikmagalur—unlike in many poorer parts of the country—it is considered inappropriate for a groom's family to make **explicit** demands. "This is seen as my 'share' of the family wealth," says Nagavi, gazing at the millions of dollars of gold jewelry. As with any Indian wedding, the gold also serves to display the value she brings to the union. "With daughters, you have to start saving gold from the day they are born," says Nagavi's father, C.P. Ravi Shankar. "It's important to marry them off well."

∧ Wearing her fortune, from gold threads in her sari to a priceless golden headpiece, Nagavi prepares for her elaborate wedding day.

# Reading Comprehension

**Multiple Choice.** Choose the best answer for each question.

**Purpose**

1. What is the main purpose of paragraph G?
   a. to show how gold production has decreased in the past 50 years
   b. to emphasize that gold is actually a very rare commodity
   c. to point out how successful giant mining companies have been
   d. to indicate that some rich new gold deposits have been found

**Cohesion**

2. Where would be the best place to insert this sentence in paragraph H? *For example, it stresses its efforts to reclaim the heaps of discarded rock, by covering them with soil and allowing the jungle to grow again.*
   a. before the first sentence
   b. after the first sentence
   c. after the second sentence
   d. after the third sentence

**Inference**

3. The quote from John Maynard Keynes in line 101 shows that Keynes thought that _____.
   a. the U.S. should have maintained the gold standard
   b. gold's appeal was about to end
   c. the gold standard was out of date
   d. no one still believed that gold gives eternal life

**Detail**

4. Today, the country that consumes the second largest amount of gold jewelry is _____.
   a. China
   b. India
   c. the United States
   d. Indonesia

**Application**

5. Given the information in paragraph N, approximately how many tons of gold are held in the central bank of India?
   a. 450    b. 775    c. 18,000    d. 720,000

**Cause and Effect**

6. Which of the following causes Nur Piah the most job-related stress?
   a. the difficulty of finding gold
   b. the low wages she receives
   c. driving her truck in bad weather
   d. spending long hours at work

**Detail**

7. Which of the following is true about Nagavi?
   a. Her husband used to work on her father's coffee plantation.
   b. She got married after she graduated from university.
   c. Her family is from a very poor part of India.
   d. She is her father's only daughter.

## Critical Thinking

**Analyzing:** Why do you think the author focuses on the personal stories of Nur Piah and Nagavi? Do the stories effectively support the main focus of the article?

**Discussion:** Imagine that a mining company has found a rich deposit of gold near your hometown. The company has promised to bring 4,000 well-paying jobs to your town if it is allowed to mine the gold. Would you favor the company's plan or oppose it? Why?

# Identifying Coherence Devices

Authors use a number of devices to achieve coherence. These expressions join together paragraphs, sentences, and parts of a sentence. Coherence makes an article feel unified and whole. Examples include:

**Personal pronouns** (*it, he, they,* etc.): Newmont is an American mining company. It is based in Denver, Colorado. (*It* links the second sentence to Newmont in the first sentence.)

**Demonstratives** (*this, that, these, those*): Only about 160,000 tons of gold have ever been mined. And about half of that has been extracted. (*That* joins the second sentence to the first by referring to "about 160,000 tons of gold" in the first sentence.)

**Forms of *other*** (*another, other, others*): One place mining companies have looked for gold is in the lowlands of Ghana. Another is in the mountains of Peru. (*One place* is linked to the word *Another* in the second sentence.)

**Conjunctions** (*and, but, or, yet,* etc.): Gold is not vital to human existence, yet it is one of the world's most valued commodities. (*Yet* joins the two sentences and shows the contrast.)

**Signal words** (*therefore, however, in addition, for example,* etc.): The gold ore that is found on Sumbawa is all shipped overseas. Therefore, no one on the island sees any pure gold. (*Therefore* links the two sentences by showing the relationship of cause/effect.)

**Synonyms:** Aside from its cultural significance, gold is also the bedrock of the Indian economy. "Gold is the basis of our financial system." (*Bedrock* and *basis* are synonyms; so are *economy* and *financial system*. The use of these synonyms links the two sentences.)

**Scanning and Classification.** Look again at the first page of the article (page 261). Scan for one example of each coherence device and note them in the chart.

| Type | Coherence device |
|---|---|
| **Personal pronouns** | |
| **Demonstratives** | |
| **Forms of *other*** | |
| **Conjunctions** | |
| **Signal words** | |
| **Synonyms** | |

## Vocabulary Practice

**A. Definitions.** Read the information below and match each word in **red** with its definition.

Mongolia has some of the Earth's largest high-**grade** gold, copper, and uranium reserves. At present, the mining industry makes up two-thirds of Mongolia's export transactions. For many, such a mining boom marks an **auspicious** time in the growth of the country's economy.

But as mining companies rush to extract Mongolia's vast deposits of gold and other minerals, government regulations—including laws that **explicitly** state that mining may not be done near rivers—are being violated or ignored. Many rivers now run dry, or are polluted, making it difficult for nomadic herders to find water for their animals.

In addition, many of the mining sites abandoned by larger companies due to protests **filed** by local activists, or because their resources have been **depleted**, have been taken over by illegal miners known as "ninjas." Such ninja miners **convene** in remote settlements, where their unofficial status has allowed for the **unrestrained** use of mercury in the mines, which pollute and poison nearby rivers. Environmentalists are concerned that the situation is grim for the survival of nomadic herders. They will face additional **hardships** since they are the ones who depend on the Mongolian land and its waters for their way of life.

∧ A father and son pan and sieve for gold from the extracts of soil taken from underground in the Sharygol district of Mongolia.

1. _____: clearly and directly

2. _____: favorable, lucky

3. _____: reduced in quantity

4. _____: level of quality

5. _____: made as an official complaint or request

6. _____: uncontrolled

7. _____: come together

8. _____: pain and suffering

> **Word Link**
> The suffix **-ship** has the meaning of *state* or *condition*: e.g., hard**ship**, friend**ship**, intern**ship**, court**ship**, partner**ship**, scholar**ship**, relation**ship**, member**ship**.

**B. Completion.** Complete the information by circling the correct word in each pair.

In India, gold is an important element in the **1. (merger / reprise)** of two families through marriage. In the wedding transaction, it is usual for the groom's family to make **2. (auspicious / explicit)** requests for the bride to bring gold jewelry into the family. Even relatively poor Indian families are required to provide gold for a daughter's wedding, sometimes **3. (reprising / depleting)** the process if they have more than one daughter. When the families finally **4. (convene / deplete)** for the wedding, the gold is worn by the bride to publicly display the value she has brought to the marriage.

# VIEWING The Art Smuggler

## Before You Watch

**Matching.** You will hear these phrases in the video. What do you think they mean? Match each phrase (**a–f**) to its meaning.

**a.** . . . [He] does not deny that he has **bent the rules** . . .

**b.** . . . he's had a very **colorful** past.

**c.** . . . knowing you have a stolen object. You have **laundered** it, and you can sell it . . .

**d.** . . . the tomb walls have been **stripped bare**.

**e.** . . . but justice does sometimes **prevail** . . .

**f.** . . . give hope that something can be done to **stem** the trade . . .

1. _____ to stop or hold back

2. _____ lively and exciting

3. _____ to win out over, or against, someone or something

4. _____ did something that is not usually allowed

5. _____ removed everything

6. _____ disguised the source or nature of something, for example, illegal funds, by channeling them through an intermediate agent

## While You Watch

**A. Completion.** You are going to watch a video about a former art smuggler. As you watch, choose the correct words to make the sentences true.

1. Michel Van Rijn used to be an art smuggler, but now he's an (**art historian** / **art theft consultant**).

2. The two parts of smuggling art that are mentioned are moving the artifacts and (**making them appear legal** / **finding a legitimate buyer**).

3. One legitimate tool that is often used by smugglers to hide an object's tracks is the (**Art Loss Register** / **Gallery Owners' Database**).

4. Some collectors justify their illegal transactions by saying they are (**then able to identify the smugglers** / **saving endangered antiquities**).

5. Richard Ellis states that when an object is illegally excavated, it loses its (**value** / **context**).

6. In 2006, the United States returned some vases to (**Greece** / **Italy**) after it was proved that they had been looted decades earlier.

**B. Completion.** Watch the video again and complete the summary using the correct words from the box. Two words are extra.

| | | | |
|---|---|---|---|
| context | convene | deny | deplete |
| expose | fake | formula | illusion |
| recovery | transactions | valid | value |

Michel Van Rijn was once an infamous art smuggler. He does not **1.** _____ his colorful past, nor that he has bent the rules. Today, Van Rijn works as a consultant, helping the police to **2.** _____ art crimes. So far, he has participated in the **3.** _____ of several valuable works of art around the world.

Van Rijn explains that it is often quite easy for smugglers to give stolen art and artifacts the **4.** _____ of legal status before shipping them elsewhere to be sold. These pieces are usually sold in major cities, such as New York and London, where art smugglers and buyers often **5.** _____.

One way to make a piece of stolen art seem legal is to create a **6.** _____ paper trail. For example, if only the smugglers know a piece of art exists, they can send a photo of the object to the Art Loss Register. They may then receive a **7.** _____ letter certifying that it does not match any record of known stolen art. From then on, the **8.** _____ involved will seem to be perfectly legal.

Sadly, the profitability of the illegal art trade continues to motivate people to steal art and artifacts. By completely removing items from their original **9.** _____, art theft often prevents historians from discovering their true histories, and with it, their true **10.** _____ as artifacts of the past.

## After You Watch

**Discussion.** Discuss these questions with a partner.

1. Do you think former criminals such as Michel Van Rijn should be allowed to help with police investigations? Should it depend on the nature of the crime?

2. What do you think should happen to people who are caught selling stolen art? What about people buying stolen art? Do you think one crime is worse than the other?

3. Think of some works of art and historical pieces that are extremely valuable. Why are they worth so much money? Is it due mainly to their beauty, rarity, fame, or another reason?

# Photo Credits

**1** Sasha Gusov/Axiom Photographic Agency/Getty Images, **3** David Boyer/NGC, **4–5** Paul Nicklen/NGC, **7** Robert Harding World Imagery RF/Alamy, **8–9, 15–17** (t) Paul Nicklen/NGC, **11** f9photos/Shutterstock.com, **12–13, 16** Juan Velasco, NGM Staff. Art by Hernán Cañellas. Sources: Guillermo De Anda, University of Yucatán; Arturo Montero, University of Tepeyac, **17** hannahgleg/iStockphoto, **18–19, 24–26** (t) Paul Chesley/NGC, **20** Craig Lovell/Eagle Visions Photography/Alamy, **23** Scott S. Warren/NGC, **26** Pete Mcbride/NGC, **27** Paul Chesley/NGC, **28** (tl) (tr) (bl) (br) National Geographic, **29** ALMA ESO/NAOJ/NRAO and NASA/ESA Hubble SPA/NGC, **30–31** Babak Tafreshi/NGC, **33** (t) (c) (b) Dave Yoder/NGC, **34–35** Jason Treat/NGC, **36** Dave Yoder/NGC, **37–39** Dave Yoder/NGC, **39** (cr) Dorling Kindersley/Getty Images, **40–41, 46–48** (t) JPL/NASA, **42–43** Art by Sean McNaughton, NG Staff. Sources: Extrasolar Planets Encyclopaedia Database; NASA Star and Exoplanet Database (August 2009 Data), **45** ESA, P. Kalas and J. Graham (University of California, Berkeley) and M. Clampin (NASA/GSFC)/NASA, **48** (cr) JulienTromeur/Shutterstock.com, **49** Art Directors & TRIP/Alamy, **50** (c) Art Directors & TRIP/Alamy, **51** Simone Perolari/LUZ/Redux, **52–53** Robert Clark/NGC, **54** Robert Clark/NGC, **56–57, 59–61** (t) Robert Clark/NGC, **58** Sources: Richard A. Lange, Johns Hopkins Hospital; Peter Libby, Brigham and Women's Hospital; Eric J. Topol, Scripps Clinic; Thomas Thom, National Heart, Lung, and Blood Institute. Art by Bryan Christie, **61** (cr) Robert Clark/NGC, **62–63, 68–70** (t) Todd Gipstein/NGC, **64** Alila Medical Media/Shutterstock.com, **66–67** gorillaimages/Shutterstock.com, **70** (cr) Education Images/Getty Images, **71** (tl) John Foxx Images/Imagestate, **71** (tc) Dr. Cloud/Shutterstock.com, **71** (tr) Jctabb/Shutterstock.com, **71** (cl) Fabio Alcini/Shutterstock.com, **71** (c) John Bill/Shutterstock.com, **71** (cr) Mazzzur/Shutterstock.com, **71** (bl) Creatas/Jupiterimages, **71** (bc) Freya-photographer/Shutterstock.com, **71** (br) David Robertson/Alamy, **73** Nick Kaloterakis/NGC, **74** Jodi Cobb/NGC, **75** Joe Petersburger/NGC, **76** Design Pics Inc/NGC, **78–79** Marco Secchi/Getty Images, **80–82** James P. Blair/NGC, **81** (cr) Island Images/Alamy, **82** Bloomberg/Getty Images, **83** AP Images/Charles Sykes, **85, 90–92** Danielle Richards/Sipa Press/Newscom, **88–89** Frans Lemmens/Getty Images, **89** (br) Niels van Kampenhout/Alamy, **92** (cr) Philip Scalia/Alamy, **93** Edwin Remsberg/Alamy, **94** The Washington Post/Getty Images, **95** Erin Patric O'Brien/The New York Times/Redux, **96–97, 102–104** (t) Tyrone Turner/NGC, **100–101** Brent Winebrenner/Getty Images, **104** (cr) Chris Fitzgerald/Candidate Photos/Newscom, **105** Michael Melford/NGC, **106–107, 112–114** (t) David Nunuk/All Canada Photos/Alamy, **108–109** Michael Melford/NGC, **114** (cr) Thomas Trutschel/Getty Images, **115** National Geographic, **117** Rodrigo Buendia/Getty Images, **118–119, 124–126** (t) Paul Sutherland/NGC, **126** (cr) Brian J. Skerry/NGC, **127** Joel Sartore/NGC, **128–129** AP Images/International Rhino Foundation, **131** Joel Sartore/NGC, **132** (tr) (cl) (cr) (bl) (br) Joel Sartore/NGC, **133** (tl) (tr) (cl) (cr) (bl) (br) Joel Sartore/NGC, **134** (tl) (tr) Joel Sartore/NGC, **135** (tl) (tr) Joel Sartore/NGC, **136** (tl) Joel Sartore/NGC, **136** (cr) Mark Bowler/Nature Picture Library, **138** (t) (b) (c) National Geographic, **139** Mark Thiessen/NGC, **140–140** Robert Clark/NGC, **142–143, 147–149** (l) Pasieka/Getty Images, **145** Robert Clark/NGC, **146** AKG Images, **149** DigitalStock/Corbis, **150** Bryan Christie Design/NGC, **151** Mark Thiessen/NGC, **152–153** Mark Thiessen/NGC, **154, 156–158** (t) Mark Thiessen/NGC, **157** (br) Fabrice Coffrini/Getty Images, **158** (cr) Mark Thiessen/NGC, **159** Brian Snyder/Reuters, **160** Aurora Photos/Alamy, **161** Thomas Dressler/age fotostock, **162–163** Minden Pictures/SuperStock, **164** Bazzano Photography/Alamy, **167** James L. Amos/Science Source, **168–170** LilKar/Shutterstock.com, **170** (cr) Beverly Joubert/NGC, **171** Amazon-Images/Alamy, **173** Frans Lanting/NGC, **174–175, 178–180** (t) Dr. Paul Zahl/Science Source, **176–177** Bence Mate/Nature Picture Library, **180** (cr) skynetphoto/Shutterstock.com, **181** (cl) Le Do/Shutterstock.com, **181** (c) Lisa Thornberg/iStockphoto, **183** DEA Picture Library/Getty Images, **184–185, 191–193** (t) WorldPhotos /Alamy, **186** Print Collector/Getty Images, **189** DEA Picture Library/Getty Images, **190** World History Archive/Alamy, **193** (cr) James L. Amos/NGC, **194** Victor R. Boswell, Jr/NGC, **195** artform/Shutterstock.com, **196–197, 200–202** Paul Colangelo/NGC, **199** Paul Nicklen/NGC, **202** (cr) Michael DeFreitas South America/Alamy, **203** (bl) (br) National Geographic, **204** (tl) (tr) (cl) (cr) National Geographic, **205** David Boyer/NGC, **206–207, 212–214** James P. Blair/NGC, **209** Peter Essick/NGC, **210** Peter Essick/NGC, **214** (tr) Eric Isselee/Shutterstock.com, **215** RIA Novosti/Alamy, **216–217, 222–224** isak55/Shutterstock.com, **224** Everett Collection/SuperStock, **225** National Geographic, **227** Omar Salem/AFP/Getty Images, **229** ihsan Gercelman/Shutterstock.com, **230, 235–237** Funkystock/Getty Images, **233** James L.Stanfield/NGC, **234** Roxelana, Suleyman's wife (oil on canvas), Unknown Artist, (16th century)/Topkapi Palace Museum, Istanbul, Turkey/Sonia Halliday Photographs/Bridgeman Images, **236** Suleiman II (oil on canvas), Italian School, (16th century)/Kunsthistorisches Museum, Vienna, Austria/Bridgeman Images, **237** age fotostock/Alamy, **238, 244–246** Nils-Johan Norenlind/age fotostock/Getty Images, **240** Jeff Mauritzen/NGC, **243** Cornfield/Shutterstock.com, **246** (cr) View of Toledo, c.1597–99 (oil on canvas), Greco, El (Domenico Theotocopuli) (1541–1614)/Metropolitan Museum of Art, New York, USA/Bridgeman Images, **247** (tl) r.nagy/Shutterstock.com, **247** (tc) Paul Brighton/Shutterstock.com, **247** (tr) SEUX Paule/hemis.fr/Shutterstock.com, **248** SmileStudio/Shutterstock.com, **249** Randy Olson/NGC, **250** Dinodia Photos/Alamy, **251** Leonid Plotkin/Alamy, **252, 257–259** Robert Harding Picture Library Ltd/Luca Tettoni/Alamy, **255** David Evans/NGC, **256** aodaodaodaod/Shutterstock.com, **259** (cr) Buena Vista Images/Photolibrary/Getty Images, **260** Design Pics Inc/NGC, **265** Randy Olson/NGC, **266–268** Dabarti CGI/Shutterstock.com, **268** (cr) Jonas Gratzer/LightRocket/Getty Images, **269** National Geographic

NGC = National Geographic Creative

# Illustration Credits

**14, 110, 192, 242** National Geographic Maps, **86** Ryan Morris, NGM Staff. Sources: Felix Landerer, NASA/JPL; M. Perrette et al., 2013; Organisation for Economic Co-Operation and Development, **87** Lawson Parker, NGM Staff. Sources: Josh Willis, NASA/JPL; John Church and Neil White, Commonwealth Scientific and Industrial Research Organisation; Andrew Kemp et al., 2011; R. Steven Nerem et al., 2010; NOAA, **99** Sean Mcnaughton/NGC, **120–121** Map: Ryan Morris, NGM Staff. Source: Barbara Block, Stanford University. Graphic: Fernando G. Baptista and Lawson Parker, NGM Staff; Shizuka Aoki. Sources: Barbara Block, Stanford University; Bruce Collette, IUCN Tuna and Billfish Specialist Group; Don Stevens, University of Guelph, **123** Maps and Graphic: Ryan Morris, NGM Staff. Illustrations: Kirsten Huntley. Sources: FAO Fisheries and Aquaculture Department; International Union for Conservation of Nature and Natural Resources; Shana Miller, The Ocean Foundation, **181** William E. Mcnulty/NGC, **220–221** John Tomanio, NGM Staff; Tony Schick. Consultants: Paul Karol, Carnegie Mellon University; Roger Henderson, Lawrence Livermore National Laboratory. Sources: International Union of Pure and Applied Chemistry; National Nuclear Data Center, Brookhaven National Laboratory, **228** Lisa Bignzoli/NGC, **263** (t) (b) Charles M. Blow. Sources: Nick Laird, Sharelynx Gold (prices); World Gold Council (uses),

# Text Credits

**9–14** Adapted from "Secrets of the Maya Otherworld," by Alma Guillermoprieto: NGM August 2013, **19–23** Adapted from "Diving Angkor," by Richard Stone: NGM July 2009, **31–36** Adapted from "Cosmic Dawn," by Yudhijit Bhattacharjee: NGM April 2014, **41–45** Adapted from "Worlds Apart," by Timothy Ferris: NGM December 2009, **53–58** Adapted from "Mending Broken Hearts," by Jennifer Kahn: NGM February 2007, **63–67** Adapted from "Misery for All Seasons," by Judith Newman: NGM May 2006, **75–79** Adapted from "Vanishing Venice," by Cathy Newman: NGM August 2009, **84–89** Adapted from "Rising Seas," by Tim Fogler: NGM September 2013, **97–101** Adapted from "It Starts At Home," by Peter Miller: NGM March 2009, **106–111** Adapted from "Plugging Into the Sun," by George Johnson: NGM September 2009, **119–123** Adapted from "Quicksilver," by Kenneth Brower: NGM March 2014, **128–133** Adapted from "Building the Ark," by Elizabeth Kolbert: NGM October 2013, **147–146** Adapted from "Brain Science," by Carl Zimmer: NGM February 2014, **151–155** Adapted from "Bionics," by Josh Fischman: NGM January 2010, **163–167** Adapted from "The Genius of Swarms," by Peter Miller: NGM July 2007, **172–177** Adapted from "Edward O. Wilson: From Ants, Onward," by Tim Appenzeller: NGM May 2006, **185–190** Adapted from "A Man for All Ages," by Kenneth MacLeish: NGM September 1977, **195–199** Adapted from "The Power of Writing," by Joel L. Swerdlow: NGM August 1999, **207–211** Adapted from "The Pollution Within," by David Ewing Duncan: NGM October 2006, **216–221** Adapted from "Element Hunters," by Rob Dunn: NGM May 2013, **229–234** Adapted from "The World of Süleyman the Magnificient," by Merle Severy: NGM November 1987, **239–243** Adapted from "When the Moors Ruled Spain," by Thomas J. Abercrombie: NGM July 1988, **251–256** Adapted from "The Power of Money," by Peter T. White: NGM January 1993, **261–265** Adapted from "The Real Price of Gold," by Brook Larmer: NGM January 2009

NGM = National Geographic Magazine

# Acknowledgments

The Authors and Publisher would like to thank the following teaching professionals for their valuable feedback during the development of this series:

**Ahmed Mohamed Motala**, University of Sharjah; **Ana Laura Gandini**, Richard Anderson School; **Andrew T. Om**, YBM PINE R&D; **Dr. Asmaa Awad**, University of Sharjah; **Atsuko Takase**, Kinki University, Osaka; **Bogdan Pavliy**, Toyama University of International Studies; **Brigitte Maronde**, Harold Washington College, Chicago; **Bunleap Heap**, American Intercon Institute; **Carey Bray**, Columbus State University; **Carmella Lieske**, Shimane University; **Chanmakara Hok**, American Intercon Institute; **Choppie Tsann Tsang Yang**, National Taipei University; **Cynthia Ross**, State College of Florida; **David Schneer**, ACS International, Singapore; **Dawn Shimura**, St. Norbert College; **David Barrett**, Goldenwest College, CA; **Dax Thomas**, Keio University; **Deborah E. Wilson**, American University of Sharjah; **Elizabeth Rodacker**, Bakersfield College; **Emma Tamaianu-Morita**, Akita University; **Fu-Dong Chiou**, National Taiwan University; **Gavin Young**, Iwate University; **George Galamba**, Woodland Community College; **Gigi Santos**, American Intercon Institute; **Gursharan Kandola**, Language and Culture Center, University of Houston, TX; **Heidi Bundschoks**, ITESM, Sinaloa Mexico; **Helen E. Roland**, ESL/FL Miami-Dade College-Kendall Campus; **Hiroyo Yoshida**, Toyo University; **Hisayo Murase**, Doshisha Women's College of Liberal Arts; **Ikuko Kashiwabara**, Osaka Electro-Communication University; **J. Lorne Spry**, Contracting University Lecturer; **Jamie Ahn**, English Coach, Seoul; **Jane Bergmann**, The University of Texas at San Antonio; **Jennie Farnell**, University of Connecticut; **José Olavo de Amorim**, Colegio Bandeirantes, Sao Paulo; **Kyoungnam Shon**, Avalon English; **Luningning C. Landingin**, American Intercon Institute; **Mae-Ran Park**, Pukyong National University, Busan; **Mai Minh Tiên**, Vietnam Australia International School; **Marina Gonzalez**, Instituto Universitario de Lenguas Modernas Pte., Buenos Aires; **Mark Rau**, American River College, Sacramento CA; **Max Heineck**, Academic Coordinator/Lecturer, King Fahd University of Petroleum & Minerals; **Dr. Melanie Gobert**, Higher Colleges of Technology; **Michael C. Cheng**, National Chengchi University; **Michael Johnson**, Muroran Institute of Technology; **Michael McGuire**, Kansai Gaidai University; **Muriel Fujii**, University of Hawaii; **Patrick Kiernan**, Meiji University; **Philip Suthons**, Aichi Shukutoku University; **Renata Bobakova**, English Programs for Internationals, Columbia, SC; **Rhonda Tolhurst**, Kanazawa University; **Rodney Johnson**, Kansai Gaidai University; **Rosa Enilda Vásquez Fernandez**, John F. Kennedy Institute of Languages, Inc.; **Sandra Kern**, New Teacher Coach, School District of Philadelphia; **Shaofang Wu**, National Cheng Kung University; **Sovathey Tim**, American Intercon Institute; **Stephen Shrader**, Notre Dame Seishin Women's University; **Sudeepa Gulati**, Long Beach City College; **Susan Orias**, Broward College; **Thays Ladosky**, Colegio Damas, Recife; **Thea Chan**, American Intercon Institute; **Tom Justice**, North Shore Community College; **Tony J.C. Carnerie**, UCSD English Language Institute; **Tsung-Yuan Hsiao**, National Taiwan Ocean University, Keelung; **Virginia Christopher**, University of Calgary-Qatar; **Vuthy Lorn**, American Intercon Institute; **Wm Troy Tucker**, Edison State College; **Yohei Murayama**, Kagoshima University; **Yoko Sakurai**, Aichi University; **Yoko Sato**, Tokyo University of Agriculture and Technology